Law and the Rise of Capitalism

Law and the Rise of Capitalism

Michael E. Tigar

with the assistance of

Madeleine R. Levy

AAKAR BOOKS

Law and the Rise of Capitalism
Michael E. Tigar

Published in agreement with Monthly Review Press, New York
for publication and sale only in the Indian Subcontinent
(India, Pakistan, Bangladesh, Nepal, Maldives,
Bhutan & Sri Lanka)

First Published in India, 2005

ISBN 81-87879-20-3 (Hb)

Published by
AAKAR BOOKS
28-E, Pocket-IV, Mayur Vihar Phase-I, Delhi-110 091
Phone : 011-2279 5505 Telefax : 011-2279 5641
E-mail : aakarb@del2.vsnl.net.in

Printed in India on behalf of M/s Aakar Books by
Mudrak, 30 A, Patparganj, Delhi-110 091

CONTENTS

ACKNOWLEDGMENTS

The first edition of this book, published in 1977, was written with the assistance of Madeleine R. Levy. I have taken full responsibility for preparing this second edition, and for writing the new material included in it. Work on the first edition was launched with grants from the Louis Rabinowitz Foundation, Carol U. Bernstein, and Stanley Sheinbaum. At Monthly Review Press, Harry Braverman believed in the book and supported its publication. The initial research for the first edition was done in France, England, and Ireland, as well as in the United States. Ms. Levy and I received assistance from professors, librarians and others in Nice, Oxford, London, Dublin, Berkeley and Los Angeles.

For this second edition, I am grateful to John Mage, Andrew Nash, Martin Paddio and all the Monthly Review stalwarts. My students have also been very helpful, providing research assistance on several topics, particularly the early history of human rights litigation in the United States. My students and colleagues at the Faculté de Droit et de Science Politique in Aix-en-Provence have given me much assistance in connection with this edition. Dean Claudio Grossman and my other colleagues at Washington College of Law, American University, have helped in many ways.

Consistent with the first edition, there are no footnotes. There is a bibliography to this second edition. In discussing Bentham, I relied on the work of Mark W. Janis. Professor Martha Nussbaum's insights on the verifiability of norms have greatly influenced me. The bibliography also contains citations to some of my own work on the themes in this book.

MICHAEL E. TIGAR

WASHINGTON, D.C., and ANNAPOLIS, MARYLAND

OCTOBER 2000

INTRODUCTION TO THE SECOND EDITION

In writing about revolution and law, I have sought to move from specific events to general principles and trends. I am aware that "such is the unity of history, that anyone who endeavors to tell a piece of it must feel that his first sentence tears a seamless web." Pollock's and Maitland's cautionary words have guided, even warned, me. This book describes the rise to power of the European bourgeoisie, and traces its struggle against hostile legal systems. I argue that legal change is the product of conflict between social classes seeking to turn the institutions of social control to their purposes, and to impose and maintain a specific system of social relations.

The most important task in studying legal history—or more accurately, jurisprudence in history—is to understand the content of competing legal ideologies and the interests from which they spring, to identify the groups whose conflict of ideology foreshadows revolutionary change, and to describe the working out, in the daily lives of men and women, of such conflict.

The proper task of jurisprudence is to explain the mechanism of fundamental change in the rules of law which, backed by the power of the state, govern our lives. If we succeed in this task, we will understand the present system of law, and how that system must and will be changed by the revolutionary challenges that now confront it. A part of any such understanding must be the acknowledgment that today's rules originated in the revolutionary social struggles of a class whose interests they serve. Fundamental change may seem more or less imminent, or even possible, at any given moment. The dialectical way in which history moves precludes strict linear development. But at any given moment, understanding legal ideology is essential, for reasons I discuss below.

I trace this book's origins to the events and ideas of the late 1960s and early 1970s. In a 1969 book review, I coined the phrase "jurisprudence of insurgency." This review became the basis for a longer analysis of the present-day movement for social change, presented under the title "Jurisprudence of Insurgency" at the Center for the Study of Democratic Institutions, Santa Barbara, California. This was followed by an essay, "Socialist Law and Legal Institutions," discussing the quite different uses of legal ideology by revolutionaries in the Soviet Union, China, and Cuba.

But my experience as a law teacher and human rights lawyer in the 1960s and early 1970s led me to see that I was taking too narrow a view. At that time, I was representing and writing about American radical and revolutionary groups. Some of these folks—of which the Weatherman faction of Students for a Democratic Society may be taken as an example—believed that fundamental and revolutionary change was imminent in the United States. They thought that American political institutions were becoming so destabilized by anti-imperialist protest against the Vietnam War, and by the struggle for racial justice, that systemic changes were "in the air." This process was, they argued, aided by the third world struggles for national liberation. You did not need a weatherman, the saying went, to know which way those winds of change were blowing.

The ideology of those groups seemed to me flawed, in two respects. First, they assumed that history usually works in some logical, linear fashion. Such an assertion is, in point of fact, at odds with the way in which past revolutionary changes have come about. As a matter of theory, these groups were ignoring the entrenched power of the bourgeoisie and of its dominant ideology, especially in metropolitan countries. That is, they had forgotten that change is a dialectical process.

I also rejected the insistence of many radicals and revolutionaries that "law doesn't matter." I thought such a view ahistorical. I noted that there were many ways in which legal ideology could be and was being deployed by dissident groups to advance their own agendas. That is, there remained contradictions between the formal guarantees of freedom and fairness inherent in bourgeois legal ideology and the reality of bourgeois state power, and some of these contradictions were resolved in favor of ideology, not power. I noted that many radicals and revolutionaries were being prosecuted for offenses that involved organizing against the state, or refusing to serve in its wars, and that law and lawyers were going to be necessary in defense of those people. In fact, some of us were achieving good results in keeping the movement's leaders out of jail. So, in the words I later wrote in a play, the law is not simply a mask the state puts on when it is about to commit some indignity on the oppressed.

Finally, it seemed to me that even after a fundamental social change, a new society would need rules and procedures to enhance justice—so that legal ideology was worth thinking about regardless of what you thought was going to happen.

At the same time, I recognized that an alternative to capitalism was not going to be found in law books. Lawyers for the people do not own nor did they invent the law. They do not stand at the center of the events by which the world is moved and changed. They are effective only if they listen to and seek to express people's demands.

It seemed to me that the only way to understand the role of legal ideology was to study its operation in history. In theory and practice, I was a dialectical and historical materialist. In a 1965 essay, I had briefly considered the upheavals in Western Europe and their contribution to changes in the law. But I wanted to test my theory of jurisprudence and insurgency by examining the bourgeois revolutions of Western Europe, and to show how the rules we live under today can be traced to specific social struggles in the rise to power of the bourgeoisie. No such legal history had been written in English.

I originally thought that the main elements of the bourgeois legal ideology had emerged in the English and French revolutions and that the main focus would be upon the seventeenth and eighteenth centuries. I learned, in moving through the primary and secondary sources in Europe and America, that the struggle of the bourgeoisie toward final victory had in fact begun centuries earlier, in the urban uprisings of the eleventh century. Not only did the story of those uprisings make an exciting chapter in the struggle for human liberation, but it modified my outlook about the relationship between law and revolution.

I had ascribed principal significance in earlier writing to the openly revolutionary phase of challenges to an existing legal ideology. In tracing the centuries-long battle of the bourgeoisie, I began to understand more deeply the role of essentially reformist initiatives in temporarily improving the position of a dissident group, in identifying fundamental conflicts and distinguishing them from those which are less important, and ultimately in sharpening the focus of struggle between an existing holder of state power and that group which will overthrow it.

I do not argue that legal change, or changes in legal ideology, *caused* the transition from feudalism to capitalism. Any social system preserves and maintains itself against its enemies, and regulates its internal affairs, through power, and thus in the last analysis through threat and use of force. Its formal rules rest on the premise that if one does not obey the commands of the state—the institution with a public force specially appointed to enforce laws and commands—sooner or later one will be either forcibly constrained to obey or punished for not obeying. Any group, such as the early businessmen, that wants to make a radical change in a society first tests the existing institutions of power to see how far they will bend, and then attacks the institutions of state power directly, setting up its own apparatus of public force, with new laws and commands designed to secure its own interest.

One way to understand history, therefore, is to trace the rise, maintenance, change in, and toppling of legal systems with their annexed instruments of violence. We must beware, however, of drawing too many hasty conclusions from such a study. In the thirteenth century, it seemed to the upper nobility possessing political power, to the Church, and to royalty that the world was in general and continual revolt. Eremitic friars, shoeless and roughly clad, wandered out of richly endowed churches and monasteries stirring up laity and clergy alike against the Roman Church. Unemployed knights carried on high-class brigandage, and runaway serfs joined them to form bands of robbers. Peasants looted their masters' houses. And merchants, town dwellers, or bourgeois—call them what you will—were advancing by open revolution, subversion, and economic chicanery ill-understood by their "betters." All four groups were either outside the law or against it.

I believed in 1977, and believe more strongly now, that studying the bourgeoisie's revolt against feudal institutions is essential to understanding today's law, and not only for lawyers, judges, and law students. Looking back nearly a quarter-century, however, it might seem that the analysis and predictions of Part Six, which dealt with current struggles, is outdated.

Because I do not believe that to be so, I have addressed that question in this Introduction to the Second Edition, and in an Afterword.

The book begins, in Part One, with an overview of the bourgeoisie's rise to power and the main outlines of bourgeois law. In Parts Two through Five, we see the struggle between feudal and bourgeois legal ideologies, beginning with the city dwellers' uprisings in the eleventh century and continuing through the French and English revolutions. Part Six, as I said, contends in conclusion that the reflection of social struggle in legal rules can only be explained and analyzed through a "jurisprudence of insurgency." I have left Parts One through Six (Chapters 1 through 22) unchanged, despite changes in the world since 1977. In this, I am following Paul Sweezy's example and counsel in not attempting to revise the text itself. To do so would take me, as Paul wrote for the reissue of his classic *Theory of Capitalist Development*, "well beyond the scope of an introduction."

The Afterword has two goals. First, it expands the subject matter of the book. The First Edition focused mainly on so-called private law, the relations of contract, property, and civil wrongs. The Afterword turns attention to public law, and particularly the public law of nations that deals with human rights. It also traces, briefly, chief features of American constitutional law. Second, the Afterword describes how the increasingly internationalist outlook of human rights advocates has helped to intensify the struggle against bourgeois legal ideology and against the subjugation of the third world.

Picking up from the French and English bourgeois revolutions, the Afterword discusses the so-called universal principles proclaimed by the victorious bourgeoisie. I sketch some more ways in which those principles were betrayed and dismantled in the eighteenth and nineteenth centuries, and how the idea of universal, or at least transnational, norms has been given new life at the insistence of popular movements in the years since 1917.

The collapse of the former Soviet Union, the continued vigor of liberation movements, and (particularly) the struggles in such places as Chile and South Africa (in both of which I was active) draw our attention. In the past decade, we have seen an unprecedented public concern with "human rights," expressed as transnational norms by which the conduct of national governments may be judged. Some of this talk is simply the false rhetoric of metropolitan countries, seeking to cloak the imposition of their will upon weaker states. But an impressive amount of this discussion has expressed the aspirations of people seeking liberation, as in South Africa, where human rights debates were central themes of anti-apartheid ideology.

In Chapter 22, I spoke of this latter kind of discussion as the basis for a "jurisprudence of insurgency." I want to bring that inquiry up to date. Some of this discussion is necessarily a defense of my own professional choices. John Mage, reviewing the autobiography of the great progressive lawyer Victor Rabinowitz, wrote that "In the U.S. system, all significant legal and political questions are given legal form. This has proved effective for its rulers, not least by limiting in advance the types of permissible answers." Mage's concern is well placed; therefore, one must understand both the possibilities in and the limits on struggle over principles of legal ideology.

I have chosen to work as a lawyer in the United States (in the words of a Monthly Review comment on my work) to "challenge and thwart the manipulation of capitalist state power." I began by defending civil rights figures and those who resisted participation in the Vietnam War. I have continued by working on behalf of political dissidents. I have even taken on the cases of mainstream clients where misuse of official power was an issue.

In recent years, I have also worked to combat persecution of people based on their sexual orientation, and to combat the death penalty. In the United States today, we have an ever longer list of state and federal capital crimes. Prosecutorial selection of those who are to face charges punishable by death is demonstrably race and class biased. The lamentable quality of legal representation, and the system's blind eye toward official misconduct, has meant that untold numbers of innocent people are condemned to die.

As of mid-1999, about 500 people had been executed in the United States since executions resumed as the result of a 1976 Supreme Court decision. In that time period, more than seventy death row inmates had already been authoritatively found and officially recognized to have been wrongly convicted, and the numbers have grown greater since then. These vindications have come from the efforts of volunteer lawyers and journalists. This error rate mocks any claim that the death penalty is applied rationally.

After all, the crimes that may carry the death penalty tend to be shocking and cruel. These are precisely the cases that the police and FBI want to "clear up" by arresting somebody as soon as possible. These are the cases where prosecutors are likely to cut corners and judges are likely to overlook such wrongdoing.

Even outside the arena of capital cases, the United States has an incarceration rate four times that of Canada and five to seven times that of any Western European country. We are seeking to solve the problems of social turmoil by filling the prisons. Disparities in sentencing between whites and persons of color abound. Sentencing and prosecution policies are tilted heavily against African-Americans.

And so I have raised my voice, as a lawyer in court and as a teacher and helper of law students and public defenders. Outside the United States, I have worked alongside brothers and sisters in South Africa, Chile and elsewhere to combat repressive state power and to help bring about social change.

These experiences have deepened my understanding of the issues raised in this book. To understand where legal ideology might go, one must understand where it has been and what have been its guiding forces. One can do this only by studying the history of legal institutions.

To say that there is a role for lawyers in struggle is not to ignore John Mage's cogent warning. Indeed, the lawyer must always know what tools to use, and what those tools cannot realistically accomplish. The history of social change is one of people moving to make change. In the process, we may use legal ideology just as we would use other forms of struggle: to ameliorate this or that onerous condition. We can also be showing just how inadequate the legal forms might be. The fact that such limits exist does not render our efforts meaningless or harmful. Indeed, the formulation of a jurisprudence of insurgency, that is, a self-conscious challenge to capitalism and capitalist state power, requires a period of struggle. In that struggle, there will be progressive victories, but one will also learn the limits and contradictions inherent in bourgeois legal ideology.

In the United States, the legal ideology of rights has come under attack from two directions. First, reactionary judges and lawyers have sought to empty democratic rights of any progressive content. They seek not only to blunt the effectiveness of such rights as equality and free expression. More importantly, they are using these concepts as affirmative devices to drown out dissent and to turn back the tide of equal treatment for people of color, women and others.

Second, tendencies variously named "critical legal studies," "deconstruction," and so on have denied that the categories of legal ideology have any real content at all. Adherents to such views argue that formal statements of "law" have no meaning aside from particular decisions in particular cases. This is, of course, a generalization about a range of opinions and arguments, but I insist that it is accurate. In my work, I seek to expose the agenda of the reactionaries, and argue against the intellectual paralysis that accompanies pure criticism. In Chapter 22 of the First Edition, I attempted to sketch a theory of legal ideology that both acknowledged the reactionary potential of legal norms and the real possibility of finding some progressive content in those norms. In the Afterword, I return to those themes.

PART ONE

LAW AND THE CAPITALIST RISE TO POWER

AN OVERVIEW

1.

THE MERCHANT AS REBEL

In 1184 A.D., in the French town of Châteauneuf, revolutionaries took control of the principal buildings, announcing that they protested taxes, exactions, and the curtailment of their freedom to work and trade. Called upon to renounce the "commune or conjuration . . . they have erected," they refused. A year passed before order was fully restored, and even so, rumors of plots, conspiracies, and secret societies persisted. The revolutionaries were, in the words of the Pope, "the said bourgeois," or in the words of the archbishop, *potentiores burgenses*—powerful bourgeois.

This story was a familiar one in eleventh- and twelfth-century Europe, sometimes with the additional complaint that the rebels had broken into the house of their lord, or bishop, drunk up the wine, molested household members, and led off the sheep and cows. Little wonder that Philippe de Beaumanoir, a learned and even gentle legal historian of the thirteenth century, referring to such uprisings, wrote that "among the greatest crimes, which must be punished and avenged, is that of associating against the common good."

This image of the medieval bourgeois as revolutionary may be surprising to us today. For the modern reader in the West, the respectability of the merchant class is self-evident. The word has become commonplace, and we use it automatically, without considering the system of laws which over the centuries has put these people in the center of economic activity.

But when he first appeared in Western Europe in about the year 1000 A.D., the merchant had a somewhat different image. *Pies poudreux*, "dusty feet," he was called, for he took his goods from town to town, from fair to fair, from market to market, on foot or horseback, selling as he went. In the great halls of the feudal lords, the merchant was an object of derision, scorn, and even hatred. Lyric songs celebrated knightly robbery of merchant bands, as well as knightly valor in battle and knightly cuckoldry. Profit, the difference between the price at which the merchant bought and the price at which he sold, was considered dishonorable in a society that praised the noble virtues of killing and revered those who lived "by the weariness and toil"—in the words of a contemporary charter—of peasants. Profit-taking was considered a form of usury, and the merchant's soul was thought to be in jeopardy. The hatred came later, when a nobility in need of cash to finance its wars and style of life discovered that the merchants had more of it than they did.

For the most part, however, the growth of merchant fortunes and merchant power was accomplished through armed conflict, and by what appeared to the established classes as nothing short of revolution, punishable—as Beaumanoir suggested—by long prison sentences and even death. In order to protect themselves and their goods from the arbitrary ravages of the nobility, the merchants felt compelled to establish conditions which permitted trade. One man, or several men, well-armed and skilled in the use of weapons, could cross Europe trading small items—like spices and silks—that were both valuable and easy to carry for cash on the spot. That would be *sale*. But for orderly and consistent *trade*, there had to be a system which guaranteed physical security and made possible credit, insurance, and the transmission of funds. *Manufacture*, as opposed to trading in imported goods, required an even more socially protected system of commerce, as well as a higher level of technology.

The relationship between the rising bourgeoisie and the law has three aspects. First, to the extent that one can speak of law in the jungle of feudal life, it was either silent about trade or hostile to it. The merchant was therefore in these terms a social outcast, who saw the legal system—the system which issued orders backed up by institutional force—as hostile and alien. The ordinary merchant, trader, or peddler sought to come to terms with this system so he could profit. As the number of merchants, and their power, increased, the legal ideologists of this *class* sought to justify the place of trade in the symmetry of the feudal system. They also sought accommodation with, and weak spots in, feudal law.

Second, as the merchant extended his field of activity to create institutions of commerce—cities, ports and harbors, stores, banks, manufactories, and so on—he came increasingly into head-on collision with the economic and political interests of the feudal masters of this or that section of territory. The merchant class chafed continually against laws and customs maintained to protect the feudal power holders. From the rules prohibiting or limiting the sale of land outside the family—which effectively prevented land from being an article of commerce—to the prohibition of most forms of bourgeois association, both political and economic, the conflict intensified and broadened until the bourgeois gradually discovered the points at which the legal system could no longer be bent to his will, accommodated at an affordable price, or evaded.

Finally, there are the laws that the merchants made for themselves, the legal system they fashioned to serve their own interests. First they set up tribunals to settle disputes among themselves, then wrested or cajoled concessions from spiritual and temporal princes in order to establish zones of free commerce, and finally—over a period of centuries—swept to power over nations. The process of bourgeois lawmaking saw the creation and application of specific legal rules about contracts, property, and procedure; these rules of law were fashioned in the context of a legal ideology which identified freedom of action for businessmen with natural law and natural reason. The men and women who fought for legal rules consistent with freer commerce did not claim to have invented the principles they sought to have applied. Respect for tradition forbade such a claim, and Beaumanoir, writing in the service of Philip III, warned that novelties not authorized by the sovereign are forbidden. Rather, the bourgeois sought old legal forms and principles, chiefly Roman, and invested them with a new commercial content.

These elements of the bourgeois relation to law do not correspond to sharply defined historical periods; they are present in each country of Western Europe from the eleventh century right up to the conquest of power by the bourgeoisie in the seventeenth to nineteenth centuries. The fall of the feudal system was a gradual process punctuated by sudden and violent upheavals. To borrow Diderot's metaphor:

> The rule of Nature and of my Trinity, against which the gates of Hell shall not prevail . . . establishes itself very quietly. The strange god settles himself humbly on the altar beside the god of the country. Little by little he establishes himself firmly. Then one fine morning he gives his neighbor a shove with his elbow and—crash!—the idol lies upon the ground.

One thing should be noted here. In this study, as the alert reader may already have noticed, "law" has no single meaning. As used by the protagonists in the struggle we describe, it means at different times (a) the rules made by the powerful to govern their subjects, backed up by organized violence; (b) the rules that some group or class thinks *ought* to be made in a godly, or at least a better, society; (c) the customs and habits of a people, which have been observed immemorially; (d) the manifesto of a revolutionary group; (e) the rules that some group makes for its own internal governance. But in daily speech, too, law means all these things, and we can only hope to make our meaning clear by context. In the final part we will attempt a fuller discussion of the meaning of law in a time when power relationships are undergoing revolutionary change.

2.

THE BACKDROP OF THE NEW LEGAL INSTITUTIONS

The eighteenth-century systems of law designed by and for the bourgeoisie take elements from, and look for authority to, six different bodies of legal thought:

1. **ROMAN LAW**, revived in various forms and carrying the authority of a civilization whose imperial military expansion left traces throughout the Western world. Roman legal thought had developed forms of legal relationships designed to accommodate and to further commerce with all parts of the Empire.

2. **FEUDAL, OR SEIGNEURIAL, LAW**: those rules defining the relationships of homage, dominance, exploitation, and protection which characterized the personal feudal tie between a lord and his vassals.

3. **CANON LAW**: the legal rules of the Western Roman Catholic Church, which claimed varying but always considerable amounts of control over the very secular business of trade.

4. **ROYAL LAW**: rules that manifest the consolidating influence of those who forced the creation of the first modern states, and of whom the bourgeoisie were early, if fickle, allies.

5. **LAW, MERCHANT**: rules derived from Roman law but adapted over the centuries to the needs of those whose business was business. The idea of a special set of rules for those with a certain status was less unsettling to the

feudal age than to our own, and the merchants fought for a law developed by and specially applicable to them in the cities and towns and in the annual or seasonal fairs held in various places during the Middle Ages.

6. **NATURAL LAW**: the bourgeois claim, developed fully in the seventeenth century though portended earlier, that the combination of rules which best served free commerce was eternally true, in accord with God's plan, and self-evidently wise.

These six categories of law reflect real patterns of power. Feudal power relationships were fragmented and patchwork, with several temporal and spiritual overlords jostling and fighting for the right to exploit each piece of arable or livable land—and the people on it. The contest was particularly keen over who had the right to judge, and to establish courts, for the fines and fees of judging were among the most lucrative sources of cash. So when a merchant of the medieval period made a contract, he would have in mind several kinds of law, and he would be anxious to know which court had enough power to make the opposite party pay up or deliver the goods.

In 1448, one Huguet Augier, a haberdasher from Grasse (in what is now southern France) who was anxious to purchase a quantity of goods from a businessman in Nice, agreed in the event of a lawsuit over the contract to submit to the jurisdiction of: the Chamber of Accounts of Aix (a royal court); the royal court of the Châtelet of Paris; a municipal court in Grasse; a merchant court in Marseille; the court of the Pope and the Apostolic Chamber; and the court of the ducal city of Nice. In each of these courts, the transaction might be judged by a different law, and the lawyer who drafted Augier's contract would have to ensure that the deal was legal, that is to say protected, under each of them.

Just as the merchant Huguet Augier could not set out to engage in important trade without some understanding of these bodies of legal precedent, so we will begin with a brief discussion of them.

ROMAN LAW

By 1000 A.D. the Western Roman Empire had been gone six hundred years, but people in Western Europe still walked on roads that dated from Augustus Caesar's time—the first century A.D. The ruins of Roman cities, Roman harbors, and Roman churches dotted the landscape. The well-educated merchant—and his lawyer—was taught that in the wake of the Roman conquest had come Roman laws and Roman commerce, including the freedom to buy and sell by means of enforceable contracts. Even those lords who claimed to apply ancient local custom in ruling their subjects were, sometimes unknowingly, handing on principles partly drawn from Roman Jurists. For the Church, and for those temporal lords who also aspired to universal overlordship, the Roman Empire provided a conscious organizational model. In order to understand the medieval merchant, we must look closely at some of these Roman institutions.

We do not claim that Roman society was the first to be regulated by law, in the sense of a system of rules backed by the power of the state. Medieval lawyers were aware that this was not so, and had access to written accounts of earlier societies, including the Athenian. But Rome, unlike earlier societies, had left a rich and diverse legal literature. Roman commerce had given rise to laws which medieval merchants and their lawyers found relevant. And Roman law came, as we shall see, to be endowed with the temporal and spiritual support of the Papacy.

The Roman legal system was created between the fifth century B.C. and the second century A.D. To shroud the law's origins in mystery and to invest it with the sanction of tradition, Roman jurisprudents purported to derive every important legal principle from the Twelve Tables. This concise collection of laws, difficult to reconstruct but of undoubted authenticity, was drawn up around 450 B.C. under the Roman Republic, apocryphally from self-evident principles but actually after study of the constitutions of a number of Greek cities. The Tables outline only the simplest of legal principles concerning property, family law, and citizenship, and they are characterized by reliance upon magic and ritual as integral parts of legal procedure and as means for the creation of obligations. This "preclassical" law guaranteed certain rights to Romans—more particularly, to the members of the clans that had founded the Roman Republic.

In the Twelve Tables we first see the emergence of legal ideas of debt, contract, and civil wrong. These ideas turn up later in countless medieval charters and custumals (written collections of customs). Early Romans, like some others in societies organized on a clan basis, dealt with murder or injury of a kinsperson by revenge upon the murderer's kinfolk. An early step away from this violent solution for the Romans was the "composition," a payment in money or goods to the victim's kin, accompanied by a solemn ceremony acknowledging the obligation to pay. It seems probable that the earliest Roman compositions took the form described in the Twelve Tables as *nexum*. *Nexum* was the bond created between a debtor and creditor by the former's promise to subject himself to the latter until the debt was paid. By the time of the Twelve Tables, the device was used to create a lien between any creditor and any debtor, no matter how the debt arose.

Bonds persisted in all their original vigor long past the time when the debtors—*nexi*—had forgotten the origins of the law that bound them to their creditors. The distinctly Roman customs of southern France yielded contracts such as one of 1362 in which Jaciel of Grasse, a moneylender, required that his debtor, in the event of nonpayment, come from Nice (thirty-five miles away) and live in Grasse to work under Jaciel's direction until the debt was paid. Municipal records show that Jaciel actually enforced this *hostagium* clause and obtained a court order requiring his debtor to lodge in the Grasse prison.

The valid sale or exchange of property required, according to the Twelve Tables, strict adherence to a precise formula of words and conduct, known as *mancipatio*:

> In the presence of not less than five Roman citizens of full age, and also a sixth person having the same qualifications, known as the *libripens*, to hold a bronze scale, the party who is taking by the *mancipation*, holding a bronze ingot, says, "I declare this slave is mine *ex jure Quiritium*, and he be purchased to me with this bronze ingot and bronze scale." He then strikes the scale with the ingot and gives it as a symbolic price to him from whom he is receiving by the *mancipation*.

The bronze ingot and scale are used, as a first-century A.D. jurist explained, because formerly only bronze money was in use; the value of these pieces was reckoned by weighing.

Early Roman procedure for the enforcement of claims was also laden with formalism. The plaintiff was required to fit his claim into a precise form and to speak the required words exactly to the magistrate. If the claim was, for example, for money, and the magistrate was satisfied with the ritual pleading of it, he would refer the matter to a delegate judge, or *index*, for decision. The *index*'s judgment would also turn on the invocation by plaintiff and defendant of formulae of claim and defense. Long past the time when clans had any significance, the plaintiff in a lawsuit was still required to swear that the demand he made for money or property was founded *ex jure Quiritium*, deriving from one's rights as a member of a Roman clan. Non-Romans were, by the Twelve Tables, rightless, without capacity to make contracts, to own property, or to bring an action to enforce debts or obligations.

The rituals of procedure and of exchange of property carried forward the myth of a clan society, and of the earlier days of the Roman Republic. Republican institutions themselves decayed during the Roman wars of conquest and expansion of the third and second centuries B.C. and came to a formal end with Augustus Caesar's organization of the Empire from 44 B.C. to 15 A.D.

With colonization on the shores of the Mediterranean in the third and second centuries B.C. came a great expansion of trade, and with it the need for a more comprehensive legal system. A legal system that gave rights only to Romans could not serve for commerce with non-Romans. And even in local transactions, rules devised for an agricultural economy did not encompass the interests of the great merchants, whose wealth was increasing at the expense of small peasants and artisans.

For Roman merchants, a new magistracy, the praetorship, was created in 367 B.C. with power to issue an annual edict stating the claims the courts would recognize in suits between Romans. At about the same time, treaties ceded commercial rights to some non-Romans and alterations were made in the ritual of procedure. Other non-Romans were permitted to allege, in pleading before the *praetor*, that they were Romans, and their opponents were not permitted to contest the allegation. (Fifteen centuries later, English courts were using the same device to obtain jurisdiction over disputes outside of England, permitting parties to allege, again incontrovertibly, if fictionally, that foreign places were in England.)

In 243 B.C. a *praetor peregrinus* was appointed to supervise the trial of cases involving non-Romans; by this action, Roman law took the step which is repeatedly and romantically referred to in the ideology of merchants for the next two thousand years. The former *praetor* took the name *praetor urbanus*, and his edicts were founded upon the existing law, the *jus civile*: in the words of Gaius, the leading Roman jurist of the first century A.D., the *jus civile* was "the law which a people establishes for itself [as] peculiar to it, . . . as being the special law of the *civitas*." The *praetor peregrinus*, on the other hand, purported to fashion and apply the *jus gentium*—in Gaius' words, "the law that natural reason establishes among all mankind [which] is followed by all peoples alike."

To regard Roman legal concepts as applicable to "all peoples" was not so formidable a conceit. Between 280 B.C. and the destruction of Carthage in the Third Punic War in 146 B.C., Rome had forcibly conquered most of the lands bordering on the Mediterranean. A village-based agricultural economy was rapidly being replaced by the class structure of the Empire, in which the dominant figures were traders, bankers, merchants, landowners, and the military power which protected their interests. The labor force which fueled this system was slave or half-free, recruited mainly from the conquered and colonized peoples. The power of the ruling class could commit the Roman state to the enforcement of a commercial law which permitted trade. The practices which they had developed in pursuing the Mediterranean trade were the most logical foundation of that law. Adoption of the term *jus gentium* reflected the conquest by the new Roman ruling class of its foreign and domestic enemies.

This "law of all peoples" was not, however, purely the product of Roman jurists, imposed by Roman might; it bears traces of those civilizations in the West with which the Romans first traded and which they first colonized. For example, the *jus gentium* recognized a contract in which the bargain was sealed with "earnest money," a small coin or other object which changed hands as evidence of agreement. The Latin word for this coin or object is *arrhoe* or *arroe*, derived from the Greek *arrhabon*.

Gaius' term "natural reason" is more difficult to understand. Writers of the Middle Ages and after have seized upon this phrase and found in it the natural-law philosophy of free trade capitalism and constitutional democracy. By making "natural reason" read "natural" or "God-given law," the legal ideologists of the sixteenth and seventeenth centuries made claims of universality for Roman ideas of free contract. The authors of the Code Napoléon claimed to have rediscovered in the *jus gentium* the true natural-law principles of freedom, and a celebrated nineteenth-century Supreme Court Justice, Joseph Story, held that the courts of the United States could apply it to fashion a "natural" interstate and international law.

Gaius probably had no such inflated idea. To him, natural reason more likely meant those customs which had been used by many peoples over time and had been found reasonable to the trading and lawmaking classes.

The changes introduced by the *praetor peregrinus* ratified and permitted expansion of Rome's emerging commercial hegemony, while the coexistence of the *jus civile* and *jus gentium* led to subtle and pervasive changes in the former as regards the law of contract, sales, property, and procedure.

By the time the *praetor peregrinus* was established, Roman law already recognized *unilateral* binding promises: X could promise (*stipulatio*) Y to deliver some goods on a certain day, and for breach of that promise the law would provide a remedy. A contract to do a thing in the future is called executory, and underlies all modern commercial transactions. Prior to this, Roman law, like early Anglo-Saxon law and other early legal systems, had recognized only *executed* contracts, those that involved face-to-face dealings, with an exchange of the property concerned at the moment the deal was made and according to a prescribed form. (This, in Roman law, was the ritual of *mancipatio*.) There is no need for such law to deal with unfulfilled promises; the only rules needed are those concerning stolen goods, and perhaps those concerning the quality of goods sold. Recognition of unilateral, binding, executory promises was one step toward freedom of commerce, for it gave merchants greater flexibility in commercial dealings.

The next step was the recognition of *bilateral* executory contracts, including those encompassing complex, long-term business associations. The *jus gentium* ratified and elaborated bilateral contracts regarding sale, hiring, deposit, and partnership, as well as commercial concepts of fiduciary relations—those of special trust and confidence. The distinction between the unilateral binding promise and the bilateral contract with obligations on both sides is of great importance. The unilateral binding obligation was created by the person *assuming* the obligation—to deliver goods, to pay money, and so on—by repeating a set speech that was essential to the validity and enforceability of the promise. If the promisor failed to perform, the beneficiary of the promise could sue to enforce the deal or collect damages for nonperformance. Such a contract seldom reflects the reality of even the simplest commercial transaction, for usually one party promises to deliver and the other promises to pay on condition the goods arrive and are in satisfactory condition. If a legal system admits only unilateral promises, these two obligations must be assumed separately, and separate lawsuits are required for the enforcement of each promise. To pursue the example, if Aulus Augerius (Rome's John Doe) does not deliver the promised cloth, and therefore Numerius Negidius (Rome's Richard Roe) does not pay, each has a valid lawsuit against the other, for the system is concerned only with whether or not the obligation has been honored. But for both buyers and sellers, the "natural reason" of commerce would seem to demand a system of *mutual* promises, so that in the event of default the state will intervene through its courts and order each party to pay the other what is due, setting claims against one another if necessary. This concept was among the great reforms carried out by the *praetor peregrinus*.

In addition, the *praetors* greatly increased the range of their authority, adding to the types of bargain for the breach of which they would give remedy, adapting the forms of contract to the needs of commerce, and introducing rational methods of allegation (pleading) and proof.

These procedures, insofar as they dealt with contract and exchange, were extended to the enforcement of the contract *bonae fidei*, literally "in good faith." The contract *bonae fidei* was the most elastic contractual category in Roman law and was originally limited to a few relationships based on special trust and confidence, such as those of guardian and ward, involving bilateral agreements with mutual assumption of obligations. The *praetors* came, however, to recognize under the heading of *bonae fidei* a great variety of commercial arrangements also assertedly based upon good faith, such as the business society or partnership, permitting pooling of capital and spreading of risk. Fiduciary relationships could be included in a contract *bonae fidei*, as when Aulus Augerius, having a quantity of money but no access to a market, gave the money to Numerius Negidius to use on his behalf. If a party to a contract *bonae fidei* failed to perform, or if Aulus wanted an accounting, procedure before the *praetor peregrinus* permitted enforcement of the obligation, the assessment of damages, or an official order to settle accounts. These remedies were based upon the *formula*, a system of pleading remarkably similar to that used in Western courts today.

The *formula* was a statement of the case by the *praetor*, based on the parties' allegations, in a form which, though rigid and overlain with ritual, was far more adapted to rational fact-finding than what had preceded it. This statement was also the *praetor*'s reference of the case to a trial judge, or *iudex*. It began with the appointment of the iudex and was followed by a summary of the controversy (*demonstratio*), a statement of the issue (*intentio*), and an instruction to the *iudex* to decide the case after hearing evidence (*condemnatio*), or else a direction to adjust the conflicting claims by determining the worth of each and awarding a net judgment (*adjudicatio*). Between the *intentio* and the direction to give judgment (*condemnatio* or *adjudicatio*) the *praetor* would summarize pleas raising defenses or counterclaims—the *exceptio*, *replicatio*, *duplicatio*, and so forth. Gaius gives us a simple example of the *formula* in a case involving sale of a slave, the parties being Aulus Augerius and Numerius Negidius. This lawsuit involved the contract of sale, *emptio venditio*, the most basic and important of the contracts *bonae fidei*.

> X is appointed *index*. *Demonstratio*: Whereas Aulus Augerius sold the slave to Numerius Negidius. *Intentio*: If it appears that N.N. ought to pay A.A. 10,000 sesterces. *Condemnatio*: Do thou, *iudex*, condemn N.N. to pay A.A. in 10,000 sesterces. If it does not appear, acquit.

To the Romans medieval lawyers owed the concept—which has continued to present times—of the corporation as a fictitious artificial person, entitled to buy, sell, and enforce its claims in the courts. Corporate organization permitted a pooling of interests and therefore an accumulation of capital far greater than in an individual enterprise or a partnership. The distinction was this: a partnership, formed by the agreement of its members, remained in the law's eyes an amalgam of individual rights and duties. To sue the partnership and get a court judgment enforceable against its members' assets one had to bring all the partners before the court. And if the partnership itself came to court, it had in general to have sued in the name of all its members. A corporation, however, swallows up the identities of its shareholder-owners in the common, artificial personality of itself, and is sued and sues, has rights and obligations, on its "own" account.

The other striking feature of the corporation, in the form it began to take in the medieval period, is that shareholders or members were not obligated beyond the amount they put in for their shares—the notion of "limited liability." A wealthy individual could put a part of his or her wealth in a corporation and not risk—if the corporation failed—invasion of the balance of his or her personal fortune to pay the insolvent corporation's debts. It is doubtful that the corporation existed in this form for business enterprises in Rome, and there was great resistance many centuries later to general recognition of the limited-liability principle in Western Europe, but medieval bourgeois ideologists could look back to the words of a leading third-century Roman Jurist, Ulpian, and not care that he probably wrote only of a special class of corporations created by the Roman state to serve special ends. Ulpian wrote: "*Si quid universitati debetur, singalis non debetur; nec quad debet universitatis singali debet*"—roughly, the property and debts of a corporate body are not the property and debts of each individual member. Ulpian goes on to underline the point by saying that even if the corporation consists of one member, it is a distinct legal entity from that member.

The corporate character of institutions as diverse as a company of merchants, a medieval city, and the entire Roman Catholic Church led to Ulpian's words being perhaps the most commented-upon in all Roman jurisprudence.

The *jus gentium* also gave to the Roman courts, and specifically to the *praetor peregrinus*, the power to adjust disputes in a rational way by ordering judgment on counterclaims made in the same action. Thus, if A.A. and N.N. had a series of dealings on account, with mutual purchases and sales, and A.A. complained of nonpayment on a particular purchase, N.N. could bring into the same lawsuit claims about money due him on some other transaction in that series of dealings. Or, if N.N. had not paid for some goods on the ground that they were shoddy, and A.A. sued for payment, the *praetor* might order that the amount of the debt and the quality of the goods be determined in the same action and a judgment be given against N.N. only for that which he ought in justice to pay. This seems elementary, for it is hard to conceive of a rational legal system which would require two lawsuits in either of the cases above, yet both the English common-law courts until the eighteenth century and the majority of the French secular courts until perhaps the seventeenth century did not permit counterclaims to be heard. Not until the revival of the Roman law, trumpeted as "natural equity" and "conscience," did the right to counterclaim revive.

The naming of the *praetor peregrinus* was one of those devices by which a rising class without power to sweep away old institutions is able to create new ones alongside the old to serve its special needs. The old form, created to serve an earlier and different set of social relations, is then more quickly emptied of the substance it once contained. The rules it administers are penetrated by borrowings from the new institution while retaining the popular regard imparted by their antiquity. Thus the Roman *jus civile* retained the fiction that it carried forward the principles of the Twelve Tables and the legislation of the Republic, while being progressively overwhelmed by the *jus gentium*, tool of the newly rich and powerful merchants. By 150 B.C., procedure before the *praetor urbanus* had become the same as that before the *praetor peregrinus*.

In about 150 A.D. there began the prolific production of Roman legal writing that was to become the basis of medieval knowledge of Roman law. These writings, by emperors and legal scholars, grew progressively more arid and decadent as the Western Roman Empire drew to a close. Periodically, these great outpourings were codified, excerpted, and arranged by subject matter. The emperor Gregorius made one such codification in 294 A.D., covering the period from Hadrian (117–138 A.D.) to his own reign. The emperors Constantine and Theodosius II also ordered codifications which bear their names.

The best-known, most complete, and to the medieval bourgeoisie most influential, codification was the *Corpus Juris Civilis*, compiled under the direction of the Eastern Roman emperor Justinian in the sixth century A.D. It consists of three parts, the Code itself, a collection of imperial edicts from Hadrian's time to 533 A.D.; the Digest, a similar work, but consisting of opinions by imperial Rome's leading jurists and legal thinkers, all of whom lived from the first to the third centuries A.D.; and the Institutes, a synopsis of the Code and Digest for law students. Though none of the edicts and legal opinions excerpted in the Code and Digest date before the first century A.D., many of these reach back into still earlier classical Roman legal concepts to cite the antiquity of a particular rule or practice. This is particularly so of the earliest jurists, like Gaius, whose work is quoted in the Digest.

Justinian's codification was not, therefore, innovative; it performed the signal service of sorting through the thousands of imperial edicts and legal treatises, eliminating contradiction by choosing the practice or rule which was current in 533, and systematizing the whole under titles corresponding to the areas of law: contracts, property, family law, procedure, crimes, and so on. Most of the sources from which the *Corpus Juris* is taken are lost: we know of them only from its pages.

Justinian was, however, an Eastern emperor, sitting at Constantinople. His work does not appear to have influenced commercial practice in Western Europe until the eleventh century. This is not to say that Roman legal concepts did not survive, although there was little commercial life in most of Western Europe which would have called for their use; they subsisted in local customs, canonical practice, and in such works as a partial codification, the *Lex Romana Visigothorum* of about 506 A.D., attributed to the Visigoth leader Alaric II, who had a power base in Spain. The monasteries remained centers of Roman law and Latin learning. At the same time, there is no question that with the death of commercial life attendant upon the fall of the Western Empire in 476 A.D., the technical, artfully constructed precepts of Roman classical law, and the structure for applying them, fell into disuse.

FEUDAL LAW

On August 11, 1789, the French National Assembly, in the first flush of revolutionary victory, decreed that it "totally abolishes the feudal regime." The draftsmen of the Code Napoléon, fourteen years later, spoke of the "many vestiges of the feudal regime which still covered the surface of France," and which the Code laid to rest. Yet for some eight hundred years a good number of merchants had lived and even prospered in the midst of this feudal regime. Why was it suddenly found necessary to destroy it at whatever cost? It is important to examine some aspects of feudal society in order to understand the merchants' centuries-long oscillation between accommodation and rebellion.

Even at its high point, in the first three centuries A.D., the Roman commercial and military empire contained the contradictions that were to bring it down. Slave labor undercut free labor, throwing artisans and small farmers out of work to roam the cities and create foci of unrest. The revolutionary doctrines of the young Christian church spread disaffection among the lower classes and spurred the authorities to brutal repression of its adherents. On the borders of the Empire, groups driven out of Central Europe by the advancing Huns added to the administrative problems of an increasingly overburdened and expensive bureaucracy. Communication, the ability to protect the wealthy, and the security of commerce began to diminish in the third century A.D., and with them went the prosperity of the Empire.

For the large latifundia in the area closest to Rome, one solution to the labor problem was to rent out part of the latifundist's domain to freemen or slaves, exacting rent in kind in the form of an obligation to toil on that part of the domain reserved for the latifundist's personal use and profit. On the borders of the Empire, to help keep the invaders at bay, free Romans were given land and the status of *coloni*, under the supervision of a landlord with governmental authority. These colonists paid rent in kind and in labor and were required to participate in the defense of the Empire's borders. Wherever possible, the invaders were bought off by being invited into federation with the Empire. The *federati* were given land to till, swore an oath to defend the Empire, and adapted their social organization to the system practiced by the latifundists and the *coloni*, but they were allowed to maintain their own laws in disputes within the group.

The "fall" of the Western Empire in 476 was only the last step in the process of disintegration. (By this time, the Roman emperors had embraced Catholicism—Constantine had been the first to convert in 313 A.D.) Episcopal and archepiscopal cities as well as Roman administrative centers survived; but large regions occupied by latifundists, *coloni*, and *federati* became autonomous, professing only nominal allegiance to the distant Eastern emperor in Constantinople. The need for survival and military defense, the lack of a Roman governmental presence and of the Roman legions, made possible and necessary a manorial system in which one finds the origins of what later writers were to term feudalism.

In places not under Roman rule, such as in Scotland, Ireland, Scandinavia, and Germany, surviving records indicate that feudal forms were developing as well, adapting the needs for food and defense to local social organization.

Throughout Europe in this period, particularly in Germany and southern France, there were farmers and peasants who were neither Romans nor *coloni* and *federati*, but who had in the past looked to Roman officials as their governors. Possessors of plots of various sizes, called allods, they were swept into the feudal system by the need for protection or by force. Europe was a battleground, the scene of successive invasions—from the Hungarians in the East, from the Moors in the South, and from Scandinavians in the North.

In the part of Europe once ruled from Rome, therefore, feudalism represented the retreat into the manor and village of a ruling class deprived of protection by a decayed and dying imperial government. Elsewhere, it was a change from a pastoral, nomadic, and war-directed existence to a more stable agricultural life (although still warlike enough). The various measures of land are one witness to the principal economic concern of the manor, for the standard, whether the *mansio* of Gaul or the *hide* of England, was that which could support one family, and its size varied depending on the region and the fertility of the soil.

At the root of the feudal relation was the act of homage, supplemented from the time of Charlemagne (ninth century) by the oath of fealty. Two men, one stronger (the lord), the other weaker (the vassal), face one another. As the French historian Marc Bloch describes it, the latter

> puts his hands together and places them, thus joined, between the hands of the other man—a plain symbol of submission, the significance of which was sometimes further emphasized by a kneeling posture. At the same time, the person proffering his hands utters a few words—a very short declaration—by which he acknowledges himself to be the "man" of the person facing him. Then chief and subordinate kiss each other on the mouth, symbolizing accord and friendship. Such were the gestures, very simple ones—eminently fitted to make an impression on minds so sensitive to visible things—which served to cement one of the strongest social bonds known in the feudal era.

The essence of the feudal relation was this personal nexus, originally enduring only for the lifetime of the vassal, and later extended to the vassal's heirs in the male line. For the vassal held the land he tilled, and virtually all his movable possessions, "of" his lord. The oath-bound relation of dominance and subordination, from the tiller to his lord, and through the latter's pledge of homage to some more powerful seigneur, constituted a system often described by its ideologists in pyramidal, symmetrical terms.

Death and mayhem were common enough in feudal society, and retribution swift and vengeful. But violence offered to one's lord was a special sort of misdeed. Witness these words from *The Murder of Charles the Good*:

> "Whom did you slay, and why, and when, and where, and how, you most evil Borsiard?" asks Walter of Therouanne of the man, then dead, whose sword first struck Count Charles as he knelt in prayer on March 2, 1127. And his own brief reply follows: "Your lord, because of his concern for justice, in Lent, in church, and in violation of the reverence due him," adding "your crime was worse than that of the Jews!"

Few lived outside the feudal system. The Church participated, as feudal lord. Local priests were attached to a village or manor. Those who did not live in homage of mouth and hands were few—pilgrims, wandering friars, itinerant merchants, troubadours, and other social outcasts.

If we look at a map of Western Europe in about 800, manorial society predominates. Trade slowed to a trickle of luxury goods. Manors were self-sufficient entities, and commerce mainly local. Inside the manor the quality of life was regulated by the lord's administrators and by his seigneurial court. The lord's power, and that of his court, included everything of concern to his vassals.

The law applied in feudal tribunals rested in the main on two sometimes inconsistent principles: personality of laws and customary law applied over a given territory. The former principle arose because former Roman subjects and those groups which had, in the last days of the Western Roman Empire, adopted Roman law were accustomed to being ruled by Roman legal principles, but each group had its own customary law as well. The pattern of conquest often brought a victorious group with one legal system in control of lands occupied by tillers with another legal system. The late Empire established the legal principle of the "personality of laws." In the courts, and in dealings among themselves, each member of each group was in theory entitled to "his own" or "her own" law, that is, to the law of her or his group: Roman, Burgundian, Visigoth, and so on. As the Archbishop of Lyons remarked, it was not unusual that of five persons gathered together, each would claim the right to be judged by a different law.

The principle of personality of laws did not survive, except in isolated cases, but gave way to the uniform application to all persons within a given area of the same law, dictated by the seigneur and based in major part upon customs or immemorial usage. The feudal relation was seen as justifying enforcement of the same rules against all vassals of a particular lord within a particular territory. The court with power to decide and to state the rule of decision, says Philippe de Beaumanoir in 1283, is "that where sleeps and arises" the defendant.

There were, moreover, practical impediments to the personality of laws: intermarriage made inquiries about origins difficult; the legal systems of different groups were incomplete and most contained no reference to feudal social relations; most judges were untrained in the laws they were to apply, and even illiterate.

The notion of a "personal" law survived only for those—such as the merchants—who had a special status and who fought to have it recognized.

The displacement of the personality of laws, which had occurred by the eleventh century, left Western Europe under the rule of a patchwork system of local customs, influenced in varying degrees by Roman law. In Germany, the Low Countries, and the northern two-thirds of what is now France, the old customs furnished the basis of law, although a few legislative decrees of territorial overlords may have been acknowledged. England, despite its Roman occupation, had never been brought into the Roman legal orbit. A feudal system of land tenure was functioning at the time of the Norman Conquest, but English law after 1066 was heavily infused by northern French—more precisely, Norman—customary law.

Southern France, Italy, and non-Moorish Iberia retained nominal allegiance to Roman law. The Visigothic compilation of Alaric, the *Liber Judiciorum* of 654, and a few local works were copied and studied, but the contracts and other writings of the period display ignorance of Roman legal principles, and the feudal legal relation was, of course, not regulated by Roman law.

In all of these regions, procedure in the secular feudal courts was uniformly slow, arbitrary, and unfair to the lower orders of society. It was characterized by reliance upon an oral tradition of custom maintained by the lord and his officers and judges. An inquest might be held to determine the content of the customary law, with a sort of jury whose members were called "inquestors," *coutumiers*, or (by a French ordinance of 1270) *turbiers*. The presence of such persons may have provided some protection, but it also multiplied the opportunity for fraud and bribery. Appeal for denial of judgment, or false judgment, was in theory possible, but the hierarchy of appeal was blurred until the establishment, much later, of strong monarchies. And careful attention to custom was no guarantee of justice. Pope Urban II wrote to the Count of Flanders in 1092: "Dost thou claim to have done hitherto only what is in conformity with the ancient custom of the land? Thou shouldst know, not withstanding, the Creator hath said: My name is Truth. He hath not said: My name is Custom." Beaumanoir regretted the incidents he witnessed in which worthy people of small means lost through delay all they might have gained if they had won in court.

The life of the tiller in this milieu was regulated by the round of feudal obligations. The family worked on the lord's domain, tilled its own plot, obtained its necessities from the manor, and had the right to use common and waste land. (This last right would assume great importance in the centuries to come.) The family was obliged to provide troops or provisions for the lord's armed retinue. It was bound to the land, and could not sell either the land or most movable goods, or transmit them to a future generation, or marry, or trade, without the consent of the lord and perhaps the payment of a tax. The lord had obligations, too, and in years of bad harvest his storehouses were to be open to ensure that his vassals did not starve. The legal system was a world apart, run by men who spoke "*Moult bele: le Latin.*" and who knew words, as one French custumal says, which the ordinary man does not understand though they be spoken in French.

Such a social system did not need a law of commerce. The "great towns" were little more than large fortified villages, great in southern Europe only because a greater lord than any other in the region resided there, and great in the north—where lords lived in the countryside—because a bishop or archbishop had his seat there. Trade between the years 500 and 1000 consisted of goods for the ruling class: silks, spices, jewelry, and other items light in weight so that a small caravan could carry merchandise of a great total value over land routes from the Orient.

Under pressure from artisans and petty traders in the feudal hierarchy, and from traveling merchants who acknowledged no direct feudal tie, lords were forced beginning in the twelfth century to codify and regularize the chaotic and uncertain body of customs they administered. In Provence, in the south of what is now France, an area which was then a battleground for Mediterranean domination, a book of legal rules for magistrates was published, drawing mainly upon Roman sources. In about 1150, a legal writer, probably at Arles, wrote a similar work, notable for its practical flavor, in the Provençal dialect. In 1283, a royal official of astounding sagacity wrote the *Coutumes de Beauvaisis*, the first of many compilations of the dozens of customary law systems at work in the patchwork of French feudal sovereignties. The author, Philippe de Beaumanoir, notes that he relied for authority first on the customs of his region, and if custom was silent, on the custom of a neighboring region and then, if all else failed, on the prevailing custom in the *pays du droit coutumier*, the north of France. Beaumanoir never openly embraces Roman law, but his discussions of contracts, civil wrongs, and royal power echo Roman texts.

At the same time, the noble class began reluctantly to accept some merchant practices, at least if the lord of the manor could make money through tolls and taxes. Provisions in many collections of local customs regulated merchant dealings, providing a market area and an occasional market fair within which exchange could regularly occur, monitored by the lord's men. In 1283 in Beauvais, the fine was five sous for beating up a fellow-citizen, but it increased to sixty sous if the citizen was in or on the way to the market.

Putting the *coutumes* in writing, originally authorized by an *ordonnance* of St. Louis in the thirteenth century but systematically undertaken only much later, was a sign of the consolidation of feudal rule and of the emergence of a king or prince at the head of the feudal hierarchy in a particular region. The study of the *coutumes* signaled the rise within the feudal system of a social stratum of lawyers, whose special task it was to discover, study, and state the law. Later writing of the *coutumes* was sponsored by the two groups which had both the resources to pay for such studies and an interest in ending feudal particularism: the Church and royalty.

CANON LAW AND THE ROMAN CATHOLIC CHURCH

For if a man consider the original of this great ecclesiastical domain, he will easily perceive that the Papacy is no other than the ghost of the deceased Roman Empire, sitting crowned upon the grave thereof. For so did the Papacy start up on a sudden out of the ruins of that heathen power.

Thomas Hobbes, in *Leviathan*, was right: by the beginning of the fifth century the Papacy was holding together what remained of the dismembered Empire. The primacy of Rome in the Western Church was established by Pope Innocent 1 (402–417); by the accession of Leo I (the Great) in 440 the Pope's temporal authority around Rome had become considerable. Little more than one hundred years had passed since Catholicism had been legalized by the Empire in the Edict of Milan (313).

The Church's claim to temporal hegemony was betokened by Pope Leo's crowning, on Christmas Day 800, of Charlemagne as Emperor of the Holy Roman Empire. The Empire, built by exaction of homage from lesser lords, had little claim to be holy, and no claim at all to be Roman. Within a few years after Charlemagne's death in 814, it had also ceased to be an empire.

The Pope's claim to have placed Charlemagne in the line of Roman emperors rested upon two of the Church's dominant ideas. The first of these myths was that the Roman Empire had been prophesied in Scripture, as the last of the four kingdoms to reign before the final conquest of God's armies and the Last Judgment. "The world is growing old," wrote a contemporary scholar, "we live at the end of time." If this were so, then the Church temporal was logically, historically, and as veritably as the Scripture, the successor to the Roman Empire, a view maintained by men as diverse in time and temperament as Pope Leo III and Dante.

Second, the Church ideologically and organizationally reflected feudal society, at once exacting loyalty from its myriad sovereignties and providing their ideological foundation. John of Salisbury wrote, as Barrows Dunham has reported, that

> the husbandmen were the feet of the body politic—nearest the ground and needing guidance, but essential alike to movement and repose. . . . One must understand that when John of Salisbury described husbandmen [in this way] . . . he thought there really was such a body with precisely such feet. After the same manner, the assertion that the Church is the body of Christ was intended quite literally.

As it expanded its temporal power and gained new converts, the Church built an ideology which saw in the pyramid of feudal obligation, with the husbandmen as tillers at its base, a parallel to its own pyramidal organization, with the tillers as the mass of faithful.

The Church's law claimed jurisdiction coterminous with the Church's concerns. The ecclesiastical courts coveted the power to decide all disputes involving the welfare of souls, and pressed the secular courts to apply canon law to all such disputes as well. The conflicting claims of secular and canon law courts is a recurrent issue in the eleventh through the fourteenth centuries. By contract, too, as we have seen, the Church's tribunals might be chosen as forums for purely secular disputes. The Church's libraries and monasteries were centers of learning and study of Roman law texts. Indeed, each diocese claimed—and enforced in the ecclesiastical courts—the right to license all teachers of the liberal arts.

The Church, after the fall of Rome, had fallen victim to the same centrifugal forces as the other institutions of Europe: the primacy of the Roman see was metaphorical, communication with outlying bishoprics absent. Yet ecclesiastical courts did sit, and the Church had centers of power removed from Rome. At Salzburg, for example, a bishopric was founded in 739, and a cathedral was begun in 767. From the monasteries and episcopal residences came manuals of ecclesiastical law, probably based on the Theodosian Code of 438, on abridgments of the Code, and on memories of

Roman law and customs. The English historian Sir Paul Vinogradoff has written of a "constant, though thin, stream of legal learning running through the darkest centuries of the Middle Ages, that is, from the fifth to the tenth." That stream runs from and through the centers of churchly learning.

And the Church had power, even when it did not have troops to enforce its will. It was a feudal overlord: from early in the feudal age, prelates had accepted the homage of tillers, knights, and petty nobles, and added to its wealth through property left it by the wealthy and pious. The secular courts could inflict death, but the ecclesiastical tribunal could excommunicate and thereby condemn souls. The Church's centralization and temporal authority reached their apogee during the Crusades. To the revival of law study in this period, the Roman law searchers of the later bourgeois revolution owe almost all their accurate knowledge of the Roman texts. Renewal of interest in Roman legal learning progressed with the Church's fortunes, taking a qualitative leap in the reign of Pope Gregory VII (1073–85), the "merchant Pope." The Catholic Church was the state church of the emerging Western European monarchs and other feudal overlords, excepting only the remaining Moorish holdings on the Iberian peninsula.

The beginnings of royal centralization and the return of trade spurred economic growth. A royal entourage and a centralized Church at the "head" of the feudal body required the lower parts to supply it nourishment. Not to tax the analogy, the tillers and producers produced more than enough to support the manorial economy and the reviving cities, and their temporal and spiritual masters could expect more of the surplus to fund their own activities.

A part of the economic surplus was channeled to lawyers and legal researchers. Pope Gregory VII, with the support of the merchants whose favor he courted, founded a law school at Bologna which began to reassemble the texts of Justinian, great portions of which were rediscovered in a Florentine manuscript. The words of Justinian were invested with Papal authority, and upon these "ruins of that heathen power" the structure of canon law was erected. The "Four Doctors"—Bulgarus, Martinus, Ugo, and Jacobus—their teacher Irnerius (d. 1135), Azo, and Vacarius (who even taught at Oxford) wrote copious glosses, or notes, on the words of Justinian. The name "glossators" is given to this movement, and the principal figure is Accursius, who in the thirteenth century assembled all their work into one great gloss.

At the same time, scholars of the Church's own internal law collected the laws, decrees, opinions, and rulings of Church authority. In about 1140 Gratian published his *Concordantia Discordantium Canonum* ("The Concordance of Discordant Canons") which attempted to systematize and rationalize ecclesiastical legislation up to that time. It formed the first section of the *Corpus Juris Canonici* in 1528, which until the nineteenth century remained the fundamental document of the canon law, and was indeed the basis of all future codification of ecclesiastical law. From this beginning, canon law developed by Papal decree, official interpretation, and the process of litigation in the ecclesiastical courts.

But the Church, having saved the texts of the old Roman law, and having claimed to inherit the mantle of the old Roman Empire, found itself too easily embarrassed by the interpretations of Roman law made by able lawyers in the service of merchants or the secular state. The Roman texts as interpreted by the canonists, and the Church's own decrees, texts, and opinions were legislated into primacy: the study of civil (that is, Roman) law was forbidden to monks in 1180 and to priests in 1219; in 1234 Henry III ordered the sheriffs of London to close the schools of civil law.

Throughout the Middle Ages, canon lawyers struggled with the problem of reviving trade. We have seen that Roman law, which underlay much of canon law, was solicitous of the interest of merchants. For the canonists, however, a central problem was resolution of the Roman texts with the Church's moral teaching. A religion which began as the faith of persecuted victims of commercial Roman civilization had for centuries maintained that being a merchant was suspect if not immoral. That this same Church should also claim to inherit Roman law was, during all of capitalism's rise, the weakest point in the armor of the Church intellectual.

One aspect of the problem was that it was difficult for the Church to sanction a legal system built upon the ideal of "law" in the sense of highly structured rules for administration by a rigid system of secular and ecclesiastical courts. Saint Paul, in the First Epistle to the Corinthians, had preached charity instead of justice and had recommended resort to arbitration by a pastor, or by friends, as being far preferable to litigation. Saint Augustine said the same. It was not until the twelfth century that the dilemma was resolved.

By then, the revival of the Roman law had become an important aspect of the Church's consolidation of secular and churchly authority, and the Church abandoned any pretense of creating an apostolic community of the faithful. St. Thomas Aquinas defended this decision; he argued that Roman law, like the works of Aristotle and certain other pre-Christian writings, was based upon reason, and was therefore independent of religious belief.

The Church maintained that it cared for the soul, and defined its claims for temporal power as well as its decisions in particular cases upon that concern. In the law of crimes, for example, the Church revived the extensive and, for the times, enlightened Roman law about the element of intent in criminal justice: a person could not be punished for committing a crime unless that person had the capacity to choose between good and evil and had in fact chosen evil. Children, lunatics (they are punished by the fact of their madness, the Roman text had said), and those who did wrong by accident were not punishable. Imprisonment, the Church taught, might be preferable to capital punishment, as giving the offender a chance to reflect on his or her wrong. In the midst of legal systems dominated by customary practices of vengeance and blood feuds, this was an innovative spirit.

Procedure in canon-law courts was more regular and predictable than in the arbitrary feudal tribunals. Written demands and defenses were normal practice much earlier than in secular tribunals, and written records of testimony and judgments were similarly more common in ecclesiastical courts. Written demands tended to focus the dispute, particularly in commercial cases, and a record of testimony permitted analysis of the versions given by different witnesses. The Christian courts even permitted cross-examination.

But the written procedure of the ecclesiastical trial was not universally approved. Some critics regarded it as dangerous. "Any pen will do to recount anything whatsoever," observed a German nobleman during a lawsuit. Forged documents, charters, and donations abounded, and charges of fraud and chicanery were often leveled against ecclesiastical judges. The detailed and extensive written contracts favored by merchants, particularly in the south of France and in Italy, may have been designed as a response to fears of perjury or fraud in court, and to avoid any question as to what was actually agreed upon.

After centuries of thinking of oaths as sacrilege and blasphemy, the Church accepted in the eleventh century the view that testimony under oath was the most satisfactory means to find out the truth. The oath insured divine retribution for the mendacious. Resolving disputes by sworn testimony was surely more rational than trial by battle and trial by ordeal, which had—along with other mystical means of determining truth—found support in the secular law of entire countries. The Church also encouraged the search for other means of determining truth. In criminal matters, this view led by a grotesque logic to torture as being the best means to induce the accused to tell all.

Merchants, in their contracts, often designated an ecclesiastical court as the forum for any eventual dispute. And once the Church had sanctioned the oath, it was used to seal bargains as well and thus gave the canon-law courts jurisdiction over a breach of contract whether or not the parties had chosen to have the dispute judged there.

Canon law adopted in large measure the Roman law of contracts, again with singular emphasis upon the moral element of bargain. For the Church's lawyers, the oath of fealty was a prime example of a binding and godly contract. Unilateral binding promises of all kinds, even those for which the promisor received nothing in return and which were therefore invalid under most secular legal systems, could be enforced under canon law. In fact, this was so common that if the unilateral promise were made under oath, and the promisee sued, the promisor could not set up a counterclaim, for to satisfy the promise by canceling it with a reciprocal debt departed from the letter of the promisor's oath.

The monasteries and bodies of clergy also provided precedents for the revival of merchant societies organized according to the Roman law of corporations; when the rights of these bodies were challenged by secular authorities, the merchants fell back upon the Roman law.

Many historians have discussed canon law of the Middle Ages as though its only concern with business was the problem of usury—lending money at interest. Such narrowness of vision is unfortunate and ill-informed. The Papacy itself, not to mention the thousands of churchly overlords of lesser rank, was a creditor and debtor of the rising merchant class. And Roman law, revived in clerical garb, proved ready to abandon earlier positions when the revival of trade demanded it. Of the early Church's attitude, Tracy Westen has written:

> In 325 the Council of Nicaea prohibited the taking of interest by clerics. St. Jerome and St. Ambrose both preached against it. In the fifth century Pope Leo extended the prohibition against clerics by using it to censure lay usurers morally. By 850 laymen exacting usury faced excommunication. Charlemagne's capitularies also prohibited the taking of interest. Finally, in 1139, the Second Lateran Council universally prohibited the taking of usury.

More legal talent was spent in devising means around these prohibitions than in drafting their terms, particularly as the Church's position as creditor grew. In the chapters that follow, we will discuss these evasions as they appeared in various countries at various times. The merchant had no need to defy the Church's proscriptions and thereby risk his soul: there was enough written doctrine in the Church's own storehouse to find a way around the most onerous proscriptions. The Church was especially likely to tolerate evasion on the part of the wealthy, since it stood to benefit when they succeeded in business. R. H. Tawney, in *Religion and the Rise of Capitalism*, remarks upon the history of the canon-law codes' prohibition on usury:

> The ingenuity with which professional opinion elaborated the code was itself a proof that considerable business—and fees—were the result of it, for lawyers do not serve God for naught. The canonists who had a bad reputation with the laity, were not, to put it mildly, more innocent than other lawyers in the gentle art of making business. The Italians, in particular, as was natural in the financial capital of Europe, made the pace, and Italian canonists performed prodigies of legal ingenuity.

"I will not enumerate the devices usurers employ," wrote Beaumanoir, "so as not to give counsel to such people on evading the law."

Casuistry was essential in construing the canon law; skillful evasion was preferable to direct disobedience, for the latter risked one's soul. The rising merchant class was weak enough and harassed enough without facing the threat of eternal damnation, which seemed to that age real enough. Later, when business was more confident, Dante recalled one version of the fate facing "the sorry throng" of usurers:

Thus farther yet, the utmost verge
along of that same Seventh Circle,

did I go, and all alone, where sat
the sorry throng.

Out of their eyes is bursting forth
their woe: now here, now there,
with hands they agonize against the
flames, against the soil aglow.

The Church had the power to excommunicate, as well as the power to burn at the stake, but burning was reserved for heretics; the doctrinal deviations of merchants were treated rather more kindly.

The canon-law courts, then, often decided disputes about trade and commerce, as well as matters more obviously related to salvation. With the demise of the personality of laws, each forum—feudal, religious, royal—applied its own rules. Not uncommonly, more favorable law and a more propitious procedure might await a litigant in one court than in another. When trade had developed to the point that large-scale "fairs" were held for sale and exchange, and port cities became international trading centers, this problem was solved by the merchants establishing their own courts. But earlier on, the choice of forum was crucial, and it remained of no small importance.

The background to the conflict over "jurisdiction," the power to render a binding judgment, lay in the personal nature of the feudal relation. A judgment to pay money or to deliver goods in one's possession is worthless unless there is a means to enforce it. The victor must be able to have at his command the force of someone with the authority of a sovereign in order to take, by force if necessary, that which the court says is owed. The problem was that feudal property was not "owned" by anyone in the sense that property is owned in bourgeois societies. All the possessions and rights of enjoyment which a vassal had were bound up in the feudal relationship of fealty. Feudal overlords coveted their judicial power in all controversies involving claims against any of their vassals. This was because any order against a defendant to pay money or do something else immediately and directly threatened the lord's overriding interest in the vassal's possessions and services, whether the vassal was an ordinary farmer or a minor lord being sued in the seigneurial court of his overlord.

This jurisdictional covetousness lay at the bottom of conflicts between ecclesiastical, seigneurial, and royal courts during the centuries before the bourgeoisie overthrew the feudal-royal regimes and put an end to the powers of ecclesiastical tribunals. Judicial business also meant fees for the class of court officials that an increasingly prosperous ruling class supported.

An example of the overlapping of secular and ecclesiastical jurisdictions is given by Beaumanoir. The case is a simple one: a cleric sues a layman, the vassal of the duke, for a debt of twenty pounds. The layman claims he paid the money back. Oh, no, replies the cleric: you may have given me twenty pounds, but that was a *loan* to me, not a discharge of your debt. I want judgment for my twenty pounds. If you want your twenty pounds, you must sue me before my monastic seigneur in an ecclesiastical tribunal. The account continues:

> We before whom these pleas are contested say to the cleric that if he does not respond to the layman's plea that he has lent the cleric something after the debt of twenty pounds was incurred, we will not constrain the layman to pay the twenty pounds, for he was not making a counterclaim when he said that he had lent the money with the intention of discharging the debt; but if he demands of the cleric something due at a time before the debt was made, or if he claims of him horses, or other beasts, or grain, or wine, or other things having no connection with the twenty pounds, we will oblige him to pay the twenty pounds and make his claim before the cleric's ordinary.

There is a great deal of medieval legal history in this short description. First, the cleric seems to be saying that the debt owed him could not be discharged by his debtor lending some money in return, the debtor having the apparently unstated intention of setting one debt against another. The layman had promised to *pay*, and the cleric apparently relies on the canon-law rule that a promise must be fulfilled to the letter. A bookkeeping entry is not fulfillment of the promise. This casuistry does not work, however, for whatever the canon-law courts might think of it, secular courts did not follow the Church in attaching such importance to the letter of the promise. The cleric next points out that in reality, the defendant-layman has raised a counterclaim, which the secular courts would not, in the customary-law region, recognize. Indeed, Beaumanoir, just a page or so before, has told us that "counterclaims do not arise in the secular court as they do in the Christian court." In the secular courts, the rule was that A had to sue B in the court of B's lord—where B *couchans* and *levens*—goes to bed and gets up. Neither A nor A's seigneur would tolerate B's lord adjudging a claim against A that B might want to bring up in the same lawsuit.

In the Christian courts, on the other hand, the Church's claim of jurisdiction over all the faithful, at least in certain matters, made it possible to recognize counterclaims, though not without some opposition from the secular lords. So the cleric, knowing the rule in the secular courts, turns it to his advantage by saying that the layman should sue him for his money before the Christian court held by the cleric's feudal seigneur or ordinary. Beaumanoir sees through this as well, for he distinguishes between an offsetting claim that is a *payment*, in effect and in intent, and other kinds of claims that might be raised in opposition.

The Church was, as we have sought to suggest, and as we shall see at dozens of different points below, an omnipresent force in European financial and legal development. As the largest landowner in Europe, it was committed to the defense of feudalism and with all its authority aided in the suppression of the peasant revolts which swept Europe. Those who wished to restore the image of a communal, apostolic church it denounced as heretics or shut up in monasteries.

The Church recognized clearly that free trade conducted by those who were vassals to no one, or vassals only in a technical sense, was profoundly corrosive of social stability. If ancient doctrine taught that trade was sin, the new political reality taught that traders threatened the feudal system. Yet the Church could not ignore the great wealth that trade accumulated, for only by tapping that wealth could ecclesiastical rulers build cathedrals and universities and live in the style to which they had become accustomed. The *potientores burgenses* might in some cases be unbearable, but there are instances of the Church supporting them against monarchs or feudal lords. And so, as we shall see, it sought to bring commerce within its universal system of theology, morals, and law. Within that system dwelt the Church's claim to have revived Roman law.

The Church translated Roman "natural reason" into "natural law" and set up God rather than the common consent of humanity as the arbiter of that law. But God rarely spoke directly to human beings; the casuistry of the canon lawyers put this divinely sanctioned law to practical secular use. The Church required good faith and equity in dealing; the emerging capitalists took over these terms and claimed that they meant the good faith and equity that a merchant would show according to the custom of the marketplace. If "honor among men" is the maxim, but thieves make the rules, then "honor among thieves" is the rule in practice. The Church tolerated only the "just price" and required payment of the "just wage," but if feudal bonds were destroyed or weakened and the forces of a market were at work, "just" could easily mean "what the market will bear."

ROYAL LAW

For every king is a sort of fountain, from which a constant shower of benefits or injuries rains down upon the whole population.

Thomas More's characterization of a king's power, though written in 1516 to begin a sharp attack on kingship, was typical of thought in the late Middle Ages. Five hundred years earlier there had been no kings in the modern sense of sovereign over an entire territory. The idea of royal power, and in particular of the absolute power to make laws and enforce them, began to develop in the eleventh century. Throughout this period, relations between monarchy and merchants were more often than not cordial, for the aims of both were often served by the same policies of consolidation.

Imagine the merchant of 1150 or so, criss-crossing Europe from Italy to the Low Countries, buying and selling. With a few other merchants, his caravan is equipped for travel and fighting. Private wars of vengeance and conquest make the journey dangerous, and danger is redoubled by knightly brigandage. In the chateaux he passes, troubadors sing of Girart of Roussillon. This outlawed knight wandered through the country with his wife and met a band of merchants. Girart's wife attempts to belie the merchants' suspicion that they have recognized the two. "Girart is dead," she says, "I saw him buried." "God be praised," reply the merchants, "for he was always making war and through him we have suffered many ills." Girart didn't have his sword, or he would have killed them on the spot. The Song of Girart summarizes the plight of the poor knights who in the wake of the Crusades have no work save private war and therefore turn to robbing merchants. They justify their brigandage by characterizing the merchants as usurers and engrossers.

In addition to outlaw knights, the merchant faced roads in disrepair, the wide Roman highways and bridges having long ago fallen into ruin. And, as he passed across the country, he was likely to be met with a hundred demands for tolls and taxes from petty local seigneurs. For his physical safety and that of his goods, every traveling merchant was a fighter.

Merchants and artisans in the cities had also to fight for their right to practice their occupations and engage in trade. Their uprisings against local seigneurs gave them the reputation of being "right puissant in arms."

Little wonder, then, that this class of traders came to rely upon powerful overlords and protectors. The Italian cities could amass fortunes and navies large enough to wrest control of Mediterranean trade routes from the Arabs; a smaller prince, duke, or duchess could concede merchant privileges to a city within his or her domain; an archbishop ruling an ancient city could sponsor trade within its walls; but the larger territorial overlords—the kings—were the longest term, firmest, and richest friends the merchants had.

The kings united their lesser nobles behind the Crusades and won control of important trading centers in the Eastern Mediterranean. They began to insist that the roads be kept up. The power to legislate, fallen into disuse since the ninth century, was revived in order to establish systems of national law and national courts. Royal legislation forbade private war, with varying success but with unvarying purposefulness. The cities, originally a product of bourgeois revolt and noble concessions, were brought under royal control and patronage. Merchant dealings were regulated in order to protect citizens against competition from foreigners and to enhance foreign-exchange revenues; the foreign policy of monarchs included establishing consuls abroad to protect the merchants. For the merchant, the king could be an important ally; for the king, the merchant could be an important means of raising money, and of ensuring a surplus of gold in the balance of international payments. For, though the mechanism of international trade was not well understood until the seventeenth century, the importance of a net surplus of gold was perceived early on.

There is a crucial distinction between unified royal power and the feudal system it first led and then helped break down. The feudal relationship rested upon personal homage, and combined in one person or institution the roles of owner and landlord, chief military defender, and lawgiver. This suzerainty, with its immediate personal possession of the land, may be contrasted with the notion of the state as a separate, *sovereign* entity, with only a distant, regulatory interest in the land.

This separation of ownership of the land from direct political control is a dominant theme of the Middle Ages. To give an example, the monastery of Lerins was overlord of vast domains just inland of Cannes, on the south coast of what is now France. Peasants, lesser nobles, and merchants did homage to the abbots, litigated in their courts, paid their feudal dues in kind, and lived in a society owned, governed, and defended by the monks and their armed retinue. By 1400, however, the role of the monastery had begun to change. It still controlled a great deal of land, including about half of the major trading city in the region, Grasse. But the courts, the policing function, and the business of military defense had passed into the hands of secular nobles, and by the end of the century were to be under the control of the French crown. The monks became landlords, collecting rents in money and goods from farmers and merchants, while certain noble families continued to exercise all the historic functions of suzerainty right up until the French Revolution, attesting that royal claims to power were incompletely realized.

In the thirteenth century legal writers begin to speak of kings as "sovereign," and to ascribe to them the authority attributed to emperors in Roman law. Ulpian's maxim, "What pleases the king must be taken for law," appears in Beaumanoir as a dictum of customary law—without attribution of its source—and Beaumanoir's discussion of sovereignty is among the first recognitions in France of a new sort of state power.

It is in England, however, that we gain the clearest idea of the fundamental notion of royal law and its relation to the demands of the rising merchant class. William, bastard Duke of Normandy, relying on a dynastic claim to the throne of England, crossed the Channel in 1066 and established the first modern state in Europe. On William's death his French possessions became less important, but the consolidation of central power in England, and its extension to Wales, Scotland, and Ireland in succeeding centuries, is remarkable.

With the power to govern, reinforced immediately by requiring all lesser nobles to take an oath to the king as their feudal overlord and they as tenants of his land—that is, of all England—came the power to pass laws governing the entire kingdom. To enforce these laws, royal officials took the place of local feudal officials, beginning the separation of landlordism from state power. Royal courts were armed with the power to dispense the king's justice, and they began by upholding the forcible dispossession of many nobles who had adhered to the cause of William's rival.

With this, feudal barriers to trade were struck down, though several centuries more were needed before the royal courts fashioned and applied laws which at all resembled eighteenth-century notions of contracts, property, and procedure.

A merchant and artisan class arose largely in the towns, which began to grow separately from the manorial economy during the reign of King John (1199–1216). Over a period of centuries the town burgesses established themselves on land nominally in the hands of feudal barons, but in reality increasingly controlled by the Crown and its officers. In the thirteenth century a "town" was considered to be all its inhabitants with equal status, but later the centralization of wealth and power in the hands of a few merchants and employers led to a separation of the "town"—the legal entity governed by these wealthy people—from the totality of the residents. The municipium, the lawyers argued, quoting the passage on corporations from the Roman Jurist Ulpian, is a legal entity capable of making contracts, selling its land to benefit the local government, and making its own laws.

While English "common law," applied by the royal courts, provided only scant and tortuous assistance to a merchant with a dispute about a contract, other courts that looked for their law to mercantile custom were established with the Crown's blessing. When, for example, the crown authorized a trading fair, drawing merchants from many countries, it also authorized a "fair court" to settle disputes arising between merchants at the fair. In the great Channel cities, originally five in number and in the eleventh century called the Cinque Ports—Dover, Hastings, Hythe, Romney, and Sandwich—special courts of marine and merchant law were established by port officials under royal auspices.

In 1361, in a port-city lawsuit, the defendant attempted to defeat a claim against him by invoking the common-law forms of trial. The court overruled the defendant, "since this court, which is the office of the admiral, will not be so strictly ruled as the other courts of the realm which are ruled by the common law of the land, but is ruled by equity and marine law, whereby every man will be received to tell his facts . . . and to say the best he can" in defense.

Basic principles of marine and merchant law—which came to the same thing in a country so dependent upon sea commerce—made great inroads upon common law, although the takeover was not completed until the bloody and tumultuous social upheavals of the seventeenth century.

The English pattern was repeated, with variations, elsewhere: an alliance between crown and merchants, the latter supporting the legislative and judicial power of the former in order to obtain uniform laws favorable to trade throughout a large area. The merchant repaid this debt by paying taxes and customs duties and in many cases by making huge loans to the Crown to carry on military policy abroad. These military policies might in turn—and usually did—benefit the merchants at home.

Scotland well illustrates this development, because the comparative wealth of its cities literally kept the Scottish monarchy in operation during the long years of struggle with England, and because Scots law borrowed heavily from both Roman and English ideas. Scotland was often swept by invasions from the sea, and coastal towns had become important by the eleventh century—an instance of towns achieving a special position due to monarchical needs for defense or territorial ambition. At the same time, the Scottish monarchy gained a firm hold on the clans and established a hereditary principle of succession. Through the towns, often with Flemish and English merchants as middlemen, passed Scotland's exports of wool, leather, and fish; in came simple consumer goods, largely from the Netherlands. The economic importance of the towns was recognized in a series of royal laws which granted them self-government and a monopoly over the export of goods, and which exacted in turn taxes and customs duties. The towns were recognized in the Scottish parliament, and by the fifteenth century their representatives were of equal status with the feudal barons. That which custom had established the Crown made into law, and in 1504 it was provided that only merchants could hold office in the towns.

Scotland developed a legal system separate from that of England, having had an alliance with France since 1295. This "Auld Alliance " brought with it French legal scholarship, and Scottish legal writing shows, both in the texts written by Scots lawyers and in the acts of the Scottish parliament, a great familiarity with Roman and canon law. Scotland, prior to the union with England, and largely to this day, applied rules derived from the Roman law. For the merchants of the Scottish towns, therefore, an alliance with the

Crown meant not only special privileges but a favorable law enacted and promoted under royal sponsorship.

What we see here is that royal aspirations toward territorial control coincided with the needs of merchants for a unified trading area. The ensuing alliance was a crucial factor in both the lawmaking of the rising bourgeois class and in the progress from merchant to industrial economies. This alliance was never consistently peaceful, for with the crown's help went Crown control, whether in the form of the "state capitalism" of the English Tudors, or the heavy taxation imposed by the French Bourbons. These measures either angered the unprotected, who moved outside the royal sphere of special protection to build positions of power from which to bring down the royally sponsored system of privilege, or weighed upon the rising class as a whole, fomenting angry discontent and spawning the teaching that good government governs little in the field of financial affairs.

LAW MERCHANT

Differing legal systems for different classes did not seem odd in the Middle Ages—no more so than differing systems erected upon different territorial bases. Nobles had extra rights; churchmen had their own set of privileges. The word "privilege" appears with great frequency in custumals, charters, and lawbooks, and usually denotes access to a special court or the right to a special favorable rule of law. The custumal of Amiens uses it to describe those who are "privileged" to sue and be sued in the royal court, where a more systematic and less delay-ridden justice awaits them.

It should not surprise us, therefore, to find that merchants had law of their own, brought back into Europe with the rebirth of trade. The "law merchant" was a form of international law, whose fundamental elements were the ease with which it permitted binding contracts, its stress on security of contracts, and the variety of devices it contained for establishing, transmitting, and receiving credit.

Throughout the Middle Ages, the application of merchant law to disputes about trade spread through the royal courts, the ecclesiastical courts, and even the feudal seigneurial courts. For the international merchant and trader, the law merchant was indispensable. The law merchant was, at least in theory, uniformly applied to dealings between merchants of every nation. As such, it promoted the consciousness of the bourgeois that he was a member of a class. The transformation of this international law into national law must therefore be a major theme of our discussion.

Perhaps the clearest analogy is to the present-day law of admiralty. If a Dutch and an English ship collide on the high seas and lawsuits result, any court—English, Dutch, or other—will apply the law of admiralty, a body of international law which is customary where not modified by treaty. This law determines matters from rules of the seaways, to rights of seamen to ownership of cargo, to the rules of jettison in the event of shipboard crisis. The very universality of this law encourages the reference of maritime disputes to special arbitration tribunals, rather than to courts whose judges may or may not be experts in the complexities of admiralty. Some countries have special courts of admiralty jurisdiction. These same features characterized the law merchant.

In 1622 the English courts were willing to summon merchants to testify about their customs and help the court to resolve a dispute. By late in the eighteenth century, Lord Mansfield said for the Court of King's Bench that the traders' law was not a special, unusual customary law, but was known to and would be applied by all of His Majesty's judges: "The law merchant is the law of the land."

NATURAL LAW

"Natural law," as the term came to be used by the bourgeoisie, meant divine sanction for using force and violence in a certain way. The idea that natural law might mean something different from the Roman Catholic claim of divine sanction for its own laws goes back to the communal urban uprisings of the eleventh and twelfth centuries; when a number of revolutionaries in cities across Europe banded together to establish the right to trade within a certain area, they bound themselves by a communal oath. Invoking the name of God, they pledged that they would stand together as a single body. This rudimentary claim for divine sanction is the beginning of the bourgeois, *burgens*, burgess ideal of natural law, in opposition to that of the Church and feudal hierarchy.

The self-conscious development of a secularized natural law begins somewhat later, however. In the sixteenth century at Bourges, a group under the leadership of Cujas began to reinterpret the Roman texts in light of "humanism" and under the influence of Renaissance philosophy. At the same time, Calvin and his followers at Geneva sought to establish an ecclesiastical state which brought the Vulgate Gospel and the pursuit of wealth into harmony with one another. The radical Protestants who followed, in Geneva, in France, in the Low Countries, and in England, refined and developed the notion of a self-evident order of the universe which mandated freedom of contract and property.

In the 1600s and 1700s, a succession of writers united this form of natural law with the principles of Roman commercial law. Domat, whose *Les Loix civiles dans leur ordre naturel* was written between 1689 and 1697, proclaimed that Roman law as reinterpreted in France contained "natural law and written reason."

In seventeenth-century Scotland, Lord Stair published *The Institutions of the Law of Scotland*, a natural-law-based treatise relying on revived Roman law. Zeiller, an Austrian born in 1753, published *Das naturliche Privat-Recht* early in the nineteenth century, comparatively late but in time to have an impact on the Austrian Civil Code of 1811, of which he was principal draftsman. Pufendorf's *Law of Nature and of Nations* was widely translated, appearing in England in 1722, and the works of Hugo Grotius, proclaiming the social contract, freedom of the seas to all commercial maritime nations, and the principles of free commerce, appeared early in the seventeenth century.

This array of dates and countries reflects the outpouring, from the sixteenth century on, of prodigious efforts to state and justify a legal system which would accommodate the needs of a prosperous and strong merchant class. These efforts looked backward to old customs and, more often, to "rediscovered" Roman law. They looked forward to the liquidation of feudal obligations and to the creation of civil societies based on freedom of contract and of property. And they laid the basis for the waves of legislation to assure these ends which accompanied and were necessary to further the bourgeois revolutions.

The blend of history with ideology was evident and powerful; the class whose interests these writers represented meant to take power, and were already—or were soon to be—convinced of the historical necessity for doing so. Yet this blend reflects the truth that revolutions do not do away with all old institutions, but keep two kinds of rules derived from the past: those which reflect concessions wrested by the now-victorious class from the old regime, and those which—as in the case of France with marital customs—

reassure the populace that nothing too drastic has been done. After the people have done their work in ousting the old regime by force of arms, the new regime has need of rules to force the people to return to their homes and stop fighting before the revolution endangers the interests of the newly dominant class. The Cromwellian reaction against the Levelers and the White Terror of the French Revolution are two examples of this. We shall have occasion later to examine the proclamation of the Code Napoléon, which ably combined, in the rhetoric of a firmly Bonapartist Conseil d'Etat, the natural-law ideals of the Revolution with assurances that while everything had changed, everything had remained the same.

PART TWO

THE MERCHANTS SEEK A PLACE IN THE FEUDAL ORDER (1000-1200)

3.

INTRODUCTION

Cutting history into slices is a risky business. If we say that generally in the year 1000 the economy of Western Europe was rural and agricultural, we must add that in the same year cities like Venice and Amalfi were engaged in active trade with Byzantium and other places, their ships plying the Mediterranean between Constantinople and Alexandria, selling slaves and other goods and buying products of Byzantine manufacture and luxury items brought over the land routes from the East. There was a substantial change in the patterns of trade, and therefore of bourgeois life, between 1000 and 1200 in Western Europe. The changes can be enumerated: trade routes were opened into Italy from the East and from Italy westward throughout Europe; mercantile law favorable to trade continued to spread; agricultural production was reorganized to enhance productivity; the bourgeoisie in dozens of urban centers rose up to gain the liberty to partake in the profits of trade.

The Crusades, which called on the seapower of the Italian city-states, opened a new phase in Western European commerce. Italians displaced Arabs and Byzantines as the dominant seafarers of the Eastern Mediterranean. Italy became a nexus: entrepôt for Eastern goods passing westward and for Western goods moving east, as well as banker for merchants, seigneurs, princes, and many others with a stake in trade. In France, England, the law Countries, and the Baltic region, new systems of exchange and distribution developed; from Italy, Eastern goods passed north and were traded for goods from these regions. This trade was carried on at markets and fairs, of which the most important took place in Champagne, 120 miles from Paris. Four small towns—Lagny, Bar-sur-Aube, Provins, and Troyes—held a succession of trading fairs throughout the year. Flemish cloth made from Scottish wool; French wheat, wine, and cloth; Scandinavian timber, tallow, iron, and copper; and English grain and wool were the principal moneymaking commodities of Western Europe. Luxury goods—spices, silks, gold, and jewels—were the principal imports from the East.

With the growth of trade came a revival of mercantile law, in the forms of rediscovered Roman law and the law merchant practiced at fairs and markets. Here, we will show how this revival was spurred by the Crusades, for the Byzantine Empire and Arabic civilizations had been a repository of the Roman legal learning and mercantile practice that had fallen into disuse in the West. We can trace, year by year and, thanks to the survival of many valuable documents, almost contract by contract, the increasing sophistication of merchants and their lawyers in institutionalizing the legal rules essential to their success. The focal points of this development were the Italian commercial city-states and the other cities along the Mediterranean littoral which were the first to be touched by the flow of commerce after the Crusades.

In the realm of agriculture and other "primary" economic activity, the period 1000 to 1200 saw great increases in absolute production and in individual productivity. Not only was the total acreage under cultivation increased, but seigneurs—mainly churchly ones—advanced the means of farming. Mines and forests began to be exploited systematically. These activities produced a surplus above what was needed for local consumption and fueled the growth of trade in two important ways. First, there was now something other than scarce silver and gold to trade for goods coming from the East. Second, the profits from selling these goods were applied by the Church, the bourgeoisie, and (to a lesser extent) seigneurs to further the growth of legal education and to support a growing class of lawyers and other professionals.

The spread of trade and the separation of artisanal from agricultural pursuits gave impetus to demands that artisans and merchants have a separate legal status—neither lord nor vassal. The word "bourgeois," as a term of art recognizing this status, appears in a charter of 1007. A few seigneurs, sensing that they might profit from fostering commerce, acceded to these demands.

Most were not so pliant, and yielded only after armed clashes with the city dwellers. The towns in which the bourgeoisie had acquired a measure of freedom from feudal constraints became nodal points along trade routes. They remained centers of discontent with feudal law.

We here take up these four themes—the growth of commerce, the spread of mercantile law, the systematization of agricultural production, and the bourgeois uprisings—and show the unifying force of legal ideology in the struggle of the bourgeoisie. In our discussion, we emphasize the primitive character of bourgeois social relations and bourgeois ideology. At this early stage, bourgeois ideology was constrained by the technology of production to seek a place for small-scale, cooperative enterprises, and for relatively simple devices for commerce. The bourgeois sought recognition of a theoretically homogeneous class of workers, proprietors, sellers, and buyers—many of them former serfs—who wished in general to remake rather than overthrow feudal society. The deep and violent antagonisms among elements of this new class, and its appreciation of its irremediable conflict with the feudal structure, came later.

4.

THE CRUSADES: SEIZURE OF TRADE ROUTES AND SPREAD OF BOURGEOIS IDEOLOGY

The motives and means of the Crusaders were various, but the results of two hundred years of crusading in the Holy Land are clear. They are visible on the map of the Mediterranean, in the history of the Italian merchants, seafarers, and bankers, and in the revival of mercantile law in Italy and southern France and thence in the north and west. In sum, the Crusades were crucial events in the bourgeois remaking of Western Europe.

To describe these results, one must begin with a brief summary of the motives of those who preached participation in the Crusades and the tactics of those who went to battle.

The period of which we speak begins in 1095, when Pope Urban began to preach the First Crusade, and ends in 1291, when the last Christian territorial outpost at Acre fell to Sultan Qalawun. Crusading combined two worthy objectives—making the Holy Land safe for merchants and for religious pilgrimage—with a worthy means of accomplishing them, namely, getting an increasingly restive, violent, and socially unproductive class of soldiers, knights, and petty nobles out of the way.

The Holy Land had to be made available to Western merchants. The Byzantine (Eastern Roman) army had been defeated by the Seljuk Sultanate at Manzikert in 1071. The Fatimid Caliphs dominated Egypt. A number of other major entrepôts fell into Moslem hands, though Constantinople remained an important commercial center under Christian dominance. Moslem seapower was raiding Western shipping on an increasing scale. Yet, the demand for Eastern goods was increasing and had to be met.

There were religious reasons for undertaking a Crusade as well, for the Seljuk control of Christian shrines in the Holy Land was accompanied by Seljuk intolerance of Christianity and of Christian pilgrims. These pious motives were not unmixed: earlier, the Church had begun to preach the purifying effect of pilgrimages, in contradiction to earlier texts, but only after the Amalfitans had constructed a hostel in Jerusalem, and after it became apparent that transporting, feeding, and lodging pilgrims was good business.

The crusading army was recruited from that portion of the feudal ruling class which was most actively battling with the merchants. The Church and some of the more powerful seigneurs, aided by the nascent bourgeoisie, had already begun to struggle to curtail private feudal warfare and the impediments to trade posed by feudal tolls, tariffs, and outright brigandage. Seizing goods from itinerant merchants had become standard practice among the nobility: Pope Gregory VII, for instance, threatened King Philip of France with excommunication if he did not restore merchandise his agents had seized. Philip relented; he did not need to risk his soul for so little.

Crusading was a means of diverting private warfare to a different territory while promising a solution to the urgent problems of the poorer nobility and its knightly retainers. One such problem was that of distributing estates under the system of primogeniture. Primogeniture—whereby land went to the eldest son—had, in feudal law, replaced the system of parceling out family estates to all children equally on the death of their parents. Once primogenture was instituted, younger sons either took service as knight-vassals of another lord, entered holy orders, or were pensioned off with a small estate and a few peasants to till it. Such a petty noble on a small estate acquired an income almost entirely in kind, inadequate in a time of inflation and the increasing use of money. One response was to grind the peasantry further. A deed of the time refers to "all compulsory services . . . and . . . all those things which by violence knights are wont to extort from the poor." The class of petty knight-nobles settled their quarrels by private war, often occasioned by a personal insult, but with the object of gaining land or booty. Tolls charged to merchants for the right to cross the lord's land were another means of enrichment, and many lords also discovered that a castle provided a useful headquarters for a band of knightly robbers.

The Crusades offered this class personal salvation and a chance to fulfill the knightly duty of fighting while also winning treasure and acquiring estates in the Holy Land. It was an opportunity of the same kind, but of a greatly different order, as that offered in the earlier battles against the Moslems in Spain and Provence. Its results can be seen in the complete dominance of the feudal government established in Palestine by the land-hungry younger sons of nobility. From the upper reaches of this group came the feudal overlords, and from its lower orders came the knights—the troops on horseback. The foot-soldiers were drawn along by their noble masters, or by the same economic and demographic forces which pushed new lands into cultivation and increased the populations of urban centers. Political control of the Crusades began in the hands of the feudal nobility, checked by the efforts of the Papacy to pit one group against another.

The direct intervention in Palestine of the Italian merchants began in 1098, three years after Pope Urban issued the call to arms. In that year, Genoa was ceded a market, a church, and thirty houses in Antioch, agreeing in return to assure communications with Italy and to support Antioch's over-lord, Bohemond.

Before this, the Italian cities had grown by making economic treaties with both Christian and Moslem powers rather than by directing large-scale conquest, and so their diplomacy had not been altered by Byzantine reverses. By 1098, however, the Crusaders had made substantial land gains in Palestine and Syria. Genoa then sought its concession in Antioch. Next Venice sought to add to its established power in the Eastern Mediterranean, built in long association with the Byzantine Empire. Pisa sought to maintain in the East the competitive position that consistently characterized its relationship with Genoa.

Soon, Pisa and Genoa were actively trading in the Christian areas, making deals with various feudal lords. The Eastern trade, conducted almost entirely by sea, was in their hands. The other Italian cities contended with Venice's favored position in Constantinople, and developed trade between Italy and the Nile delta, assuring sources of products from all three Eastern Mediterranean outlets to the West.

The Western Christian feudal princes, however, failed to hold onto their Palestine fiefdoms; the last Christian outpost fell in 1291. The Italian city-states lost ships and men in support of Christian military efforts, but managed to retain the right to trade in the region. The fighting orders of knights—Templars and Hospitalers—suffered battle casualties but retained their role as bankers. There is persuasive evidence that the mercantile and banking interests in Palestine were actively doing business with both sides. Such activity was unavoidable if trade for goods coming from the East by caravan was to be carried on at all. Some Italian merchant combines carried the matter further, however, and sold quantities of war materiél to the Moslem princes.

The Crusades represented, therefore, an economic opportunity, quite apart from which side was militarily victorious. The opportunity represented by the increase in Eastern trade could not, however, be exploited without legal and institutional forms to permit the pooling of capital to fund large sea and land enterprises, to assure a protected market for the merchants who did gather the necessary capital, and to provide for the distribution of goods from the East in exchange for those from the West.

Few records remain that could give us an indication of how people's lives were affected by these changes in law and in legal institutions. Only Genoa has left us a rich collection of contracts concluded among merchants in the mid-1100s, in which we can read something of the life of one group, and try to infer what the lives of the other groups must have been like.

In 1099, just as the Crusades had opened the East and Genoa was beginning a period of phenomenal economic growth, the city's leading merchants and capitalists formed an organization, the Compagna, under an elected leader. The Compagna was not a business organization; it was probably more like a corporation, possessing a fictitious "personality," and members bound themselves to the organization for a short term, perhaps a year. The organization may have been secret. Its members in time came to believe, if they did not at the beginning, that they were the vanguard of a new class. Soon the Compagna seized political power and installed itself as the commune—the oath-bound leadership group—of Genoa. The party had become the government; the government was the party.

We find mention at this time of a new group of professionals, identified principally with the large merchants, but also working for and with smaller entrepreneurs and even at times with the peasantry. These were the lawyers. There are distinctions in their formal titles: notaries (*notarii*) generally drafted contracts and other business papers while advocates pleaded in court, but other names are used too, such as *magister*, from the Latin "master," an official, and *scribus*, scrivener, scribe. Whatever the name, suddenly increasing numbers of them begin to appear, and they begin to use techniques adapted to new economic needs, and to show signs of new legal learning. By 1100, the majority of northern Italian contracts were drafted by trained lawyers.

The presence of lawyers, and the increasing use of standard forms of words to spell out various types of agreements, indicates the existence of a legal system—rules of law and courts to enforce them—which would give a predictable legal effect to certain types of contractual promises. For those who fulfill the terms of a contract willingly and without question, the written version of the agreement is necessary only as a reminder of the obligations each party has undertaken. But when one person gives a large sum of money to another to outfit a ship, on condition that the latter raid the Moslem coast and return to divide the booty, the writing must make it possible for the merchant to get his share of the loot, and for the sailor to limit the merchant's percentage to whatever it was they agreed.

It follows, therefore, that if many contracts from a certain period use new legal terms and record new types of business association, the system of state power has recognized or is about to recognize these terms and forms. The best-educated lawyer would not fill a contract with his or her learning if the judges were still unaware of such things.

Beginning in Genoa at the time of the Crusades, and spreading to the Mediterranean littoral and northward along the trade routes, a new law gradually came into use, specially adapted to the needs of the merchants. This law required the presence of persons skilled in the drawing up of contracts, so lawyers appear and identify themselves as such. Before, charters and contracts had been drafted by men possessing no apparent formal legal training, often employees of a religious house or minor government officials. In even more distant times, the term notary referred to employees of the early Frankish kings, the men who wrote out legislation, edicts, and charters and worked under the direction of the Chancellor, always a cleric. As evidence of the improved formal training of the new notaries, their contracts are drafted in a Latin which is more refined, accurate, and consistent than before.

(The first contracts written in the everyday language of the people also date from this period—particularly in southern France—but they are generally ill-informed about legal categories and ideas.)

Other more significant changes appeared at this time: modes of association permitting the combination of capital by two, three, four, and soon dozens of participants; methods of transporting credits from one port to another, the forerunners of letters of credit and letters of exchange in international commerce; the refinement of contract law and the elaboration of methods of sale and exchange; the techniques of banking, permitting the pooling of thousands of small amounts of capital in the hands of an investor, a merchant banker.

The devices for amassing capital in an expanding economy deserve study first. In the eleventh and twelfth centuries Genoa developed the *societas marts*, similar to devices used in other cities under other names at about the same time (*commenda, colleganza*). One partner would advance from two-thirds to all of the capital for a round-trip sea voyage out of Genoa. If the voyage failed, each party bore his or her own loss. If it succeeded, the profits were divided in an agreed proportion, guaranteed to provide a rate of return of up to 150 percent. This sort of contract was in reality a disguised loan or deposit. It bears clear marks of Roman origins, specifically the Roman contract of mandate, but more closely resembles the Byzantine conception of this sort of agreement.

In 1163, a merchant named Stabile mandates Ansaldo Garraton in a *societas maris*:

> Stabile and Ansaldo Garraton have formed a societal into which, according to their declarations, Stabile has brought a capital of 88 lire, and Ansaldo 44 lire. Ansaldo takes this capital, to cause it to increase, to Tunis or wherever else must go the vessel which he will take—that is, the vessel of Baldizzone Grasso and Girardo. On his return, he will remit the profits to Stabile or to his representative to be divided. Deduction being made for the capital, they will divide the profits in half. Done in the house of the Chapter, the 29th of September 1163.
>
> And further, Stabile gives Ansaldo the authority to send his money to Genoa by whatever vessel he wishes.

Within a very short time, two elaborations of this simple two-party association developed: the association of *loci* and the merchant bank. *Loci* were shares in a ship. With the coming of large vessels, and the need at the same time to draw into commerce the liquid savings of many people, division into shares was a logical development. In essence, in the *loci* a number of shareholders mandated a ship captain to make a voyage. The shares themselves were movable property, and could be sold, exchanged, or pledged as security for debt. Often many small amounts of money would be pooled to buy one share. The backers' control over the use of the mandated capital is typical of maritime contracts of association.

In the inland cities of Lombardy—which became clearing houses for the goods brought by sea into Venice, Pisa, and Genoa—more generalized forms of money-gathering developed. Small capitals and large were gathered from those of every class—from the landed estates of seigneurs, the small workshops of artisans who sold for cash, the cash hoards of peasants whose land was held of no seigneur, the little sums of money a worker or peasant could get by selling off a valued possession—and given to a merchant banker, who would in turn finance buying and selling trips to the fairs and markets. Entrusting money in such a way bore close resemblance to the Roman contract of deposit.

Commercial contracts also begin to change during this period, reflecting the infusion of new legal ideas and the growing power of a class that possessed capital and the means to increase it. The contract of sale becomes important as a source of rights rather than as a mere adjunct to possession. In the uncertainty of feudal society, possession of property was the essence of ownership; paper rights were worthless without a system to ensure their speedy and unquestioned recognition. The farmer on his plot, the peasant with a herd of sheep, the small artisan with his supply of wool—all regarded possession as the primary token of their rights. Similarly, the contracts of sale along the Mediterranean littoral prior to 1000 are really nothing more than receipts given by the seller to the buyer to acknowledge payment of the price and to transfer physical possession of the property. Often, these briefest of documents mention no legal provisions at all, and some simply warn that anyone disturbing the acquirer's possession shall "incur the wrath of God and suffer with Judas the torments of eternal hell." Others mention that "ecclesiastical and Roman law" require a writing to evidence the sale. These primitive documents were little more than "fossil remains" of Roman legal tradition.

By the end of the eleventh century, however, in northwest Italy and later along the trade routes that led north and west, the Roman notion of sale had begun to reappear in contracts. The single most important legal idea to come out of this period is that of the contract as a uniting of wills, reflecting promises of one, two, or more people, which, *because of a legal system which exists to enforce them*, are binding without any other formality. Specifically, the newer contracts do not require *tradition*—the handing over—of the object sold or of some ritual portion of it to validate a sale. A contract of sale is entered into and reflected in a writing. This contract obliges the seller to deliver the item contracted for, and the buyer to deliver the price. That is the essence of the Roman-law contract of sale, which was bilateral and rested upon good faith, and sharply separated this contract from the delivery of the item sold and the payment of the price—the *agreement* to do these things was its essence.

So remarkable was this change that some early contracts are not content to adopt Roman legal language for a contract *emptio venditio*; they go on to say, for example, that "by the sole authority of the contract" the buyer may enter into possession of the thing sold.

If a sale is concluded only after the money and the land or goods are exchanged, the parties need only protect their rights to what they have acquired. Willing conclusion of a sale which creates, by mutual consent, the *obligation* to deliver land or goods and to pay money presupposes that sellers, buyers, or—more probably—their lawyers are conscious that some system exists to compel fulfillment of the reciprocal obligations.

The contract of sale also creates the possibility of continued trade relations. Because title does not pass when the contract is signed, parties can agree to sell future goods—the fruits of a harvest to come, the cargo of a ship not yet arrived. The sale can involve even more intangible items: one can agree to sell to another all his produce for a certain term, or to buy the stock of certain goods from a certain merchant or company of merchants. Here is perceptible movement away from the feudal idea of power being exclusively personal and immediate, implying the armed presence of the lord or his subaltern at every turn.

Another, even more revealing, indication of the presence of Roman legal precedents in emerging bourgeois institutions is the new consciousness on the part of lawyers of the possibilities of protection against fraud and coercion in sales, exchanges, and gifts. Were we to study only the records of the courts, picking up here and there a hint that such principles were applied to prevent overreaching, we would have a different picture than the actual contracts show us. In many contracts of the period, particularly in those areas of southern France and Catalonia associated with Genoa and Pisa, we see peasants, artisans, and other poorer folk selling, exchanging, or pledging for debt some item of property, usually land. Some of these contracts state that the sales are intended to raise cash to finance a trip to the Holy Land; they are records of the beginnings of pilgrimages, or of foot-soldier peasants following the example of a nearby powerful lord. For countless other contracts of sale, no motive is apparent: in the areas opening up to commerce at this time there seems to have been a wave of sales by poorer people to richer ones, particularly to ecclesiastical bodies. Perhaps some of the contracts reflect disguised loans, the item sold passing to the lender with an implied agreement to reconvey it when the loan was paid. The small amount realized in many of these sales seems to bear out such a hypothesis. Or perhaps small landholders, the last holdouts against the feudal system, were being driven to sell their lands and rent them back in order to raise capital with which to enter an increasingly cash-based economy. The insistent growth of cities as market centers, the monopolistic tendencies of urban culture, and the extensive changes in agriculture by the working ecclesiastical orders allow for this possibility.

Indisputably, though, the weak are making contracts with the strong, and the lawyers are working for the strong. We know that lawyers were beginning to come upon the provisions of the Roman law that served to protect the rights of weaker parties, because in the 1100s these provisions begin to be enumerated in contracts. However, the enumeration of the weaker party's rights is almost always the prelude to a term in the contract renouncing—waiving—these rights: protection for minors is waived; all rights based upon sex are renounced; the seller promises not to resist delivery of the thing sold on the grounds that he did not receive all the purchase price, or on the grounds that the price paid is pitiably inadequate; or the seller recites that if the value of his land should be greater than the price paid, he freely makes a gift of the difference to his buyer.

There must have been motives for inserting such clauses in contracts. In order to write them, the lawyers—most often in the 1100s notaries—would have to know that such Roman legislation existed, and they would have to have had some notion that the courts, in which the contract might be challenged, might apply these principles to invalidate the sale. The lawyers' attention to the possibility of litigation is shown in the parties' renunciation of procedural delays—to which Roman law gave them a right. Finally, in almost all the cases we know of, the contracts are written in Latin, another indication of the removal of the law from the control and consciousness of ordinary people.

We can thus reconstruct from surviving contracts and records three effects of the Crusades. First, merchants in the Italian city-states begin to struggle for governmental power or protection to permit them to trade. Second, this power is used to sanction devices, such as the *societas maris* of Genoa, which permit exploitation of the financial opportunities provided by increased trade with the East. Third, Roman-law principles of contract and property reappear to provide a framework for the expanding relations of trade. These developments appear first and most clearly in Italy, but they soon spread along the routes of trade to other places in the Mediterranean. We first describe, then seek to explain, the linkage of revived Roman law with the spread of trade.

At the beginning of the 1100s, or perhaps a bit earlier, there appeared a book entitled *Exceptiones Petri*. It had been written in Provence, the Dauphine, or in Lombardy—the absence of printing in that period meant that all books were hand-copied, so discussion of the "original" becomes problematic. But the plan of the *Petrus* bears closer resemblance to Justinian's codification than to compilations of Western origin, such as the Theodosian Code. It appears to have been used by lawyers in Catalonia, though not in Provence.

During the 1100s, the practice book *Lo Codi* appeared in Provence. Whether it was an official collection of rules or a private undertaking is a matter of dispute, but what is important is that its counsels agree in most particulars with surviving contracts of the time. Where there is a difference, *Lo Codi* chooses a Roman-law solution to a problem—such as that of the marketability of land—and ignores feudal restrictions.

In the light of books like *Lo Codi* and the *Exceptiones Petri*, and more fully through the surviving contracts of the time, we can measure the progress of the Roman law of commerce as it spread east and north from Italy. Early in the 1100s, as we have noted, Genoa and Pisa had developed competence in Roman law and a class of people to apply it. Roman law arrived later in those cities where the pace of trade began to quicken only when the First Crusade was well along. In Marseille and Aix, consciousness of Roman legal practice appears in the last half of the 1100s. For a brief period in the 1100s, Marseille enjoyed some independent financial power in Palestine, having been granted a trading concession by Fulk of Anjou, then King of Jerusalem, in 1136. The treaty was renewed in 1152. But the Marseille merchants, by comparison with the Italians who controlled the Palestine trade,were minor figures. By about 1160, Marseille had trading establishments in four Palestine cities, most of them ports, while in the same period the Genoese had their establishments in eleven cities. Marseille also had a shipbuilding industry; Richard the Lion Hearted embarked at Marseille for the Crusades in 1190.

Arles, a city which had never been entirely deserted during the early Middle Ages, shows a growth of population, an increase in trade, and a revival of Roman law a dozen years after the Marseille-Aix region. Other cities in Provence and Catalonia follow, reflecting the spread of trade through the areas which were in earliest contact with the Crusades and with the Crusading traders of the Italian cities and Marseille. From southern France, Roman law makes its appearance in commercial contracts at intervals well into the 1200s, all along the routes from the Western Mediterranean littoral to Flanders. It followed after the rise of the cities whose charters, statutes, and fundamental laws do not rest upon recognizably Roman principles. Roman law came later, with the spread of systematic and long-distance trade. It arrived in response to a clear need for its capital-pooling, trade-facilitating provisions, and it arrived under the sponsorship of those political and economic groups with the capital to fund centers to study it and to train acolytes in its mysteries.

Thousands of contracts survive from this period, and we have a very good picture of the spread of Roman legal ideas. We see the emergence of legal technicians laboring for a new class—the merchants—and for their allies in the feudal system—those ecclesiastical and secular seigneurs with cash and the desire to increase it through trade.

(The participation of Italian noble families in trade is common in this period; the French, on the other hand, retained the view that participation in trade was inconsistent with nobility, and a noble who did so lost his or her noble status. This did not, however, prevent French nobles from putting up capital as silent partners.) And we can guess at some of the effects of the resurgence of trade upon the rural working population. We do not always know exact prices, destinations, and goods shipped, however, because among the foremost counsels of the merchant at that time was that one must hide the details of one's business from one's competitors, and this included writing minor falsehoods in contracts.

In addition to thousands of private contracts we have charters and "statutes" of many cities. These fundamental documents often contain provisions of private law as well as details about administration. In addition, there are diaries, histories, and the records of the Italian universities with their faculties consecrated to the study of law.

Considerable debate exists over the question of where the Roman-law revival of the 1100s began. We think that the Roman law—not all of it, but whatever was convenient and necessary to commerce—was primarily borne along the routes of trade, and that the academic study of the surviving texts was then stimulated and financed by the financial and political powers. We reject the view that the study of Roman law in the universities was the primary source of doctrinal change in the houses of merchants and the offices of lawyers. The universities were instruments of Papal or secular political policy, and as such were supported or opposed by spiritual or temporal powers in the measure that their study took one or another practical direction.

Nor can we credit the view that the law evolved in a "natural" progression, building upon trade and representing essentially the rediscovery of forgotten Western Roman concepts. It would be conveniently ethnocentric to take this view, for it makes commercial civilization from 1000 onward a Western invention. But the myth of Western supremacy falls when we read the chronicles of the Crusades. The voyagers east discovered a civilization—indeed, civilizations—far more advanced than their own. They discovered Arab science, including medical learning. They discovered, and we know that they brought back, a system of mathematics based upon nine numbers and zero, which replaced the cumbersome Roman numeral system. A bit later they brought back rudimentary double-entry bookkeeping. And St. Thomas Aquinas erected his neo-Aristotelian philosophical system upon an Arabic translation of that philosopher.

The traders who returned from the East brought Roman law, too, or at least a more systematic and commercially usable version of it than had survived anywhere in the West. There is a good deal of evidence to support this. With the exception of Venice and, a bit later, Amalfi, there was no sustained trade between the Eastern and Western Mediterranean between 500 and 1000 A.D. Boats called at Marseille and other ports, and goods were exchanged, but the activity in the West required neither devices for pooling capital, the means to carry on sustained trade, nor the myriad other legal devices which surround, protect, and extend commerce. Things were different in the East; active trading continued after Constantine moved his capital in the face of internal and external danger. In the Eastern Mediterranean, the Roman legal system continued to reflect the dominant themes of commercial practice, including the practices of the Egyptian-Palestinian littoral. This law of trade, a *jus gentium* in the Roman sense, was there when the Western traders came East with the Crusades.

The law which began rapidly to acquire currency in the 1100s contains not only the elements of Roman mercantile law as it existed when Constantine moved from Rome, but also explicit references to legal provisions enacted by Justinian at Constantinople in derogation of the former Roman law.

In the opening decades of the Crusades, the friction between Byzantium and the West—which later developed into warfare over trade routes and money, conducted in the name of religion—did not exist. Byzantium was an early and helpful, if not enthusiastic, ally of the Crusaders, and there was no Western resistance to learning of Byzantine provenance. When the break between the two was cleanly and clearly made in the thirteenth century, the economic growth of the West had already permitted establishment of institutions to guard and extend the legal basis of the economic order.

Not that the businessmen, as opposed to the feudal overlords and perhaps, for the sake of appearances, the Papacy, were averse to adopting heretic, even infidel ideas; the vigorous trade quickly established with Moslems as well as Eastern Christians attests to that. It is likely, indeed, that much Arab commercial usage as well as scientific knowledge passed to the West. We know that in the 1100s Italian cities struck both Byzantine and Arab gold coins, since these were the recognized currencies of Mediterranean trade. The Italian merchants of the 1100s, and perhaps even those in the previous century, were familiar with a book by the Arab al Dimisqui entitled *The Book Relative to the Beauties of Commerce and to the Knowledge of Good and Bad Merchandise and of the*

Falsifications Which Cheaters Commit Concerning Them. The Arabs were also familiar, perhaps through Mediterranean traditions going back to the high point of the Roman Empire, with the ideas of partnerships involving pooling of funds, sales on credit, and letters of exchange. Some researchers have found words of undeniable Arabic origin in the lexicon of commercial practice of the 1100s and 1200s.

We certainly do not claim that Byzantine and Arab trading practices and legal systems were the sole basis for the Roman-law revival in the West following the Crusades: the following chapter underscores the role of Venice and Amalfi in this process, and there were surely parts of Roman legal teaching and writing which were called back into service as the need arose. But the influence of the East is greater than most have supposed.

It is ironic that the Crusades, ostensibly launched against the "infidel" and soon turned against Byzantine Christians, should have been the occasion for such extensive borrowings from the legal learning and mercantile practice of the Arab and Byzantine civilizations. In fact, every stated purpose of the Crusades seems to have paled into insignificance alongside the real and lasting effects of the expeditions to Palestine.

In 1095, the Crusade was called a Holy War, and supported by elements of the nobility as a means to solve insistent and violent social problems within the feudal system. The Crusaders did not, however, establish a lasting military presence in Palestine, nor did their feudal estates bring them much profit or glory. The most significant and permanent beneficiaries were the merchants of the West, who established trading outposts which could and did survive military and political changes. These outposts could be profitable to whoever ruled the region, through duties, taxes, and tolls.

The merchants and bankers profited financially and learned new techniques of trade and new legal and institutional forms. Their trade continued profitably until the Mediterranean was displaced as the principal avenue of commerce by voyages around Africa and to the American continents. And, as we shall see, the economic forces fueled by the Crusades hastened the ruin of the very feudal institutions some had thought they might help to save.

5.

VENICE AND AMALFI: BETWEEN EAST AND WEST

In this year the Pope crowned Charles the King of the Franks, . . . in the temple of the Holy Apostle Peter, smearing him with oil from head to foot, and putting . . . a crown on him. . . .

This is the way in which a contemporary Byzantine historian ridiculed the coronation of Charlemagne as emperor of the Western Roman Empire in 800. The Byzantine may have had a right to mock the Franks. Even four hundred years later, when the Byzantine Empire was but a shell, the West had still produced no city that could remotely compare with Constantinople. Villehardouin of Champagne, a leader of the Fourth Crusade, first saw the city from the sea on June 24, 1203:

> Now you may know that those who had never before seen Constantinople looked upon it very earnestly, for they never thought there could be in all the world so rich a city; and they marked the high walls and strong towers that enclosed it around about, and the rich palaces, and mighty churches—of which there were so many that no one would have believed it who had not seen it with his own eyes—and the height and the length of that city which above all others was sovereign. And be it known to you, that no man there was of such hardihood but his flesh trembled: and it was no wonder, for never was so great an enterprise undertaken by any people since the creation of the world.

And Villehardouin was speaking of a decayed and decadent shell of the great city that Venice had earlier courted; he had come with the Venetian squadron to steal the last of Constantinople's treasures.

But if we seek the sources of the economic and legal ideas which underlay the urban uprisings of the bourgeoisie, we must consider the position of Venice and Amalfi, port and merchant cities, vassals of Byzantium, through which passed the goods, money, and learning that first penetrated and then began to break up Western European feudalism.

The geographical situation of Venice contributed to its role. The lagoons and marshes provided protection from land invasion and directed the inhabitants toward the sea. From the sixth century onward, chronicles refer to Venice as a sailing and merchant town, though commerce was surely at a virtual standstill in the rest of Western Europe. In the next century, Venice became an important link in the Byzantine trade network, its galleys supplying the Empire with slaves, timber, iron, and other "primary products." Even Papal interdictions did not seem to stem the traffic in Christian slaves. Charlemagne himself acknowledged the suzerainty of Byzantium over Venice.

Amalfi, too, profited by its nominal vassalage to Byzantium. Lying on the western side of Italy, Amalfi traded to the west—with the Moslem cities in Africa and on the Iberian peninsula—as well as with the East. By the end of the 900s, Amalfi was, in the words of an Arab merchant of the time, "the most prosperous town in Lombardy, the most noble, the most illustrious on account of its conditions, the most affluent and opulent."

As the Byzantine Empire decayed and Byzantine power faltered in the Mediterranean, Venice and Amalfi made direct contact with Moslem and Fatimid rulers. In 992, Venice concluded a favorable commercial treaty with Byzantium. By 1000, the long-distance trade and naval defense of Byzantium were in the hands of Venetian shipping; in 1000, Dalmatia did homage to Venice, transferring its nominal allegiance from the Byzantine Emperor. Collapsing under the weight of guild privilege and high taxation, Byzantine merchants seemed unable to finance costly trading ventures by sea. Indeed, the resentment of Byzantines against the privileged position of the Italian merchants eventually reached such a point that in 1180 there were riots and massacres of Latins in Constantinople.

By about 1030, Amalfi had a prosperous colony of merchants in Fatimid Jerusalem, where an Amalfitan hostel—the Hospital of St. John—had been built. Claiming exemption from taxes as vassals of the Byzantine Emperor, and engaged in a mutually profitable trade with the Moslems, this enclave survived even the eclipse of Amalfi's commercial prosperity. In 1071, the Norman conquest of Amalfi put an end to its role as trading center.

Venice, however, continued in its position of strength, acquiring suzerainty over small outposts along the Mediterranean. When Italian seapower was enlisted in the aid of the Crusaders and the battle for revived Mediterranean trade began, Venice was challenged by latecomers Pisa and Genoa, with their links to the growing urban movement to the west.

Venice and Amalfi played an important part in the growth of Western capitalism. The *societas maris* of Genoa in the 1100s is probably adapted from the Venetian *colleganza* of much earlier. The law of the sea, essential to the Mediterranean trade and later to the Atlantic seaborne trade, traces its origins to Byzantium by way of Venice and Amalfi. Amalfi published its maritime rules perhaps as early as 954, no later than 1010. About 900, the old Roman and pre-Roman maritime usage had been revived by the Byzantine emperors and probably governed Venetian sea-borne commerce. The crucial parts of this law apportion the loss when a part of the cargo is lost, regulate disputes between the owner of the goods and shipowner, and above all provide a common body of rules for use in all ports and entrepôts.

Banking techniques and activities must also have played a major role in the development of Venice and Amalfi. Corporate banks did not appear until the 1300s, but there are signs of enormous personal and family fortunes in architectural remains and in contemporary accounts of life in both cities. While the precise banking techniques of the 900s and 1000s are not clear in the sources that remain, we can reconstruct them through the facts that are known. Carrying large quantities of gold coins or bullion to settle accounts for galley-loads of merchandise would not have been practical, and it is harder still to imagine merchant caravans carrying large quantities of cash. This presupposes institutions of credit, at least for larger purchases among *mercatores*—those who made their living buying and selling. The only possible hypothesis is that the banking industry in and around Venice and Amalfi predates our earliest records of it.

We are left, therefore, with a picture of Venice and Amalfi as staging areas for an economic penetration of Western Europe, a penetration that both encouraged and later profoundly influenced an indigenous revolutionary urban movement. From Venice and Amalfi, and later Genoa, Pisa, and their network of allies, came legal and commercial techniques fashioned by Roman international trade, developed in Byzantium, and transmitted to the West as the Italian cities took over the warehousing, shipping, and banking activity of the Byzantine merchants.

6.

SOME ORIGINS OF URBAN CULTURE

In the unrest of the eleventh century, family ties to a particular manor began to weaken. One typical contemporary story tells of Godric, an English serf who systematically gathered goods and other objects washed up on the beaches until he had enough to join a caravan of merchants. Traveling and selling his merchandise, Godric gradually amassed a grand fortune. We know about him because his life story was written down in a church account which praised Godric for finishing his days as a devout.

As trade spread, distinctly "unfeudal" ideas spread with it. Pilgrims, travelers, merchants, and runaways returned with tales of the Italian cities, and even of Byzantium and Alexandria. Every seigneury of any size already contained a group of artisans and traders, working under the lord's direction and for his account. In the ecclesiastical cities, where bishops made their diocesan headquarters, the educated officials charged with buying and selling began trade on their own account. No doubt the message was received in different ways and acted upon differently in different places, but the result was the same: producers and traders understood that the process of making and selling could be broken out of the feudal economy and made a separate activity, centered in the cities.

Many cities already existed as crumbling fortifications left over from Roman times, which still provided shelter in case of warfare; often these Roman remnants also had been maintained in feudal times as a center for the lord's business with his vassals. In Provence, feudal lords themselves had directed construction of fortified hill villages from which vassals ventured each day to till the fields on the lower slopes; this contrasted with the lords of the North on their country manors. The diocesan cities, usually those the Romans had used as administrative subcapitals, were also centers of active urban life; many medieval merchant cities grew on the site of a bishop's seigneury. The urban movement of the 1000s and 1100s encouraged breakaways from the feudal system who had settled on the territory of the old cities to create new legal institutions protective of their economic role.

Cities were newly constructed as well, sometimes around a manor house or church. Most of these, however, came into being later, and were sponsored by lords or monarchs for special reasons. For example, King Louis IX, about to embark on a Crusade and seeing France's need for a seaport on the Mediterranean, ordered construction of a port at Aigues-Mortes, because Marseille was not then in French hands.

In the main, the urban institutions of the 1000s and 1100s came into being in the struggle against the restrictions of feudal life. Artisans and purchasing agents, who were part of every lord's household, demanded the right to trade for cash on their own behalf. Tillers of the soil sought the right to sell some of their produce for cash, in order to buy the goods and supplies which were not available on the manor or which were being sold by traders and artisans who had themselves worked free of the feudal system. Tillers, artisans, and traders alike sought to restructure or abolish the taxes on goods sold at markets in their lord's domain.

Itinerant merchants who traveled from fair to fair and town to town in a particular region often needed to seek protection from different sources. Sometimes the Church stepped in to reason with the lord, which resulted in apologies such as the following:

> I, Landru the Fat, seduced and tempted by the greed that often creeps into the hearts of worldly men, admit that I have stopped the merchants of Langres who passed through my domain. I took their merchandise from them and kept it until the day when the Bishop of Langres and the Abbot of Cluny came to me to demand reparation. I had kept for myself a part of what I had taken and restored the rest. The merchants, to obtain this remainder and to be able in the future to cross my land without fear, consented to pay me a certain sum for tribute. This first sin suggested to me the idea of a second, and I undertook to impose and to cause to be imposed by my officers, an exaction called a toll on all those who crossed my territory for business or pilgrimage . . .

Landru gave up his claim to a toll in exchange for a one-time payment of three hundred sous.

But when intercession by the Church or the civil authorities did not produce results, the grievances of the artisan and trading class went unsatisfied. The Italian merchants, wiser in the economic forms of trade and the political forms of merchant-run enclaves, must surely have spread the news to the north. The roadways were also peopled with an assortment of travelers whose role was not so well defined—pilgrims, students on their way to a university to study, runaway serfs looking for a place to settle—who were harassed by the imposition of tolls, by robbery, by feudal warfare.

The last line of resistance for the artisans and traders in the towns was to organize against the common enemy, and the form of organization they chose reflected a new legal concept, or at least a new version of an old concept. They formed groups within the walls of the Roman and feudal cities and bound themselves together as co-swearers (conjurationes), equal among themselves and pledged to mutual aid. The oath, the foundation stone of the feudal relation, became the distinctive feature of the revolt against feudalism.

The first groups united to campaign for an end to feudal warfare, brigandage, and illegal exaction of tolls. Often supported by the Church, or at least by the monastic orders, they were semi-mystical associations and often had a special reverence for the Virgin Mary—symbol of the Church as peacemaker, not the Church militant.

The more powerful oath-bound groups went even further, demanding of the seigneur that all manufacturing and trading functions be separated from the body of feudal life and put outside feudal relationships. The oath to struggle for such a severance of feudal bonds was called "communal," and the term "commune" variously described the oath, the oath-swearers, and the area in which the right to work and to trade was claimed.

Typically the commune—a collection of several dozen to several hundred artisans, lords' officials, minor clerics, peasants, runaway serfs, and others—demanded rights within the territory of the city, including the right to make laws and administer justice. They demanded the right to hold a regular market, free of tolls, and a periodic fair to which merchants from afar might come unhindered. They demanded the right to regulate the work of artisans within the city walls. And they generally wished it understood that serfs who made it to the city gates were free upon entry, or after a period of residence.

More than anything else, this last condition reflected a general dissolution of feudal obligations working in favor of all within the city.

The members of the commune also agreed to pay the lord some kind of regular tax, provided the commune itself was charged with its assessment and collection, and provided it was not too heavy. The commune's degree of independence from the lord and his officials varied significantly from one location to another. The earliest surviving French city charter, dated 967, simply accords the inhabitants freedom from serfdom. Other limited charters grant only the freedom to hold a fair or market. Later charters generally show greater concessions to the new class, which at the same time becomes more conscious of its need for a systematic law defining its status within the feudal system. The term "bourgeois"—in Latin, *burgens*—first appears in a French charter of 1007, and soon passes into other European languages. The "communes" were truly autonomous; they claimed to replace their erstwhile seigneur in the feudal ladder, or even to owe no feudal obligation at all. In many cases, particularly in Provence, the communes claimed to be small republics, on the model of the Italian city-states. The commune's members were often freed from all military obligation to the army of any lord, themselves exercising the power to make war and to conduct foreign relations. Many of the Provençal communes were allied at various times with Genoa and Pisa.

A "free city," by contrast, was governed by a seigneur (who might be a king or emperor) and enjoyed a special status and special rights of trade, commerce, and manufacture. The charter of a free city might be won by purchase or popular uprising, but it left no doubt of the city's continued submission to the seigneur.

City charters from the 1000s or 1100s, whether from northern France, southern France, England, the Low Countries, or Scotland, display remarkable similarities of form and even of language. In part, this is because the texts of charters and news of the uprisings which had produced them were carried along the routes of trade. In part, the similarities reflect development of parallel forms of social organization under the same material conditions. In any event, we see from this evidence the development of a new international *class* of merchants conscious of its status as such.

In each case the city charters reflect the extent to which the seigneur was constrained to accede to the demands of the new groups. The charters tell us, too, of the geographical spread of the bourgeois revolution. For instance, the charter won by the bourgeoisie of Lorris in 1155 spread throughout the center of France; that of Rouen was copied in all the French domains of the Plantagenet kings of England; the charter conceded to Beaumont by the archbishop of Reims was copied in what is now eastern France.

After the Norman Conquest, many English, Welsh, and Irish towns were granted charters quite similar to those of the Norman French towns, most notably that of Breteuil. The Breteuil "liberties" appeared in England at the close of the 1000s in the town of Preston, where they are a constitution in miniature, providing for exemption from many feudal exactions and setting limits on the fines for criminal offenses prosecuted by the seigneur. Tolls are "fixed and moderate." The markets of the town are entitled to the protection of a special court of law merchant. Any person who lives in the town for a year and a day is safe against pursuit by his or her former feudal master; and although newcomers must have the unanimous consent of the burgesses in order to remain, such consent is presumed if the burgesses fail to register a challenge for the year and a day. Reflecting the burgesses' solidarity, and their desire that the town's credit be good, Clause 33 provides that if any burgess fails to pay a debt, the town is to pay it and recoup from the goods of the debtor. This provision avoids the possibility of having any foreign creditor (including a seigneur jealous of the town's liberty) claiming the right to seize goods or property within the town. Preston does not appear to have had a commune.

Another surviving charter is that of Saint-Quentin, in France, which was also copied widely. It provides that a villein is free of feudal obligation immediately upon entry into the city, although any movable goods left behind remain the property of the former seigneur. A person may become a member of the commune on entry, and he or she is thereby under the obligation to respect the mutual oath and to remain in the city unless called outside by business or needed for the sowing and harvest seasons on holdings retained outside the city. Indeed, the dual lives of city dwellers—in urban houses and as rural peasants—contributed to the general weakening of the ties of feudal obligation, for tillers who had ties to a commune were not bound to the land. The "manor" began to lose any geographical significance it might have had, and even given rural areas might be under several different lordships. Rural peasants were bound to their neighbors by proximity and by participation in common agricultural practices; in the city, artisans or traders took part in the group life of the bourgeoisie. In the scheme of feudal duties, they might owe formal allegiance to several masters, but any sense of personal duty was gone.

The essential feature of the commune charter, therefore, was the lord's recognition of the town as a unit, a collective vassal. This recognition conceded the commune's essential characteristics—the unity and equality of its members, and its right to internal self-governance. Implicitly, the charter conceded that this class of bourgeois, like knights, sergeants, monks, abbots, archbishops, and all other members of closely defined social groups, had a law proper to it and a status of its own.

The grant of a charter did not, however, insure an end to the bourgeoisie's struggle. Sometimes a charter would be granted by a lay seigneur or sovereign, leaving the ecclesiastical portion of the city, often widely scattered, under the Church's authority. In Marseille, for example, the bourgeoisie gradually and amicably purchased from the viscount the liberty to trade and run the harbor in the lower city. But the bourgeoisie coveted the archbishop's suzerainty on the hill, and a series of violent clashes erupted.

In other areas, questions of taxes, property, or jurisdiction—particularly the last—remained unsettled for years, and summoning a member of the commune before the lord's tribunal, in ostensible disregard of the charter, could provoke an incident. When a young man of Celles was imprisoned in the abbey of St. Crespin during a fight between the local church and the bourgeoisie, the latter built bonfires outside and kept watch to prevent his being removed for trial outside the bourgeois courts. To keep their fires going, they cut trees in the vicinity of the abbey. One Sunday the curé condemned the cutting from the altar, saying the trees belonged to the monks of the abbey. A bourgeois, Jean le Vacher, stood up and said that the trees were in the territory of the commune and could be cut; indeed, he added, if there were monks standing in the commune's territory, he would think it right to cut them down too. To unravel the dispute, Queen Blanche of Castille, in whose territory Celles then was, appointed a nearby abbot to conduct an "inquest," a sort of inquiry under compulsion to which persons might be summoned and ordered to give evidence. The commune met and swore an oath that all bourgeois summoned before the inquest would swear they knew nothing and would otherwise remain silent.

At Laon, in the territory of the King of France, a commune was conceded certain powers in about 1108 by the bishop, then suppressed four years later by the same bishop and King Louis VI. The order of suppression was quickly followed by a cry in the streets of "commune"; the bourgeois came together and forty of them swore to kill the bishop. Led by a former serf named Ysengrin the Wolf, they found the bishop hiding in his wine cellar and cut off his head. To protect themselves against the anger of King Louis, the bourgeois then formed an alliance with a local brigand lord. It was not until 1128 that an accord was reached, including a new royal grant of commune and amnesty for all.

The struggles in Celles and Laon testify to something more than communal militancy; both also demonstrate the hostility shown the communes by the Church. This hostility often arose because the city in which the commune was located was the seigneury of the bishop, containing the diocesan cathedral, and ecclesiastical seigneurs often insisted on rigorous maintenance of feudal exactions. Also, the commune represented a threat to the fundamental laws of the Church and to churchly prerogatives: The communes claimed control of the system of education, which the Church had always regarded as its special province and which it feared would be infused with lay ideals; worse, the communards were often regarded as heretics in that although they had an active religious life, they paid little attention to Church hierarchy and had little patience with tithes.

The very nature of the commune brought it into direct conflict with the organizational structure of the Church. At the center of the communal organization, usually coterminous with it, was a sworn religious fellowship. This was known as the confraternity in the Latinate lands, the "gild" or guild in the Germanic, and included either all members of a trade or all artisans and traders in a particular locality. "For friendship as well as for vengeance, we shall remain united, come what may," runs a tenth-century London guild ordinance. The oath of fellowship often bound the members to secrecy; and it expressly provided that the communal oath took primacy over all others—which called into question not only loyalty to one's seigneur but also the truthfulness of testimony at an inquest. In several communes—for example, those of Cambrai, Avignon, Arles, Digne, St. Omen Lille, and Arras—we know that the dominant group in the seizure of municipal power was a religious confraternity bound by a mutual oath and acting in secret. These groups not only subscribed to doctrines regarded as dangerous, but their form of organization challenged the rule of the Church as the only institution authorized to mediate between the Trinity and the mass of individual sinners on earth.

Not all towns were born of violence. In Provence, the seigneurs often lived in the cities, granted charters without protest, and continued to play an active role in city affairs. Further north the lay lords and the bishops helped found new towns, marking out the boundaries and supervising construction. They were encouraged to do so by the prospect of sharing in the towns' revenues, and by the wish to avoid confrontation with their vassals. In 1175, Count Henry of Troyes conceded a charter to "Ville Neuve near Pont-sur-Seine," setting a fixed rent per year for the right of artisans and merchants to live in the town and farm on the outskirts, as well as to freely sell houses, vines, and leases. Six *échevins* were to be chosen by the townspeople "to assist my provost in hearing his pleas" and to administer town business. Citizens of the town were protected from being taken back by their former seigneurs.

Churchly cooperation in founding new towns often meant an ecclesiastical declaration of a zone of truce or peace for the town's territory, ruling it off-limits for feudal warfare.

In England, the Norman Conquest brought with it—in theory, at least—an efficient, centralized system of government. Although the Norman lords initially granted franchises to many communes, all cities were soon gathered under the direct overlordship of the king, predating similar developments in France by a century. The Crown's disapproval of the lower feudal lords permitting the growth of new levels of feudal obligation was formalized by the statute *Quia Emptores* in 1290.

In 1130, the earliest surviving *royal* grant states that the citizens of Lincoln had asked King Henry I to confirm that they held their city of him, without obligation to any other lord. The same year Henry issued a charter to the city of London:

> Henry, by the grace of God king of the English, . . . sends greetings to all his faithful subjects, both French and English throughout England. Know that I have granted to my citizens of London that they shall hold Middlesex at farm for a composite payment of £300 annually, . . . with full power to appoint as sheriff whomsoever they please of their own number, and as justice anyone or whomsoever they please of their own number to look after the pleas of my crown and the proceedings to which they give rise; no one else shall be justice

> over these people of London. And the citizens shall not plead outside the city walls for any plea; . . . nor shall any of them be forced to prove his innocence at law in a trial by combat. And if any citizen is impleaded in a crown plea, let him assert his standing as a citizen of London by an oath which shall be judged within the city. . . . And let all men of London and all their goods be free and exempt from payment of any toll, passage . . . and all other dues throughout the whole of England and in all the seaports. . . .

The early development of royal control in England was made possible by the presence of a central authority that was absent on the continent, where the feudal patchwork of suzerainties lasted much longer. The provisions for independence from seigneurial justice were particularly important. No Londoner was to be called before a seigneurial court, and even claims of bourgeois status were to be tried in London. This independence is a familiar theme in this period. King Philip Auguste of France, probably echoing an earlier charter, promised the citizens of Saint-Quentin "that neither we nor anyone else may pursue someone of the commune except before their tribunal of aldermen."

The limitation of military duties played not so great a rule in the English charters as it did in France, since these duties were regulated in England by uniform national legislation. The Assize of Arms of 1181 provided:

> Every free layman who is worth 16 marks in goods or rents shall possess a hauberk, helmet, shield, and lance. Also, every free layman who is worth 10 marks in goods or rents shall possess a mail shirt, iron headpiece, and lance. Also all burgesses and freemen shall possess a quilted tunic, iron headpiece, and lance. . . .

But the English kings still feared the rising of the bourgeoisie, perhaps due to experience with their French dominions, for the assize went on to provide that "any burgess who has more arms than he ought to have according to this assize shall sell, give or otherwise transfer them to some man who will keep them for use in the service of the lord king of England."

Scottish cities developed on the English pattern under the patronage of the King of Scotland. The inhabitants kept some involvement in the farming and pastoral activities of the countryside, but turned increasingly to trade and artisanal activity. The most important Scottish towns, which received charters as "Royal Burghs," were on the seacoast, and became centers for the export of raw wool to the growing manufacturing trade carried on in the Flemish cities.

Thus by the beginning of the eleventh century, the bourgeoisie had carved out areas of autonomy within the feudal system, enclaves within which economic and legal relations were conducted differently than they were on the manors. What went on in these enclaves?

In the smaller cities, the form of municipal organization was dictated by the concessions the communards had wrung from their seigneur or seigneurs. The most important concession related to the right of a municipal assembly, elected in any of a variety of ways, to make laws and hold courts that could issue judgments binding upon all members of the community. Often, as in the cases of Marseille and Brabant, the council was selected in part by the guilds and in part along geographical lines. The guilds united members of each occupation or *métier*, often breaking down a process (such as the making of cloth) into a number of distinct operations, each of which would be done by a different *métier*. The geographical representation was by "quarters" of the city, and might often duplicate the selection by the guilds, for practitioners of the same *métier* tended to live in the same area. There were many variations: at Arles, bourgeois and nobles each chose sixty municipal councilors, and the council chose the mayor. At Eu, a locally elected council named three candidates for mayor, and the count—the city's seigneur—picked one of them. In most cities there was a municipal assembly, but its powers varied. In some cases, such as at Aurillac, the municipal assembly was composed of all persons over twenty years of age who had lived in the city for a year and a day. At its annual meeting, the assembly members renewed their communal oath of mutual support and selected the city officers.

The seigneur sometimes retained the right to designate the officer who was to preside over the local court. In the case of a more independent city, the mayor or a comparable official (consul, rector), or sometimes an alderman, would preside. The decisive judging function was usually exercised by several men sitting as a panel and called by various names—*échevins* or *scabini*, for instance. Their functions were to hear the evidence and to pronounce on the law. In some places these functions were separated and a party to a lawsuit brought persons to court to swear to the existence of a custom entitling the party to prevail. Some disputes could no doubt be settled by reference to the municipal statutes; but in the 1100s and 1200s these documents varied from a bare sketch of municipal independence to a detailed code of laws, and most cases required reference to custom—the custom of the city, of the country, or of merchants in general. To determine the general custom, there were books of law—*Lo Codi* and the *Exceptiones Petri* among them—as well as reliance upon memory and tradition.

Where the law-declaring and fact-finding functions were separate, the modern jury makes its first appearance and rationalizes the method of trial. The judicial duel—a fight to the death between the litigants in order to decide the outcome—was formally abolished in a number of town charters. To replace the duel, jurors are used as finders of fact. In the beginning they are brought by a party rather than summoned by the court; they speak from personal knowledge, rather than being sworn to hear evidence brought by others. From the custumal of four Scottish burghs, we see the confluence of merchant law and early jury procedure:

> If a burgess can be charged by a countryman for stolen goods, found in his own house . . . and can deny the theft as a free burgess against a countryman, and can say that though he has no warrantors yet he bought the goods which are challenged lawfully in the borough market, the burgess shall purge himself by the oath of twelve neighbors and lose only the goods claimed. And he shall swear that he knows not where the door opens or shuts of the house of the man from whom he bought the goods.

This provision deals with the situation in which the goods are indeed stolen, but in which the buyer in the market did not know it. The buyer forfeits the goods to the true owner, and suffers no additional penalty. His good faith in purchasing without knowledge that the goods were stolen is established conclusively, if he is a burgess, by his own oath and that of twelve neighbors.

Borough or city laws also regulated the local fairs and markets in other details. A market was a weekly or semiweekly affair to which local peasants would come to sell foodstuffs, and artisans might sell goods for the local trade. Typically, the market was free of all interference by the seigneur, except perhaps for a tax levied and collected by the municipality for the former's benefit. Where municipal statutes regulated the market, they did so in great detail, regulating the price of goods, restricting advertising or hawking of wares, providing for protection of the merchants on their way to market, and in general seeking to harness the forces of commodity sale and exchange to the needs of the community.

The spirit of competition is not present in the market provisions of the statutes, even those of a great city like Marseille. All members of the commune were to be equally protected. While kinship had provided a unifying influence under the domination of the lords, the commune forged new links against common enemies and in common pursuits. For instance, in the contracts made by peasants who borrowed money against their next harvest, the family often stood surety for the debt; in the communes, fellow citizens take the same role, even assuming collective municipal responsibility for the debts of every bourgeois.

Artisans came to the cities to be free to sell their goods and to buy their raw materials. But this was a freedom from feudal obligations and exactions, not the freedom to compete. Municipal laws usually provided that raw materials could not be bought by any artisan while they were en route to the city in an attempt to get these materials at a lower price and gain an advantage over potential competition. The same principle held with labor: statutes provided that if a master artisan had two workmen, while another had none, the first must allow his fellow to hire one of his workers. As Régine Pernoud has written: "One considered the raw material of production, or the available labor power, a little like an indivisible mass in which each person possessed rights, and just division of goods and services of primary importance." These regulations of the conditions of work and of sale persisted for centuries, principally in the occupations limited to local commerce—such as the bakers, butchers, and other purveyors of foods—where protection of a local and relatively stable clientele remained important. But in the occupations producing goods for the growing international trade—for example, cloth—and in the profession of merchant trader in the great port cities and inland entrepôts, the pressure of economic events broke down such anti-competitive rules and forced a continual reorganization of production.

The growth in trade inevitably favored some members of the commune over others. Within the cities, the struggle between the working artisans and the master craftsmen, or between the producing elements of the population and the trading elements, manifested itself repeatedly. We take as an example Cambrai, first of the communes north of the Alps, in what is today the far north of France near the Belgian border. From about 900 to about 1100, Cambrai was part of the Holy Roman Empire, a diocesan city whose local seigneur was a bishop. In 958, the inhabitants formed a *conjuratio*, an organization bound by mutual oath, against the bishop. Not until 1076, however, after a successful rising during the bishop's absence, was the co-swearers' right to form a communal government recognized. The *métiers* were organized, municipal statutes enacted, and communal life regulated. But little more than one hundred years later Cambrai had lost its unity and was divided into two warring camps, as Lambert of Waterloo, a contemporary historian, describes:

> At the beginning it [the commune] was greeted with favor, because it had been instituted by men held in high esteem, men whose lives were just, simple, honorable, and not avaricious. Each was content with what he had; justice and concord reigned among them; avarice was rare. Citizen respected citizen; the rich did not despise the poor; all shunned strife, discord, and lawsuits. . . . . What a change has come over the commune! It has suddenly become dishonorable, such fair beginnings have led to such a state of shame and perversity for reasons that are only too clear. The citizens have become numbed by prosperity; they have risen one against the other; they have left sin and crime unpunished, each thinks of nothing but his own enrichment by dishonest means. Little by little the great have set themselves to oppress the poor by lies, perjury, and open force; right, equity, and honor have disappeared. . . .

Many such condemnations appear at about this time, and although they must be discounted to a certain extent because they originate from the churches and monasteries, store-houses of hostility to commerce, their essential truth is undeniable. The municipal legal institutions, like the municipal offices, drifted into the hands of the rich. And the very institutions which at the beginning ensured respect for the shared goals and common interest—the use of *coutumiers* or *échevins* to govern and to decide disputes—became instruments of oppression where the role of appointing officers and declaring the ruling custom came into the hands of a small group.

In cities organized by occupation or *métier*, the richer masters came to dominate guild life while their poorer competitors were forced out of business, to become wage-workers. Soon the election of local officials by *métier* no longer meant election by the whole community. Alternatively, a loose-knit municipal organization came into the hands of a few families through the process of co-optation. We will take up this thread in the next chapter, but by the end of the twelfth century, its early signs were clear in the tension between rich and poor.

7.

TRANSPORT BY LAND AND SEA

Efficient, large-scale transport of goods was indispensable to the survival and expansion of merchant capitalism. Small luxury items—gold, jewels, spices, even silk—could be and were carried overland and on small ships, but the stuff that kept the economy turning—wheat, wine, wool, wood, tallow, hides, the armies of the Crusaders—required something on a larger scale.

The Romans had left a network of military roads, sixty-four feet wide, criss-crossing Europe. On the Iberian peninsula alone, Roman laborers built twelve thousand miles of roads. Even the difficult traverse over the mountains from Genoa to Nice was bridged by the Via Julia, built by forced labor under Augustus. But by 1000 these roads were hardly passable, especially in bad weather. Heavy four-wheeled carriages drawn by teams of horses or oxen frequently proved to be unusable, so the normal means of transport between Flanders and Italy became light two-wheel carts and strings of pack animals. But such small-scale transport added 25 percent to the price of lightweight goods, and 100 to 150 percent to the price of grains, wine, and salt. Banditry and various tolls and exactions added to the cost.

An early sign of the alliance between royal houses and merchants is the monarchs' growing insistence that roads passing across the lands of their vassals be repaired and improved. St. Louis, king of France between 1226 and 1270, commanded, according to Beaumanoir, that all roads over sixteen feet wide had to be kept in good repair by his tenants-in-chief, the barons. In 1285, by the Statute of Winchester, Edward I ordained:

> The highways leading from one market town to another shall be widened. Where there are trees, or hedges, or ditches within a distance of two hundred feet on either side of the way, they shall be removed, so that no one may make use of their cover to lurk by the wayside with criminal intent. But oaks and large trees shall not be felled, provided there is a clear space between them. If a lord fails in his duty and willfully refuses to fill in ditches or clear undergrowth and bushes, and robberies are then committed, he shall be liable for damages; and if it is a case of murder, he shall be fined at the king's pleasure . . . . It is the king's will that ways through his own demesne lands and woods, whether within a forest or not, shall be similarly widened. If a lord's park comes close to the highway, he shall take back the park boundary until it is clear from the highway by the required two hundred feet, or else he shall build a wall, or make a hedge or ditch which is so substantial that evildoers cannot escape across it or come back over it to commit an offense.

Beginning in the 1100s a distinction came to be made between confiscatory tolls exacted by the baron for his own private use—municipal statutes inveigh against them, and Popes decree against them—and tolls levied against the merchants by the baron for improvement of the road. Seigneurs and kings who began to improve roads and erect bridges felt inclined to tax the merchant to pay for the improvements.

Given the condition of most roads, and the danger involved in using them, such travel was not the most favored means of transport. Wherever possible—for example, over the 120 miles of rough, mountainous terrain between Genoa and Nice—trade was conducted by sea. And although there were three land routes from Western Europe to Asia through Byzantium, there too the sea route was preferred. In ships with a capacity of two hundred to five hundred tons each, Italians—and, beginning in the 1100s, Provençal and Catalan traders—moved between the Eastern Mediterranean and Byzantium, Egypt, and Palestine. Due to the lack of accurate navigation and mapping—sciences which the Crusaders were later to learn from the Arabs—most vessels stayed close to shore and anchored at night, and during the winter season sea travel was impossible because of the formidable Mediterranean storms. It might take two years to complete a cycle of trade as goods moved from Venice or Genoa to the east, back to Italy, to the north for exchange, and then to Venice. But even given the time involved and the perennial danger of piracy, the cost of carrying goods by sea from one end of the Mediterranean to the other was less than by land—2 percent of the value of the goods for wool or silk, 15 percent for grain, 33 percent for alum (used in processing silk).

Use of the seas was, therefore, of primary interest to merchants. Groups of merchants in the Mediterranean cities armed convoys of ships; merchant-controlled communal governments picked an admiral to fight the Saracens for control of the seas, or to battle other Italian cities for trading areas. Some of these sea-borne merchants were sailors as well as traders: a Venetian statute provided that on each Venetian ship all command decisions were to be made by a committee of five—the captain, the pilot, and three persons elected by the merchants on board.

Regular sea trade from the Mediterranean to the Atlantic ports of Portugal, France, England, and Scandinavia was not established until about 1300, but local trade from England, Scotland, and Ireland to the Continent, and from Scandinavia south, began much earlier. By 1200, the Normans had control of much of Ireland, and such Irish port cities as New Ross were exporting agricultural products to England. Berwick and Roxburg were Scottish raw-wool export stations, linked to Flanders. We have already mentioned trade in the Baltic and North Sea. The Italian businessmen-sailors were found in the north as well; from time to time we know they hired out to a prince or monarch as admirals.

It is logical, then, that merchants were largely responsible for the spread of techniques of sailing and naval warfare. Their own riches depended upon the former; stealing the riches of their rivals, and protecting their own, required the latter.

The system of inland rivers was also widely used to transport goods. The great river systems—the Rhine-Danube, the Po, the Flemish rivers, and the canals which from the 1100s on were built to extend them—were axes of important commerce; the Rhine, for instance, transported French wine. Being situated near a great river was a sure road to urban prosperity. A series of contracts signed by a Piacenzan businessman in Nice in the 1200s neatly demonstrates the role of the rivers in the establishment of an economic pattern for the entire region. This particular businessman, Aubertus Ruphus, sold wool and other cloth that he received from Champagne, Italy, and Flanders. This material was no doubt shipped overland from Champagne to Piacenza, an inland entrepot allied with Genoa and an important banking center. From there, the cloth was either trans-shipped via Genoa to Marseille, then back overland to Nice; or was brought directly to Nice on a ship that anchored there overnight on the Genoa-Marseille run. (From Marseille, of course, the ship could go upriver to inland towns—there are surviving contracts establishing partnerships for this kind of coastal trade. Coastal vessels of about fifty-ton capacity were in regular use.)

Ruphus sold on credit to the inhabitants of the Nice region, with payment due at the next harvest. He also purchased the results of future harvests for cash. Some of these "purchases" no doubt represented loans to the peasants; since Ruphus also sold wheat in the region and elsewhere, some of his purchases represented a form of commodity-futures trading. He also made loans which are identified as such. The pattern of his commerce follows the Var and Paillon rivers up steep valleys into the pre-Alps above Nice. Ruphus and those like him contributed to the peasantry's increasing involvement with a cash economy.

So, while the great land-trade routes were established, improved, and protected by political alliances between merchants and self-interested seigneurs and urban governments, the rivers and seas were the province of the large capitalists. And each urban area, increasingly a center of trade for the cash economy around it, was tied to its dependent trading areas by a network of smaller rivers or roads, and to its sources of supply by the greater road and river systems or by sea.

8.

POPES AND MERCHANTS

From the very first stirrings of the bourgeoisie, there were within the Roman Catholic Church influential groups that favored trade. Although it loudly proclaimed unity and universality, the Church harbored an astonishing diversity of economic interests and social views. It is not true, as modern writers are accustomed to say, that the sixteenth century splits in Christendom were sudden; nor is it the case that only the newly emergent Protestantism could accommodate a spirit of acquisition within the confines of a consistent moral theology. The role of the Catholic Church in shaping the legal ideology of merchants deserves to be examined.

Life in Western Europe in 1000 was lived in the shadow of the Church. In the villages and towns, as well as on the manors, the Church was the center of social life; it united people, telling familiar stories and promising improvement of their condition in the life to come. It should not be surprising, therefore, that the secret societies of the merchants and bourgeois took the form of religious confraternities. The uncertainty which even rich bourgeois shared about the morality of trade heightened the religious concern of the new class; in 1065 one Amalfitan merchant had two enormous bronze doors forged in Constantinople for the archepiscopal palace, and transported them in his ships. Stories abound of rich merchants who gave up their fortunes and spent their last days in monasteries. One might wish death upon the incumbent Pope, or bring it to a local bishop, or spread saucy stories of the priest's latest mistress, but one still belonged to the Church.

The Church had a virtual monopoly on education, particularly higher education in theology and law; among its clerics and lay officials were found most of the literate, not to say educated, men and women of the day. The rising bourgeoisie could not build and disseminate a formal social ideology without the Church.

For our purposes, there are four principal ways in which the Church affected the growth of the bourgeoisie: (1) it protected itinerant merchants as a species of pilgrim; (2) it applied great resources to the study of Roman law, including commercial law; (3) it entered into the dispute over the morality of trade, with results that were in the long run favorable to the bourgeoisie; and (4) it developed a system of courts and of procedure.

As part of the movements for peace which began in the 900s, the Church began to step forward as protector of the poor. Appalled by the powerlessness of local authorities, the Church legislated the peace and provided a legal structure to enforce it. In 989, for example, the Archbishop of Bordeaux ordained that it was contrary to canon law both to commit certain acts against churchmen and church goods in the course of private war, and to take goods from the poor. In 990, the protection of this "Peace of God" was extended to merchants and their goods. To strengthen such legislation, seigneurs were induced to swear an oath to abjure violence, violation of which was punishable as an ecclesiastical crime.

Blood feuds were at first prohibited on Sundays; later this was extended to include Wednesday through Saturday, in order to "prepare" for Sunday. The seigneurs were then pressured to refrain from violence for the great religious holidays, beginning with Easter. The sowing and reaping seasons were included next—"From the first day of May until All Saints' Day I will seize neither horse nor mare nor foal . . . ," went the 1023 oath of Beauvais. First legislated in each diocese, and then by Church-wide councils, the truces and peaces were supervised by "justices of the peace" who were to report violators and institute appropriate action before special tribunals. There were other means of enforcement, too: in 1038 the bishop of Bourges enlisted all males over fifteen in a militia to enforce the oaths of truce and peace, and this band of peasants burned down the castle of more than one recalcitrant lord. Elsewhere, powerful seigneurs were placed under oath to keep the peace and to try violators in their own courts, thus imposing something other than spiritual penalties. Ecclesiastical officers, knowing that they lacked the power to impose monetary or physical sanctions, asked lords, when swearing an oath, to give hostages or pledge money. If the pledge was taken before a court— secular or ecclesiastical—the oath was known as an *assuremens*. Under this name it was taken into French royal law as the Capetian kings increasingly injected themselves into the peacekeeping function. The custumals in some cities contain a more developed notion of the same device: the bourgeoisie, as part of its function of maintaining peace among its members, forced any bourgeois who seemed likely to commit violence to post a bond to guarantee good behavior. The old custumal of Amiens, for instance, contains an interesting and detailed example of such a provision. This sort of *assuremens* persists today as the "bond to keep the peace" in some American states.

The Church's researchers contributed to the systematization, legitimization, organized study of the Roman law. In large measure this was a by-product of the reform movement of Gregory VII (1073–1085), the Pope who sought to assert the primacy of the Roman bishopric over the entire Church.

To do this, he referred to a number of forged documents purporting to date from the reign of Constantine, which he attempted to invest with legality by putting legal scholars to work searching libraries and archives for supporting texts and early Papal legislation.

From the reign of Gregory VII to that of Innocent III (1198–1216), the Papacy's claims to ecclesiastical supremacy and a good share of temporal power were refined and developed. The Papal bureaucracy increased in size and authority. An alliance between the Papacy and the large merchants developed. Orders of monks, such as the Cistercians, and of fighters, such as the Templars and the Hospitalers of Palestine, were created outside of the ecclesiastical hierarchy of bishops and archbishops. The Papacy was able to receive revenues directly from the great Cistercian domains and to share in the proceeds as the Templars became the international bankers and moneylenders of Palestine. For a time the Papacy enjoyed a monopoly on the mining and sale of alum in much of the silk-producing region of Western Europe; the monopoly was farmed out to Italian merchant seafarers for an annual royalty.

The money from these commercial ventures made possible the endowment of university faculties for the study of canon and Roman law. It also made the Papacy an ally of the large mercantile interests. Pope Innocent IV, elected in 1243, was a member of the Fieschi family of Genoa, one of the city's richest merchant dynasties.

The ideology of this Papal supremacy envisaged a reborn Roman Empire, with the functions of emperor shared by the Pope and, to a lesser extent, the Holy Roman Emperor. Essential features of the Roman law were simply taken into canonical legislation, although refusal of lay sovereigns to take oaths of homage to the Emperor led to the concession that each king could be "emperor within his own domain." The centralized fiscal and administrative system of the Roman Empire was imposed on the Church, and increased both the revenue and the authority of the Papacy.

In the Theodosian Code and the rediscovered compilations of Justinian, "doctors" of canon law found the answers they wanted to questions of Papal authority. These men sought to rationalize and consolidate the internal authority of a bureaucratic Church long removed from its beginnings in revolution and martyrdom. Their efforts were capped with the appearance in about 1140 of the *Concordia Discordantium Canonum*, which is popularly ascribed to one Gratian, a professor at Bologna. It is a collection of 3,500 fragments or excerpts taken from Roman civil law, from the canonical legislation of church councils, from popularly accepted forged documents on papal authority, and from imperial legislation of the Carolingian period. Gratian's work was in no sense legislation; the fragments were merely put in a form that made them convenient to study and apply. It became, however, a manual for students and professors at universities throughout Western Europe.

Systematic elaboration of canonical legal principles began. Canon- and civil-law scholars trod separate paths and established separate university faculties; their study and theory reflected the split between secular and ecclesiastical jurisdictions. Canonical legal scholars, even today, take as their basic source a body of material both broader (because it includes strictly ecclesiastical legislation, opinions, and doctrine) and narrower (because it does not include all the secular Roman legislation) than the "civil-law" scholars, whose basic text is the *Corpus Juris* of Justinian.

But even more significant than the choice of basic material was the difference in theoretical outlook. The canonists' intricate arguments were directed toward creating a legal order infused with divine principles, a concern that led them at times to oppose all mercantile activity, at times to support restrictive legislation typical of the smaller communes, and at times squarely to support the large mercantile interests. The prohibition of usury, for instance, which we discussed earlier, was handled differently at different periods by these theorists.

The theory of the "just" price proved equally adaptable. While Roman law used the principle of the just price as a means of protecting buyers and sellers, for the early canonists it became a moral imperative. The buyer and the seller were to disregard the market price and laws of supply and demand and to seek that price which reflected the intrinsic worth of the article sold as well as a fair remuneration for the work—*stipendium laboris*—of the seller. This concern with fairness accorded with the common practice of price regulation in the communal statues. With the dissolution of feudalism, however, and the Papacy's increasing contact with large merchants and bankers, the more general principles of good faith and free will came to overshadow all others, and moral principle gave way to casuistry. The concept of just price was turned on its head by canonical theorists to become "that price prevailing in the market," whether that price was artificially elevated due to scarcity and hoarding or artificially lowered due to glut.

The principle of "good faith" infused the canonists' doctrines concerning prescriptive title to land. For instance, someone who inhabited someone else's land in good faith for thirty years without challenge was entitled to possession, but someone who during the prescriptive period discovered the true ownership and continued in possession was prohibited from taking the title. The Romans had insisted upon good faith only at the outset, but to the canonists bad faith was sinful and could not be the basis for rights.

The canonists' concern with free will revolutionized the law of contract, eventually swallowing up all other principles touching upon trade. For the canonists, to default on a contractual promise—whether or not it involved a sacred oath—was tantamount to having lied at the time of promising. The theoretical importance of this was enormous. Roman-law forms were cast aside and attention was focused on the *will* of the promisor. So long as there was a reason for the promise, *a causa*—be it something in exchange or the desire to fulfill a moral duty or whatever—it was enforceable. The scholars and judges, including the Pope himself, continued to expand the remedies which the ecclesiastical courts would allow for breach of promise.

This interpretation of the principle of free will had its most important practical effect on large mercantile ventures, where written contracts were most common. While in the marketing of essential goods, the Church's professed concern with ordinary folk and the continued vitality of communal regulation kept check on prices, quality, and (to a lesser extent) working conditions, in the written contract—a formal expression of the will—the doctrine of contractual freedom could be carried to an extreme: the presence of *causa*, if recited in the writing, was presumed, and the party who denied its presence had to prove his assertion in the event of a lawsuit. More important, the protective provisions, including that concerning just price, could—as a matter of "free will"—be bargained away. By making the writing of an agreement *prima facie* evidence of the uncoerced nature of its contents, the principle of free will not only devoured its exceptions, but in fact became a sham. This was especially true since the stronger party hired the notary and dictated the terms of the writing.

The ecclesiastical courts defined their competence by subject matter and by the nature of the persons involved. Thus they heard matrimonial and testamentary cases and those involving oaths. Their jurisdiction extended not only to clerics, but to those said to be under the Church's special protection, such as widows, orphans, and the poor. In addition, Church courts also accepted cases in which a party had pledged to submit to their jurisdiction. This prorogation, as contractual choice of forum is called, was of vital importance amidst the relative anarchy of feudal justice; from the time of Gregory VII, the Church, with its well-defined system of courts, had a vastly greater summoning power than did any feudal or royal tribunal. It diminished in importance from the 1400s on, when national courts became more regularly organized.

Beaumanoir gives evidence of the ecclesiastical courts' greater power in his chapter on jurisdiction. In the secular system, if the *bailli* of Clermont should issue a summons to someone who "is subject to the justice of another count or another seigneur, and he who is summoned has nothing in the county of Clermont, he is not required to obey the summons." In short, the plaintiff who chose the wrong court in which to sue was out of luck—one seigneur had no power to issue an order binding in another's domain. Furthermore, with the crazy-quilt pattern of seigneury in the late feudal period, finding the proper seigneurial court in which to sue could be so exacting a task as to make the lawsuit not worth the trouble. In the ecclesiastical system, on the other hand, defendants could be brought to court surely and swiftly. It also offered certain procedural advantages, which we will discuss in detail in the next chapter.

Unlike the seigneurial courts, the Church courts kept written records of trials and judgments, and at least in theory referred to a body of written doctrine as the basis for decision. The results of ecclesiastical trials were therefore often more predictable than the results of trials in the seigneurial courts, which may have been one reason contracting parties of the period agreed to submit to an ecclesiastical tribunal.

The Church courts' jurisdictional claims did not, of course, go unchallenged. Beaumanoir reflects the views of the feudal and royal lay powers: "A good thing it is and profitable . . . that those who are in charge of spiritual justice concern themselves with the spirit only and leave it to the lay justice to administer that which pertains to temporal things."

But advocates of royal power like Beaumanoir also recognized that to compete with the Church courts the monarchs would have to provide merchants with speedy and amenable justice, so that "they do not lose by delay all they might gain in the lawsuit." In truth, the ecclesiastical courts were the objects of a kind of awe-tinged respect, which evoked both jealousy and emulation. The Church's written doctrine was respected not only because the notion that temporal sovereigns could legislate was far from universally accepted, but also because of the ecclesiastical courts' preference for documentary proof, "for the memory of men slips and flows away, and the life of man is short, and that which is not written is soon forgotten."

Clerics and lawyers were regarded as members of the same class. The lawyer's Latin was generally learned in Church schools, and his legal training was obtained in large measure through the agency of the Church: either he attended a university founded by a church, or he studied with a cleric, or he journeyed to a library to read manuscript books written by the Church's legal scholars.

Latin charters, complex written rules, the pride of place given documents, contracts, and writings—all tended to push the business of counseling, pleading, contracting, and judging into the hands of a specialist class. The wealth required to train and maintain such a class could be found only in large institutions, of which the Church was preeminent.

9.

THE BOURGEOISIE IN 1200

The blending of new and old, with the mediation of law and lawyers, is evident in the bourgeois uprisings in the towns and in the system of long-distance trade between 1000 and 1200.

The great achievement of the bourgeoisie in this period was to wrest from seigneurs in hundreds of separate localities the recognition of an independent status within the feudal hierarchy. The urban movement began in the lower orders of society; many of its members were serfs. It demanded one major concession from the seigneur: a charter, drawn in accordance with the law of the place, setting out that there existed—as there had not existed before—the status of *bourgeois*, *burgher*, or burgess, and establishing that this status implied certain rights and duties.

The internal life of the towns was regulated by these collectives of citizens, according to charters written by legalists in the service of the group. The often-echoed "right freely to correct their customary laws from day to day and to change them for the better as circumstances of time and place demand" is the keystone of the charters. The framework of these rules—the basic, constitutional provisions they contain—is the most interesting feature of the urban custumals. In the early years of the communes, these provisions ensured that legal decisions addressed as judgments to individual suitors would be based upon rules fashioned by local judges from their understanding of the common consent and the customs of the place.

Internal autonomy granted a collective group—*universitas*—is not intrinsically significant. Many monastic orders had the right to make their own rules, which date from well before the year 1000. These rules, like the town custumals, reflect the internal rhythm of work and worship of a defined community, but they are historical relics, with little more modern significance than the ruined walls of the colonies they governed. It is quite otherwise with the charters of the towns.

The system of social relations established by and in the urban communes spread, and began to destroy the feudal economy of the countryside.

How could the ostensibly simple act of granting a charter, self-governance, a fair, and a market produce this profound result? After all, the burghers had originally asked only for equal rights in the feudal system. But with recognition of their status came the tacit approval of a wholly different relationship between people—a relationship that was based upon buying and selling and was inconsistent with the fundamental feudal notion of ties of fealty.

The leaders of the scattered, independent, urban uprisings did not at first themselves understand the power of this new form of social organization. In the course of their struggle for freedom from feudal hegemony, they created legal devices which were internally contradictory, and which eventually dissolved even the bonds of solidarity in the name of which they had come together. When they realized this, tardily, they warred against some of the consequences of the system they had established. This is a decisive element of the period between 1200 and 1400, to which we turn in Part Three.

So long as the economic life of the town was oriented toward small production and limited long-distance trade, the legally enacted notion of a common stock of goods and labor, of common efforts and common goals, was protected. In the communal towns, money was a medium of exchange, simply a means of taking the value of all things: the universal equivalent. Within the framework of the community's goals, it was useful as an accounting device; money as an abstract commodity never got far away from the production and exchange of goods for use and consumption. While outside the community the introduction of cash might profoundly disrupt old relations, because the peasant unlike the town-dweller had no directing role in the process of trade in which he participated, this was, at first, not so within the community.

However, technology and social stability combined with the forces set in motion by the bourgeoisie to make commerce possible—the sustained doing of business with the object of multiplying a stock of money by first buying, then selling. This trade surpassed the limits of any given town. Its financiers were interested in money for fortune's sake; the production of goods turned the producers' attention from an identifiable, largely local market to an anonymous, widely scattered group of users represented to the producer only by a sum of cash offered by a trader or wholesale dealer. The alienation of producers in the towns from their product had begun.

The legal framework created in the course of this development revived the principles of the Roman-Byzantine Mediterranean trade. While the urban collectives were originally characterized by widely varying local custumals and by internal, often non-appealable, judicial jurisdictions, the new law of commerce had a more stable, coherent, and uniform content. Consular courts established under seigneurial or sovereign grant and manned by jurists in the service of the great commercial interests, fair courts set up to handle the large-scale transactions of a transient temporary assemblage—these are the institutions of the larger units of economic activity, which came to override, or simply ignore, the local courts.

As money became an object in and for itself—the abstraction of all commodities, including human work—the town body became abstracted from its members. The corporation—*universitas*—was less and less the representative of all the townsfolk, the means for them to express their unity, and came to be regarded as a separate, fictive person, endowed with the attributes of personality the Roman jurists had ascribed to it. It held the property of town; it made the laws, held court, dealt with outsiders. The control of its destiny lay in the hands of those who had the legal power and the right to sign its name and affix its seal. In turn, this power and right was progressively gathered up into the hands of the wealthy and powerful. Whether by placing new limitations on membership in the communal body, or by making changes in the means of choosing its leadership, the corporation as the embodiment of state power became separate from the townsfolk, and a new era of commercial—*and legal*—development was underway.

PART THREE

BOURGEOIS LAWYERS, ROYAL POWER, AND URBAN DEVELOPMENT (1200--1400)

10.

INTRODUCTION

A new phase in bourgeois history began in about the year 1200. Within the space of the next two hundred years, the forces emerged which were to culminate in the bourgeois revolutions of the eighteenth and nineteenth centuries and the Western European commercial community took on the attributes that define it even today.

The 1200s witnessed the end of the Crusades, the final destruction of Byzantine power, and the establishment of Western European control over the Mediterranean. Commodity production in the West became of principal importance in east–west trade, and the first extensive minting of Western gold coins—later to become accepted international currency—was evidence of the West's increasingly prominent economic position. St. Louis, king of France (1226–70), outfitted the final Crusade and, when he was captured by the Turks, paid his ransom with loans from Italian bankers that were negotiated and to be repaid in French currency. A century and a half earlier, such a large financial transaction would probably have been negotiated in *besants* from Byzantium or in Arab currency.

Luxury trade with the East continued, but the West was buying fewer and fewer finished goods. Aside from spices and paper, raw materials became the staple items of commerce, particularly dyestuffs and chemicals needed in the finishing of cloth, timber, and tallow.

Between 1200 and 1400, the localized law of the towns—which, along with the recognition of the bourgeoisie as a separate element of the feudal order, had been the most striking legal and social development of the preceding years—responded to the needs of large-scale, long-distance trade. The cities, as centers of bourgeois power, became instrumental in the breakup of the labor-intensive, inefficient units of agricultural production. Long-distance trade, in its turn, both directed and helped form consciously national or quasi-national legal and political institutions which profited from its success and provided the framework within which it could operate. From the universities, from the newly powerful national monarchies (in England and France), from the Italian cities (Venice and Genoa), and from the Hanseatic League of German cities came a legal literature outlining and commenting upon commonly accepted mercantile and seafaring law. The civil authorities (including the civil jurisdiction of the ecclesiastical tribunals) established courts to apply this law as the merchants wanted it applied. By making these tribunals uniquely competent in certain classes of cases, and by channeling appeals to royal, ducal, or municipal courts of last resort, the temporal powers sliced through feudal jurisdiction in order to protect trade.

Seizing the power to legislate, the French and English monarchs enforced or allowed simpler, more rational methods of pleading and proof in commercial matters. From the time of St. Louis, and particularly under the reigns of his successors, Philip III (1270–85) and Philip IV (1285–1314), lawyers grouped around the sovereign developed legal theories of the separation of Church and state and of the centralization of power, to the detriment of feudal authority. If the period between 1000 and 1200 had seen the growing importance of Roman commercial law in the economic life of Europe, the period between 1200 and 1400 saw the development and adaptation of Roman public law to bolster temporal authority. (Among the notions of temporal power was that of public credit and finance, which tended to bring the more powerful economic figures directly into the government of large territorial units.) For the first time we see public authority exercised over increasingly larger units of territory, authority which rested ultimately on armed violence but was administered in a predictable way by officials appointed for that purpose. The bourgeoisie became the leading figures in this officialdom, their power began to be acknowledged and their presence tolerated; the price they paid for this uneasy truce with the royal power was in taxes, customs duties, or loans to the protector of their commerce.

The great legal and theological treatises of the period show the disparate forces at work in society. At the moment feudalism was about to die—or rather, to be done in—its form could be seen most clearly.

To evaluate the importance of the bourgeoisie, and its relationship to new concentrations of royal power, we examine a secondary commercial center, Grasse, in the south of France. We have attempted to reconstruct the life of the city, as seen by its bourgeois inhabitants and by the peasantry from the surrounding countryside, increasingly dependent on the urban economy. We open our consideration of the period 1200–1400, however, with a discussion of the framework of legal theory within which the bourgeoisie increasingly came to live.

11.

BEAUMANOIR AND OTHERS: THE THEORETICIANS OF A NEW ORDER

A SERVANT OF ROYAL POWER

By examining the life and writing of Philippe de Beaumanoir in its historical context, we can reconstruct the jurists' contribution to the unification of royal and bourgeois power. We therefore discuss Beaumanoir's writing against the background of the 1200s, and compare his work with that of legal scholars who were active elsewhere at the time.

Beaumanoir's principal surviving work, *Les Coutumes de Beauvaisis*, is ostensibly a collection of the customary laws of Beauvaisis, where he was for a time *bailli*—an agent of the French Crown charged with fiscal, administrative, and judicial duties. In fact, *Coutumes* is a masterful recasting of local custom, unified, restated, and interpreted in light of the common law of the French-speaking world. The literary and political attributes of Beaumanoir's work have assured its continued influence as much as has its apparently faithful recording of the law he administered. His clarity of expression is remarkable even to moderns who are unused to medieval literary manner isms. The scholarly commentators on the Roman law had the comfort and aid of a ready-made system—Justinian's *Corpus Juris*—to comment upon; by contrast, Beaumanoir faced the task of systematically expounding a tangled, uncertain, and incomplete oral tradition of custom and precedent. His purpose, he said, was to understand and record these customs because "the memory of man—the *escoulourjante* memory—slips away and the life of man is short, and that which is not written is soon forgotten." His political goal, however, was to assert royal prerogative in the interest of commerce.

We do not know much about Beaumanoir's life, except that he was born in Picardy and that he received some legal training. Whether he was born a knight or ennobled by royal grant, we do not know, although it is more likely it was the latter. The study of law had become a means of admission to a professional caste within which one might rise to become a royal adviser and receive a special knighthood, the *chevalier-ès-lois*. From the reign of Philip Augustus (1180–1223), bourgeois families in some number had begun to send their sons to study law at Bologna and at an allied law school at Montpellier. The study of civil law, like that of canon law, medicine, or theology, was conducted by masters who instructed their students and granted degrees. The prestige of the school and its teachers gave these degrees currency throughout the Roman Christian world. Graduates of these institutions began to take their places as councilors and civil servants in the cities of southern France. Paris and Oxford were soon added as centers of civil-law study. Vacarius, one of the glossators, came from Italy to Oxford in the mid-1100s, to teach and to write a book on Roman law for English students.

At Paris, where Beaumanoir probably studied, the university was chartered in 1200 by royal grant, the first by a secular prince. The charter codified the customary-law rule that a degree was to confer the right to engage in a certain profession. Universities soon appeared at Toulouse, Poitiers, Cahors, and Grenoble. (Much later, in 1312, perhaps under the influence of books like Beaumanoir's, Philip IV established a law school at Orléans, principally for the study of the customary law of France's different regions.) Clearly, the building of these universities represented an expenditure which only a central power—a king or the Pope—could make. It is no surprise that the university was crucial to the advancement of royal ambitions.

The charter of the University of Paris describes the legal status of students and masters. A student was free from feudal obligation, and free from arrest unless he committed a notorious crime—in which case he was to be turned over to an ecclesiastical judge, a reflection of the essentially clerical character of even secular education. The students were regarded hostilely by antibourgeois clerics, who felt they were polluting the true purpose of learning. Jacques de Vitry, a clerical writer who was a declared enemy of the bourgeoisie and later a prime force in the crusade against the merchant-led heresies of southern France, wrote:

> Almost all . . . foreigners and natives did absolutely nothing except learn or hear something new. Some studied merely to acquire knowledge, which is curiosity; others to acquire fame, which is vanity; others still for the sake of gain, which is cupidity and the vice of simony. Very few studied for their own education or that of others.

Though chartered by royal grant, the University of Paris acknowledged ecclesiastical authority as well, in keeping with the crown's concession that the Church had a direct interest in education. For its part, the Church was content to assert only a nominal authority over university affairs. By the time Beaumanoir would have arrived, toward the middle of the 1200s, this ecclesiastical authority was no longer exercised by the Bishop of Paris, but by the Pope. The name *universitas* was first applied to the masters and students by Papal decree in 1228. A Papal document of 1231 reaffirms the privileges of the university, and recognizes the jurisdictional claims of the French king, by then St. Louis; the Pope enumerates the students' protection from arrest and from other exactions, but concludes: "We . . . wish and command that after the privileges have been granted to the masters and students by our most dearly beloved son in Christ, the illustrious King of the French. . . ."

A student arriving in Paris studied at the Faculty of Arts, then graduated into a specialty—medicine, law, or theology. He was placed, based upon the region or country of his origin, into one of the four "nations" of the university—France (which included the Paris region, Italy, and Spain), Picardy, Normandy, and England. The "procurators" of the four nations elected the rector of the Faculty of Arts; the other faculties each had a dean.

The atmosphere at the university reflected the intense social conflict in which the bourgeois families of Western Europe, whose sons formed the bulk of the student body, found themselves at that time. One of these conflicts was centered in the south of France, in the urban civilization which had grown up under the leadership of the communes. Spreading along the trade routes, the idea took root that "religion [was] primarily and almost exclusively a matter of personal ethics." Believers "were interested in establishing the purity of their own lives, and they cared rather less about the fate of the Church as an organization." This anticlerical doctrine was well suited to the mercantile community; its antiorganization bias, supported with empirical evidence of the venality of the Church's officials, lent theological credence to the secret urban societies led by lay persons and to the assaults upon ecclesiastical jurisdiction within the towns. A combination of Papal and royal power finally rooted out the heresy. A crusade was preached against the so-called Albigensians, and in 1209 Philip Augustus sent an army, which massacred fifteen thousand men, women, and children at Beziers, near Marseille. "Kill them all," the Papal Legate is said to have urged, "God will recognize His own." After another campaign in 1226, the county of Toulouse, center of the heresy, passed to the King of France, greatly strengthening France's territorial base and providing an outlet to the Mediterranean.

Students at the university must also have been aware of tremors of urban conflict in the north of France. Many of the northern city governments had passed into the hands of the wealthier bourgeois, whose power was assailed periodically by uprisings of the poor. These clashes, and the financial problems of many cities, led to royal takeovers of urban governments; the status of bourgeois was thus conferred by royal grant, rather than by a pact of the communards themselves.

These conflicts were reflected in the universities, and students often fought among themselves in the cloisters and nearby streets. Their study of civil law was, however, a unifying influence, as it was designed to be. To the university came partisans of this or that position in the social conflict; from the university, or so the monarchy wished, went lawyers trained in the civil law and convinced that the crown stood as a public authority above warring factions. To put this view of royal power into practice, the monarchs recruited the graduates into the staffs of their administrative structures.

Beaumanoir joined this civil service as a *bailli*, representing the king in a part of the royal domain and exercising judicial, administrative, and fiscal duties in his name. Unlike other officials, *baillis* were paid in cash—not in land and the labor of its occupants, nor in a percentage of whatever revenue they collected. In order to prevent them from forming entanglements within their territories, they were moved to a new location every three years; nor could they serve in the region of their birth. The *bailli* was often in conflict with the local feudal lords, who were the king's vassals but were unused to interference in their affairs.

Beaumanoir's position as *bailli* typifies the movement of a section of the bourgeoisie—the lawyers—into positions of service to the central power.

There they also served the interests of commerce by helping to fashion a legal system favorable to it. The crown was beginning to see the value of acting predictably, according to a certain rationality which came to be expressed in a system of rules and maxims, for predictability is essential to commerce. Beaumanoir understood this role of the lawyer, and in his work described his task straightforwardly and authoritatively. The self-confidence of his prose is perhaps justified; he was in royal favor all his life, and served as a member of the *Parlement* (royal court) in Paris, once even undertaking a diplomatic assignment to Rome.

The personal qualities Beaumanoir extols are typical of a certain bourgeois moral stance, loyal—but not unreservedly so—to the existing institutions of secular and ecclesiastical power. In an opening chapter of the *Coutumes*, Beaumanoir notes the *bailli*'s judicial responsibilities and a list of approved virtues for a royal judge—literally a "doer of right," *droiturier*—which reflects a sense of the *bailli*'s need for tact, firmness, and attention to the goals of royal power. The "dame and mistress" of these qualities is sagacity, followed by piety, gentleness (without cruelty), patience, the ability to listen, good health, and generosity. "He must know the well from the ill, the right from the wrong, the lawful from the treacherous, the good from the bad." He must obey the commands of his seigneur. The last virtue, "which illuminates all the others," is loyalty.

Baillis and others were enjoined to uphold the king's rights and rents, to refuse gifts from suitors above the value of ten sous and to refrain from giving gifts to the king's retinue or their wives. They were to "refrain from blasphemy" and from "the game of dice" and to "keep away from taverns." They were enjoined to remain at their posts forty days after their terms were up, "so they may answer to the new *bailli* in respect of any wrong done to such as may wish to bring a complaint against them."

Beaumanoir, though conscious of the obligation to obey, qualifies it. The judge ought to obey his seigneur, "except those commands by which he might lose his own soul if he should follow them; for the obedience he owes extends to do well and keep well and in loyal justice support his lord; but *baillis* are not excused of their duty to God." And he adds, "For those sires are not good to serve who take more care to impose their will than to maintain right and justice."

The law which Beaumanoir chronicles, and which the *bailli* is to enforce, is stated in a manner that indicates that fundamental political changes are at work. He does not purport merely to record immemorial usage and custom, for to do so would have left little room for either the evolving principles of commerce or the legal theory of royal supremacy. Rather, he weaves together local customs, royal legislation, and a common law drawn from all over France. He does so in a manner which makes unmistakable his commitment to the expanding power of the crown:

> We finish the greatest part of this book with judgments made in our own times in the county of Beauvais, supplemented by customs and usages of long standing, and, where there is doubt of the rule in the said county, by the judgments of neighboring seigneuries, and by those principles of justice which are common to all the custumnals of France.

His selection from among competing customs was not random. He would have in mind St. Louis' admonition that *baillis* were to "do justice to all . . . and . . . observe such usages and customs as are good and have been approved."

The injection of royal power and interest into formerly feudal domains was the single most important aspect of the *baillis'* work. The *baillis*, a French professor has written

> showed themselves to be the most effective agents of the extension of royal power; they spent their time trespassing upon the rights of the seigneurs and the Church. The king, while congratulating himself on the results thus obtained, did not hesitate to disavow them if their often bold initiatives generated too much complaint; at the same time, he would quietly encourage the *baillis* to try again on a better occasion.

Beaumanoir clearly sought to justify and extend royal power and he makes a striking claim for absolute control over the judicial process. The power to judge—to issue binding commands—was at the center of the medieval dispute over feudal, royal, ecclesiastical, and communal power. Beaumanoir built his argument by combining an artful interpretation of feudal legal logic, principles clearly derived from Roman law, and empirical evidence of the inefficiency and crookedness of justice left free of royal control.

The argument begins with a statement of feudal principle: all lay jurisdiction in the kingdom of France is held "of" the king, as supreme feudal lord. Royal appellate power is then deduced from the lord-vassal relationship, and from this follows the principle that no vassal or subvassal of the king is immune from the obligation to appear before a royal court in which his judgments may be questioned. The *bailli*, in addition to deciding matters within the king's direct competence, can have any seigneur or his delegate judge summoned before the *Parlement* in Paris, for "there is none so grand as may not be summoned in the king's court for denial of justice or for false judgment." The extent of this power is suggested by the fact that the King of England did homage to the King of France with respect to the English domains in France.

In principle, the judgments of the feudal courts were tested in the *Parlement*, which was staffed by lawyers appointed by the king and serving as his personal representatives. In deciding such cases, however, *Parlement* applied local custom, for as Beaumanoir explains, it is the king's duty to maintain the customs under which the diverse peoples under his subjection have lived. A custom was, in theory, established when no one could cite a contrary rule having been applied, or when a previous judgment was cited that such-and-such a rule had been immemorially observed. *Coutumiers* were called to the *Parlement* to swear to the custom in the locality where a case arose. The *Parlement*, however, was the final arbiter, and the step between finding the law—*jus dicere*—and making the law—*jus dare*—was easily crossed.

Beaumanoir was not the first to use feudal legal theory in this way. In England the Normans applied the theory that all land was held directly or indirectly of the king; the growth of the power of the French kings was 150 years behind that of the kings of England in this respect. At the time Beaumanoir wrote, the barons in England were still demanding enforcement of the concessions of Magna Carta, seeking assurance that their role in the government of the kingdom would be maintained. St. Louis, and his successor Philip the Bold, were engaged in a rather different battle: they were gathering up their barons' power and authority, in part by appropriating the jurisdiction of the feudal courts.

With regard to the upper nobility, the feudal ties of dependence had lost most of their original character. As the importance of such feudal services as military duty declined, the personal tie between lord and man became attenuated, and services were transformed into money payments. Courts composed of knights would hear cases of chivalry, honor, and disputes among those of knightly rank. The lords' courts would hear matters arising in the administration of their domains—the respective duties of the lord's officials and the peasantry. (One consequence of the king's increased role was centralization of the police power, and this was reflected in an expanded royal jurisdiction over crimes.)

Beaumanoir injected into this situation the notion of the king as the sovereign, not merely the chief of a feudal hierarchy. Not only does the royal court have the authority to declare what the custom is, it has the power to legislate as well. All the nobles of this kingdom hold of me, St. Louis had said, and "I hold of no one but God and my sword." As Beaumanoir put it:

> You see that kings are sovereigns over all and have, in their own right, the guardianship of their kingdom, and for this they can make such laws as please them and for the common profit of their kingdom, and that which they enact must be obeyed.

This sentence clearly paraphrases a celebrated epigram of the Roman jurist Ulpian on the powers of the Roman emperors. It is a tentative statement, hedged with the qualification that barons may also have some limited legislative power. It is nonetheless clear that Beaumanoir has in mind the concept of sovereignty, and that the power of the king—and that of his representatives in the *Parlement* or highest court—to override local custom may be deduced from this rather than from any feudal principle. (Beaumanoir's double-edged defense of royal power is even earlier than that of Fleta, the anonymous author of an English treatise which appeared between 1290 and 1292. Fleta asserted not only that all judicial power was held of the king, but that even the manorial courts were royal courts—clearly false, but equally clearly expressive of the crown's ambitions.)

At another point, Beaumanoir places the king's legislative power on a somewhat narrower footing, but at the same time he expressly describes a wider field for its operation. Custom, he writes, cannot in general be changed:

> But in times of war, or when there is a danger of war, it is permissible for kings, princes, barons, and seigneurs to do things which, were they to do them in peacetime, they would commit wrong toward their subjects; but the times of necessity excuse them.

A mild-seeming premise this, echoing Cicero's *silent enim leges inter arma*—in time of war the laws are silent. In a century in which, as Jacques de Vitry wrote, outside the cities there were battles, and inside perpetual alarms, the "exceptional" power to legislate covered a multitude of cases:

> The king can establish new laws for the common profit of his kingdom, as where he is accustomed to order taxes to defend his territory, or to attack another who has wronged him, to provide that nobles and gentlemen have their knightly battledress, and that the rich man and the poor are provided with arms, each according to his station in life; and that the good cities perform the services they are required to perform, and maintain their fortresses, and that each one is ready to move when the king commands it: all these provisions and others which seem wise to him and to his counselors the king can make, for time of war or when war to come is rumored. And each baron may also make enactments in his territory, but may not contradict the enactments or will of the king.

Beaumanoir's statements of royal prerogative were likely to offend not only the barons; if the king held of none but God and his sword, he did not derive his power from the Pope or the Holy Roman Emperor either. This was not, however, a new idea: in 1076 Henry IV, emperor of the Western Roman Empire, claimed to be "king not through usurpation but through the grace of God." The notary Galbert of Bruges, recording the violence in Flanders in 1127, speaks of the French King Louis VI (liege lord of the counts of Flanders) as "emperor," meaning that he owed no allegiance to any other feudal lord.

To establish the king's independence of ecclesiastical authority, Beaumanoir restated the policies of St. Louis—"at once a Christian full of humility and a prince jealous of his authority"—and set out the limits on the jurisdiction of ecclesiastical courts. The secular power could not, according to Beaumanoir, impose a court of last resort upon the ecclesiastical system as with the feudal courts; instead, Beaumanoir described two competing, equally dignified, jurisdictions, secular and ecclesiastical. He prefigured an unbroken line of French legal writing on the role of the Church.

> Good cause it is and profitable, according to God and the world below, that those who are in charge of spiritual justice concern themselves with that which appertains to the spirit only, and leave it to the lay justice to administer that which appertains to temporal things, so that by the lay and spiritual tribunals justice is done to each person.

The Church, Beaumanoir says, has jurisdiction in eleven matters: heresy, marriages, gifts to the Church, religious properties, trials of persons in holy orders, trials of widows and orphans, testaments, the keeping of holy places, bastardy, sorcery, and tithes. Even in these fields, its authority may be limited by custom or grant, for many Church properties were under the protection of civil authority. Further, holy places, such as churches, may be distinguished from those ordinary lands the Church or some part of it holds as would any ordinary lord—these may fall under the jurisdiction of lay tribunals.

In any event, Beaumanoir claimed that the lay courts, particularly the *Parlement*, had the final authority to decide the ecclesiastical tribunal's competence in a particular case, and could even command the latter to relinquish its jurisdiction. Further, since the Church had no power to use force, it must call on the secular authorities to enforce its judgments (the sole exception being cases of sorcery, in which the Church court could impose and exact the penalty of death).

THE BOURGEOISIE AND THE CITIES IN FRANCE AND ENGLAND: FROM AUTONOMY TO ROYAL CONTROL

Beaumanoir's concern with the bourgeoisie, and the threat it represented to royal power, is repeatedly expressed in the *Coutumes*, as he seeks to accommodate his desire to encourage the commercial development of the towns to his commitment to subordinating the legal system of the entire country to ultimate control by the crown.

Most important in this regard is his theory that the statuses of "good city"—*bonne vile*—and "bourgeois" are conferred by the king, or, on occasion, by an overlord subject to the king. The idea that the law of the city—indeed the city's very existence—derives from the mass of the bourgeois, who have risen up to take power, is nowhere to be found in the *Coutumes*. While Beaumanoir recognizes that cities with communes and those without may have different types of charters, he writes as if there were "good cities" only. If a city has a charter, it should be observed by seigneurs and by the monarch. As for new towns, no one may establish a communal city without royal authorization, for "all novelties are forbidden." If the king wishes to establish a city, "what is to be done must be written in the charter of franchise."

This movement toward making the incorporation of cities a sovereign prerogative had reached England as well. English jurists agreed that the creation of a corporate personality required an act of sovereign power, a formal grant of the status of artificial person—*persona ficta*, in the words of a declaration of Innocent IV in 1243.

Beaumanoir was not idly spinning his theory of corporate existence. His legal conclusions had emerged from the conflict between the towns and the king and within the towns themselves. He believed there was ample reason for royal intervention. He wrote, without mentioning any particular city:

> We have had in the good cities many struggles of one group against another, as the poor against the rich, or one group of the poor against another, when they were unable to agree on a mayor or a representative or an attorney . . . We see many good cities where the poor and middle citizens have no voice in the administration of the city, but where all the power is held by the rich; because of their money or their lineage, they are the formidable power. It also happens that certain citizens are the mayors, or the aldermen, or the treasurers, and the next year they elect their brothers or their nephews or some other close relations, such that in ten or twelve years, all the rich men have captured the administration of the town; and when the time comes to audit the town records, they cover themselves by saying that certain of their number have verified the accounts of the rest. Such things must not be tolerated, for the communal finances must not be audited by those who are in charge of administering them . . . . Many discords are born in the communes due to the royal tax imposed on the city, for it happens often that the rich men who are in charge of the taxation of the citizens pay less than they ought to, and similarly exempt their relatives and the other rich men . . . thus, the entire burden of the tax falls upon the poor community. By this means, an injury is done; the poor do not wish to suffer it, but they know no good means to claim their rights but through force; from whence there have been on many occasions a number of killings.

Or, if the perceived injustice is due to conditions of work, the action might take a different form: a strike, which is defined as

> an alliance against the common profit, when workers promise . . . or agree amongst themselves that they will not work any more at the same low wage as before . . . and decide between themselves the punishments and threats they will mete out to their fellow workers who do not support them.

What had happened to the cities, that Beaumanoir could be so pessimistic? For one thing, the logic of the market had prevailed over plans for communal ventures. This is seen clearly in the first towns to be drawn into long-distance trade, the weaving towns of Flanders and the north of France. Financed by Lombard bankers, wholesale cloth merchants began operating in these cities in the 1000s and 1100s. By the 1200s, a pattern of trade was visible. Merchants imported raw wool from England and Scotland and brought it to master craftsmen working under a municipal guild system. In the ateliers of these small manufacturers the wool was worked into fine cloth and returned to the entrepreneur-financier. He in turn sold it at the local market hall, for export, or took it to a fair; in either case, the wool was sold to another wholesaler.

The intense competition over control of the trade routes—competition between families, between dependencies of this or that Lombard banking interest, between nominees and agents of this or that Italian city—had little effect on the economic life of the master craftsmen. They took the wool and worked it at the prevailing price, dictated by economic forces beyond the control of municipal regulation. When squeezed by falling profits and rising prices—all evidence points to a period of great inflation in the 1200s—they in turn put the squeeze on their workers. The large merchant did not, in the eyes of the craftsmen and their employees, work for his bread: he was simply a *compsore*, a *changeur*, a moneychanger. To escape from this pattern of life, the master artisan was required to form an alliance with larger interests, or to struggle for a position in the municipal government, where he or she could gain access to town revenues gathered from tolls and commissions on imports and exports and on sales in the local wholesale market halls.

The economic situation in the cities was aggravated by a change in patterns of farm production that accompanied the growth of differences in wealth. The richer bourgeois began to buy up land outside the city, drawing social relations in the countryside into a cash economy. Municipal regulations concerning food prices could not cope with large-scale speculation in foodstuffs, particularly semidurable ones like wheat and wine.

> *Rich bourgeois with others' money:*
> *Making a God of your paunch*
> *You like to traffic in wheat*
> *Buying cheap and selling dear,*

wrote a contemporary poet. The rich, lamented a monk of Froidmont, suck the blood of the poor.

The commonality of interests among the larger merchants was expressed in their guilds; these were not the guilds of artisans, but the meeting places of the rich. Entrance fees were high, and admission limited to those who did not work with their hands. This class with money and relative leisure succeeded to the government of the cities. Often, no change in the city charter announced this development, though it was sometimes ratified in municipal law after the fact. In 1240 the holding of municipal office in Bruges was closed to any artisan who did not first renounce his or her trade.

Small wonder that struggles began to erupt between artisans and their increasingly proletarianized employees, and between the artisans and workers on the one hand and the great families who controlled economic and political leadership on the other. These struggles provided the pretext for the intervention of royal power. In 1250, when the workers of Paris rose up against the master craftsmen, St. Louis appointed a royal civil servant to arbitrate and write out the customs of the trade in binding form. In 1233, in the commune of Beauvais, the poor rebelled against the rich. Bishop Milon took the side of the poor, no doubt due in large part to his opposition to the financial operations of the rich. The king intervened, ostensibly to restore order, but his participation was interpreted by the bishop as support for the rich, so the bishop took reprisal in the form of interdicting the royal domains, meaning that religious services could not be held there. The final victory, however, went to the king, for the matter ended with litigation in the *Parlement* over the provisions of the city's founding charter concerning matters of municipal administration. The *Parlement* annulled the charter for being too aristocratic.

The story was repeated, with minor variations, again and again during this period. At Douai, in 1245, the workers organized against their masters. In Flanders, hardly a major city was exempted from the conflict. Workers organized secretly and bound themselves by an oath ("*conjuration*"), rising up against the institutions of power.

Financial crises provided another occasion for intervention, as insolvent communes could pay neither their debts nor the taxes due the king. An *ordonnance* (statute) of 1260 established the royal right to audit municipal finances. An *ordonnance* of Philip the Bold in 1287 made all bourgeois "bourgeois of the king," with the obligation to reside in a city of their choice. (This status of bourgeois of the king was also granted to certain representatives of Lombard banking houses, whose presence was necessary for transmission of funds and loans to needy monarchs.)

In this context, it is little wonder that Beaumanoir wrote, "There is at times a great need for one to help these communes as one would a child." This kindly advice is backed up with the admonition that it may be necessary to seize the city government and install a new one, keeping the city under tutelage for a year or two.

In the end, the legal status of bourgeois was defined by superior authority and not by the united action of the bourgeois themselves. The beneficiary in each case was the central authority, which intervened as an outside and ostensibly neutral force to restore order and control.

In whose interest was this royal intervention? St. Louis sent out one commission of inquiry under orders to assure that the "poor might earn their bread in peace," a charitable enough thought which surely did not countenance any great dislocation of the power structure. Thefts, chicanery, and urban oligarchy were often targets of royal intervention, and frequent subjects of judicial decisions in the Parliament. In this process, the French monarchs were exploring, through their lawyers, the means to ensure that the laboring population was well enough treated that it would not rise up against its masters, creating internal disorder and exposing the kingdom to grave external dangers. Harried on the north by the ambitions of the counts of Flanders, and on the west by the English, the French king needed the support of the "*bonnes viles*."

These developments in France were paralleled both in England and in the English crown domains on the French side of the Channel. Royal intervention in the affairs of English cities is recorded in the 1200s, though it is more difficult there than in France to separate the element of royal interference dictated by economic changes from the process of centralization which began with the Norman Conquest. England in the 1100s was divided into "vills," administrative units which might or might not coincide with the feudal manor—one lord might hold several vills; or, one vill might acknowledge several suzerainties. The vill was, for the Normans, an important administrative unit, and it acquired a role in arming the country, apportioning taxation, and presenting and convicting criminals. The typical vill in 1200 was the center of a communal agricultural unit. It consisted of a group of houses, each household having the right to farm an irregular strip of land.

The earliest cities were simply enlarged vills. As the city dwellers took by force or were granted by sufferance a charter of liberties, the vills became boroughs, the homes of the burgesses. As early as Domesday Book, 1081–86, some of these boroughs were singled out as "shire-boroughs," and the words *Terra Regis* inscribed beneath their names, indicating that they were held of no lord but of the king directly. In the majority, however, the vill system persisted. If the land was divided in crazy-quilt fashion, the lords' domains might also be irregularly divided. Even within a single cluster of houses, half a street might acknowledge one lord, the other half another. The lord of half a street might in turn be vassal to a superior lord, and so on. Generally, the lowest suzerain on this ladder would collect rent from the householder. As vills became boroughs, these rents increasingly took the form of cash payments. The services this first suzerain owed to others above him would continue to be exacted, and these services in their turn became converted into money payments.

The impact of this hierarchy of feudal dues and services on property law was formidable. If A rented the house of B, who was suzerain of the place, and B in turn held of C, the death of B without heirs put C into B's place; henceforth, he would receive the whole of the rent paid by A. To work such an escheat (forfeiture), however, C had to hold a feudal court and declare his rights, but if he held only three or four houses in a borough, each yielding a derisory sum, he would have little occasion to hold a regular court. The smaller feudal lords thus lacked both the means and the incentive to enforce their jurisdiction over property within the borough, which gave the royal power the opportunity to intervene. The burgesses did not want to be bothered with the panoply of feudal exactions, services, obligations, and tolls; a borough in which a dozen middling seigneurs had interests was an untidy, ungovernable mess, as none of the seigneurs had the power to do anything in a governmental way. Further, royal taxation was inevitable, particularly early in the 1200s, when the Crusades bore heavily on the population, and on the vill as the unit of accountability; no one wanted to pay taxes to more than one overlord. The Crown wished to continue the Norman centralization, already the most thoroughgoing and efficient in Europe. The result was a merchant-king alliance at the expense of the lesser lords.

F. W. Maitland has studied this process in the borough of Cambridge. King John granted the city a charter which gave the municipal corporation—*universitas*—its liberty in exchange for certain considerations, including £60 per year and a one-time payment to the suzerain of the place, an earl. Later judicial interpretations of the charter held that John had intended to make the town "mesne lord" of its territory, placing it as a corporate suzerain immediately beneath him in the feudal hierarchy. The town was to hold all tenanted land as landlord and all waste land as owner. This fictive person thereby became the "lord" of some real-life nobles with fiefs within the borough. The interests of these lords were subsequently forgotten, bought off, or ignored.

Once the town was a "person," and a lordly one at that, the same process at work in the French and Flemish towns began. The town collected the rent on houses, which were held as leaseholds and willed as movable property. On the waste land, the residents of the town had the right to graze their beasts. A fair was established, and each burgess held his booth at the fair "of" the corporation as seigneur-landlord. Rents and revenues from the fairs were the corporation's property, to be used for the improvement of the town.

Gradually the corporation detached itself from the body of the people and became an object in itself. Its leaders came to view themselves alone as the corporation, and the common and waste land as theirs to enclose, lease, or sell.

The borough's charter defined the jurisdiction of its court, which used royal protection to expand its powers at the expense of the feudal lords. By defining the leasehold interests in the burgesses' houses as movable property, the courts succeeded in preempting the jurisdiction of the feudal courts. The royal power also began to grant franchises for the holding of fairs, or permitted the burgesses to hold them. The fair court often became simply a special session of the borough court.

This unity of the Crown and the bourgeoisie—in England, France, and elsewhere—fostered orderly trade and was in their mutual interest. The revenue from royal domains having become inadequate to support the royal establishment, the Crown began to perceive revenues from trade in the form of taxes. The "commune" was still recognized as an entity, bound by an oath, but that oath had become subordinate to loyalty to the Crown. Any mass communal movement of the kind that had erupted so often in the 1000s and 1100s was considered a crime and punished as such. Beaumanoir leaves no doubt about the attitude of the French king toward such *conjurationes*, and his remarks would have been endorsed by most sovereigns and seigneurs in Western Europe:

> A good thing it is that malefactors are taken and punished, each according to his crime, so that others will take heed from this example and keep from committing crimes. And among the other crimes of which we have spoken above, one of the most serious, and that which seigneurs must punish and avenge, is that of associations formed against seigneurs or against the common good.

Uprisings and rebellions, he writes, should be punished by prison terms and fines:

> Another type of association that is often made is that in which a city or cities are destroyed and the seigneur dishonored and dispossessed, as where the common people of a city or of many cities form an alliance against their seigneur to exert force against him. Thus, as soon as the seigneur is aware of such an alliance being made, he must crush it with force and imprison all members of the conspiracy for long terms. It is, indeed, an offense for which the seigneur would be justified in putting the conspirators to death, as it is a sort of treason against one's lord.

To illustrate his point, Beaumanoir recounts, inaccurately as it turns out, the uprising of the Lombard League against Frederick Barbarossa in 1164:

> It happened that all the good cities and the castellany of Lombardy were held by the Emperor of Rome, in his domain, and held of him; and there were his *baillis*, provosts, and agents for all the cities, who did justice and preserved the rights of the Emperor; and they had done homage before the Emperor as their seigneur. And it happened that, in one of the good cities, there were three rich Lombards, who did not consent to the rule of the *baillis*, one of whom had hanged one of their parents for desertion and in all justice. The Lombards banded together in bad faith, led by a man at once subtle, malicious, and well-spoken. This man, as agent of the others, went round to all the other good cities of Lombardy; and when he would arrive in a good city, he would seek out ten or twelve men of great lineage and wealth, and then speak to each one by himself and say that the other good cities were in accord privately, that they no longer wished to obey their seigneur, and that any city which did not go along with the plot would be destroyed by the other good cities. But that afterward, each city would be its own mistress, not held of another. And after these messages and travels, which required five years to complete, and at the end of the five years, one day all the cities of Lombardy rose up and took control of their own affairs, because the Emperor had not provided for such disloyalty. And when the cities were taken . . . they could make such

> laws and customs as they pleased . . . . And by this one can understand the great perils that await all seigneurs who suffer such alliances to exist among their subjects.

It was not, however, hostility to commerce or to wealth that motivated this opposition to communal independence, but, on the contrary, a recognition that with royal sponsorship the bourgeoisie would be able to develop its economic relations beyond the bounds of any single city. Beaumanoir takes care to assure his readers that he is a foe not of commerce but of disorder. An organization to do business, a *compaignie*, is clearly lawful, even when it interferes with guild or seigneurial prerogatives. We noted earlier Beaumanoir's description of new communes as forbidden "novelties":

> What we have said concerning all novelties being forbidden is to be understood as meaning all novelties that are instituted contrary to the rights of another; for it is forbidden to no one to make an oven, a mill, a wine press, a fish tank, or any other things, any place he wishes, and this would not be contrary to the rights of anyone. . . . For example, if I make a mill on my property, where I have the right to do so, and the mill of my neighbor therefore earns less, for he does not have as many customers as he is accustomed to; or because I give a better price than he does, for such damage no one can make me dismantle my mill, for it is to the common profit of each person, that each person may pursue his or her occupation and improve his or her property, without harming anybody.

This passage clearly shows the competitive ideology of the new bourgeois as opposed to the communalist spirit of the early cities or even the feudal spirit. In each generation, therefore, older bourgeois were shunted aside or crushed by competition, while new developments brought new families, new entrepreneurs, to the fore.

This new bourgeois ideology was, however, tentative and uncertain, not having a firm grip even over the attitudes of the bourgeoisie itself. No development more clearly shows the persistence of feudal ideology at this period than the decision by second- and third-generation bourgeois, grown rich in trade, to renounce artisanal and entrepreneurial activity and move to the countryside; their object was, quite simply, to acquire legitimacy and status in the feudal order and by feudal standards. They bought land, thus taking it out of the feudal system, or bought fiefs together with the services due the lord, seeking to step by purchase or marriage into nobility.

The king or emperor alone had the right to confer knighthood, a badge of noble rank. (Beaumanoir does, however, recount one instance of three knights creating a fourth, but notes that they acted unlawfully. In the south of France, it was still claimed in 1298 that the secular and lay lords, vassals of the king, could bestow knighthoods. Beaumanoir, however, makes it clear that such "novelties" are for the king alone to sponsor.) In practice, knighthoods were conferred on the richest bourgeois as they migrated into the countryside. Those rich bourgeois who were not knighted still aspired to own fiefs. Although this was forbidden in France by royal *ordonnance*, Beaumanoir demonstrates how such purchases were nonetheless accomplished; many seigneurs—financially squeezed by inflation and by the levies of men, money, and material for the Crusades—were motivated to sell their land or to marry off their daughters into bourgeois families, for a price.

The legal status of the bourgeois was firmly recognized in Western Europe by the thirteenth century, but the leaders of the movement to create that status, and their opponents, were bound up in the legal, economic, and religious ideology of their time. They did not see themselves as overturning or abolishing old ways. Far from it: the bourgeois, as we have seen, aspired to be noble. Beaumanoir's book attests to a strong current of legal thought which sought to accommodate, rather than annihilate, all the interests of feudal society, consistent with the aspirations of the bourgeoisie. The bourgeois theorists—at least those whose works have come down to us—saw contradictions between the progress of commerce and certain feudal privileges, but they did not see any fundamental opposition between the two.

PROPERTY AND CONTRACT: TRANSFORMATION OF THE FEUDAL ORDER

Because feudal categories of social status were still dominant, Beaumanoir took some care to describe each category and its relation to the law of property and contracts. Three classes are recognized, he says: nobles, freedmen, and serfs:

> Nobles are of free lineage, such as kings, dukes, counts, or knights, and this nobility is always reckoned through the father and not through the mother; but it is otherwise with the franchise of freedmen, for those of them who are of free lineage trace it through their mother; and whoever is born of a free mother, he is free, and has free power to do what pleases him. . . .

In discussing serfdom, and with it the lord's power to imprison the serf at will, Beaumanoir recognized the natural-law command that all persons are by nature free. He contended, however, that earthly society is a corruption of nature, and as evidence of this corruption he acknowledges the legality of slavery.

In treating property law, Beaumanoir stresses feudal rights, including the right of members of a family to buy back within a certain time, usually a year, any property sold to an outsider. This right, held by anyone who would have inherited the realty at the death of the seller, severely limited commerce in real estate. For this reason, many urban custumals of this period abolished this right of *rescousse* or *retrait lignager*.

In the field of contracts, the *Coutumes* gave the nobility certain privileges. A creditor was required to allow a noble fifteen days after the demand for payment before suing to collect; others received only seven days. Nobles had the right to have seals, and could therefore enter into contracts without the intervention of a notary or royal officer.

We can see in the *Coutumes* the penetration of essentially Roman ideas of free contract into northern France. Beaumanoir had no doubt studied Roman contract law, and those who have detected almost no trace of Roman principles in his work must have paid insufficient attention to Roman ideas of contract and have omitted to consider the place given to Roman law in the university Beaumanoir attended. Both the content and manner of his summary evoke Roman principles, and his discussion of commercial societies and corporate bodies indicates a familiarity with Italian business practices, which relied upon Roman-law principles. Beaumanoir's setting out as law of principles clearly derived from Roman ideas demonstrates both the currency of these ideas and the extent of their diffusion. Unlike other writers of the period, Beaumanoir described the law that was in use and did not parrot Romanisms from vanity, partisanship, or a need to fill in gaps. Further, his treatment of contract law shows an appreciation of the extent to which the notion of contract had penetrated feudal society: the feudal relationship of homage and vassaldom was beginning to be assimilated to the contract.

Beaumanoir's discussion of contracts, though evincing his familiarity with Roman law, stresses the practical, mercantile aspect of the subject. His familiarity with both Roman rules and mercantile custom is apparent from his first words. He calls contracts *convenenes*, a word which, with some variations, was in general mercantile use at the time. The word comes from *convenientia*, a noun form of the vulgar Latin *convenire*—to be in agreement. "All contracts are to be kept," Beaumanoir writes, "and for this one says 'contract makes law,' except those contracts that are made for bad causes."

In drawing this distinction, Beaumanoir is following the classification of contracts made in the 1200s at the great law schools under the influence of the glossators. Azo, author of a celebrated gloss whose works should have been familiar to Beaumanoir, began his treatment with Ulpian's maxim *ex nudo pacto, actio non nascitur*—from a naked contract, no action can be born. The "naked contract" was the simple agreement to pay or to do, unenforceable unless "cloaked." The cloak was termed *causa*, *cose* in medieval French, *cause* in modern French. Something more than a simple agreement, even if the agreement were proved, was indispensable if the contract was breached and the injured party wanted to sue; to win, he or she had to prove the agreement "plus" one of the cloaks. Following Roman law, Azo enumerated six "cloaks":

1. The thing transferred (*res*) in a "real contract." Real contracts in the civil law do not necessarily have to do with real estate. They are contracts in which an object is delivered to someone as a pledge, deposit, or loan for use or some other purpose, to be returned to the giver at the end of a specified period. We have seen examples of such contracts in treating business practices in Chapter 4. Once the object is delivered, there was evidence that an agreement of some sort had been reached; the contract was thus "cloaked," and its terms could be proven.

2. The words (*verba*) of a stipulation, which carried forward the ritual *stipulatio*. Here the parties' use of such ritual words in concluding their bargain as "*spondes-ne?*" and the response "*spondeo*," rather than ordinary speech, lent the agreement legal force.

3. The writing (*litterae*) of a contract.

4. The agreement (*consensus*) in consensual contracts. The appearance of the consensual contract, which required no particular formal wording and did not have to be in writing, came to Roman law under the influence of Rome's widening international commerce. Its application was limited to commerce, it was regarded as part of the *jus gentium*, and it gave rise to a praetorian action in good faith. Within the permissible ambit of the consensual contract, to follow Azo's logic, the cloak was that no cloak was required.

5. For contracts supplemental to an earlier contract (*pactes adjoints*), the *causa* of the initial contract would suffice.

6. Finally, an executed contract had *causa* because the doing of the act (*rei interventus*) led to a presumption that there had been a prior agreement.

Beaumanoir's discussion includes almost all of these elements, leaving out the Latin names and reference to Roman sources. He does, however, appear to confuse the notion of *causa* as a legal category with a literal translation of it as "reason" or "motive," insisting that contracts for "bad causes" are invalid. The examples he gives include contracts to pay losses at dice, usurious contracts, or others "*contre bones meurs*," such as contracts to commit crimes. He also shows the influence of either canon law or the gloss of Accursius, a follower of Azo, in recognizing an oath as *causa*. Indeed, he takes the canonist view that contracts made under oath especially are to be kept, for "in contracting between God and himself, if he does not keep the promise to the best of his ability, he has perjured himself in the sight of God."

Beaumanoir's discussion of contracts shows how a critical appraisal had begun in thirteenth-century France of the elements of the feudal relationship, prefiguring the bourgeois state. The increasing centralization of authority in the hands of the king took judicial, police, and military power away from the lords. While these changes in legal theory need not have meant any change in practice—the lord's court could have continued, subject to a new right of appeal to the king, and the lord could have been told that he held the right to judge "of the king"—the power to judge was no longer bound up in the personal relationship of vassal to lord, but was part of the sovereign authority claimed by the king. Put another way, the rules were no longer even colorably regarded as the product of an immemorial common accord; lord and vassal alike looked to the king to determine the content of their feudal relationship.

Beaumanoir repeatedly insists that homage, fealty, and feudal services are elements of a bargain that is theoretically no different from any other contract. If contracts involve a meeting of wills, an agreement, no valid consent may be the product of force or fear. Beaumanoir makes clear that he has in mind agreements extorted by seigneurs and other powerful people. Indeed,

> if I say that I made a contract because someone menaced me . . . , and it appears that he who did the menacing is not my lord, or a powerful man, such that

> I would not be able to pursue my rights against him; then, I was fearful without reason, for I could assuredly bring a lawsuit against this person and both prevent any damage to me and avoid a foolish contract.

He followed this discussion with the passage quoted earlier concerning the ubiquity of royal jurisdiction. This implied opportunity to test the feudal bond was often taken up, and the 1200s and 1300s witnessed prodigious use of the royal courts to challenge seigneurial rights.

In sum, therefore, the legal idea of contract penetrated feudal political institutions much as the fact of contract penetrated the feudal economy. The late-Roman commercial principles, applied to an increasingly robust and technologically improved commerce, had, by the time Beaumanoir wrote, passed into the common language of the law, at least in France.

Thirty years before Beaumanoir, Bracton compiled a treatise on English law, similar in scope to Beaumanoir's and likewise clearly influenced, in its treatment of contracts, by contemporary Roman-law scholars. In Italy, Roman law had been received as "common law," binding on all tribunals in all sovereignties unless displaced by a *jus proprium*—a law of the place, such as the urban statutes of the city-states, the maritime-legislation statutes of the port cities, and the monarchical *ordonnances* of Sicily, Sardinia, and Savoy. In Spain also, under the influence of the cities (*fueros*), Roman law notions of contract and procedure had taken hold. A Barcelona custumal of 1068 borrowed extensively from the *Exceptiones Petri*. *Lo Codi* was translated into Catalonian. After 1215, when a university was established at Salamanca, locally trained Romanists entered the practice of law. Roman-law borrowings appear in the kingdoms of Leon and Castile in the mid-1200s in *Las siete partidas*, a general restatement of the law which is attributed to King Alfonso the Wise.

In Germany, the wholesale adoption of Roman law came later: only in 1495 was it accepted by the German central imperial court—the *Reichskammergericht*—as the common and general law of the empire. In the 1300s, however, as the Hanse built its commercial power, Roman-law principles made their appearance in practical texts and treatises and in the universities in the Hanse towns. Certain Roman-law principles had arrived even earlier; both Frederick Barbarossa and Frederick II, regarding themselves as the Western heirs of Constantine and Justinian, enacted *novellae* as appendages to the Justinian codification.

The Roman law of the civil- and canon-law professors, the royal courts, and the marketplaces of Europe did, to be sure, vary widely. But Roman law unmistakably imposed a certain uniformity of legal technique, and crept, sometimes in disguise, into the customary law of every place touched by the commercial currents of the 1200s. Even in the north of France and in England, where it was never recognized as the "common and general law," Roman law was used without being cited. An *ordonnance* of Philip III of 1278 stated: "The lawyers be not bold enough to involve themselves in citing Roman law in those areas where govern the customary laws." They need not have been bold; Roman law had already infused the customary rules.

Beaumanoir's book is not the only evidence of the tendency of the Roman law to invade the field of contract law. Other works from the same time present a similar picture of reliance on Roman principles—and upon the glossators—without direct reference to them: Pierre de Fontaine's *Conseil à un ami*; the *Jostice et Plet* (Justice and Pleas), the *Tres ancienne coutume de Brétagne*, and the *Livres des droiz et commandemes* are other examples. Similarly, in notarial practice we find increasing use of the technical language said by the glossators to be necessary to constitute a *stipulatio* and thereby give the contract *causa*. Clearly the lowest level of the legal profession—the local scriveners—were receiving some formal training.

Beaumanoir further reflects the Roman-law influence when he treats the validity of a contract as primarily a question of legal procedure. There are some agreements that are unlawful, and to make them is perhaps even to incur liability for punishment. But the principal attribute of *causa* is not that it validates the agreement of the parties in any substantive sense, but that it gives rise to an action at law for breach of promise.

At first sight, this may seem academic and theoretical, but it was in fact an expression of a principle essential to the growth of commerce. The canonists believed that the promise was sacred, and looked to the fulfillment of the inner intentions of the parties in good faith. For the civil lawyers, however, the promise was *nudum pactum*; it might be a weight upon the conscience, but it was not enforceable without more. That "more" was in almost every case objective and evidentiary, designed to tell onlookers about the bargain, to record it, or to leave no doubt it had been concluded. This objective notion of contract is suited to a marketplace in which the contract alone unites the parties, rather than its being only one element in an ongoing relationship of family, village, commune, or guild.

Under the *jus gentium* merchants could resort to the consensual contract, the need for ease of dealing outweighing the desire for objective evidence of the bargain. They were protected nonetheless by knowing the reputation of their opposite number, by the suretyship laws of many communes, by other devices in the realm of credit, or by some token of agreement. For instance, merchant contracts were routinely upheld if the "God's penny" had been given as a token of agreement, thus taking the place of the formal "vestments" of the glossators. The God's penny would be handed over, then used perhaps as alms or, as was the custom in Arles, taken to the Church to buy a candle.

The canonists, insisting on the moral obligation to keep one's promise, exerted pressure on the civil tribunals, often taking their theoretical guidance from the Roman law of natural—i.e., moral but generally unenforceable—obligations. This pressure led the *Parlement* in France to validate contracts "*ex causa*" as a matter of equity, and was one force behind the later establishment of the equity jurisdiction in England.

There was, however, a lawyer's maxim in the 1200s, "*Dieu nous garde de l'equité des Parlements*" (God keep us from the equity of *Parlements*), which reflected an important assumption about the role of contract in a new form of social relations. Feudal relations proceeded upon the notions of superordination and subordination: some were weaker than others; the stronger would fight on horseback and lead the weaker—on foot—to battle, and so on. The early city charters, as we have seen, expressed this same view: they were protective and restrictive, with the goal of advancing the common interest of all the city dwellers who had won their partial freedom. Even later, when the guilds struggled to maintain their privileges in the face of large-scale commerce, their protective functions were frankly acknowledged, only at this time a smaller slice of society—artisans and masters—was protected, to the exclusion of the laborers.

The law of contract, by contrast, tends to treat all parties as equals. The more complex the system of commerce, the more faceless the parties become in the eyes of the law. If A sells to B face-to-face, for B's immediate consumption, there can be elements of good faith and personal trust which go beyond the letter of any bargain they make. This is simply not possible in larger-scale commerce. Take as an example the bill of exchange. Ghuglielmo Barberi, an exporter of Flemish cloth dealing primarily with the Barcelona market and living in Bruges, borrows money on short term from the Bruges representative of the Florence banking house of AIberti and Company in order to buy cloth. He sends the cloth to Barcelona in the hands of an agent who has full authority to sell it and orders him to deposit the money from the sale with the Barcelona banking house of Francisco di Marco Datini da Prato, which will in turn see that Alberti is repaid by transferring the money to his banker. The money borrowed was in French or Flemish coin; the money deposited in Barcelona will be in the currency of Barcelona.

Imagine the paperwork necessary to accomplish this transaction. The goods travel with documents, and when they arrive in Barcelona, the contract of sale drawn up in Bruges has no personal meaning for the buyer; it is only a piece of paper which says that the goods belong to a certain person. As such it represents, in an abstract sense, ownership of or title to the goods.

The operation of credit and monetary exchange is even more abstract. In Bruges, Barberi writes a letter of exchange:

> In the name of God, the 18th of December 1399, you will pay by this first letter, according to the usual delays for payment, to Brunaccio di Guido and Co. . . . CCCCLXXII livres X sous of Barcelona, the said 472 livres 10 sous having a value of 900 ecus at 10 sous 6 deniers per ecu, having been paid over to me here by Riccardo degl'Alberti & Co. Pay them in good and due form and charge them to my account. May God keep you.
>
> —GHUGLIELMO BARBERI
> Greetings from Bruges

The letter therefore involves four parties: the drawee in Barcelona, Datini da Prato, who is to pay the money; the drawer, Barberi; the payer, Alberti, who gave the money to Barberi in Bruges; and the payee, Brunaccio di Guido, Alberti's banker or agent who will collect the money in Barcelona and see that Alberti is repaid.

This use of a writing to represent a sum of money or stock of goods began to acquire importance in the 1200s and developed as the needs of commerce required. But it was not until the 1400s—for example, in the Hanseatic cities—and the 1500s in the Mediterranean domain, that the bill of exchange became entirely separated from the persons who made it and took on, through the technique of endorsement, the character of a negotiable instrument.

The writing of contracts, made necessary by the needs of long-distance commerce, reinforced the anonymity of the parties in a juridical sense. What they meant when the deal was negotiated was irrelevant, for third parties at some distance and in some future time would evaluate the arrangement on the basis of evidence left in the form of written memoranda. The formal requirements of contracting them became more important then ever, and if parties wanted to have their contracts recognized as legally binding—that is, if they wanted it clear that they meant to create an obligation—they used one of the legal forms of agreement which the lawyers told them would have that result.

This in turn strengthened the position of the lawyers and called for the development, recording, and study of legal formulas suited to the arrangements merchants wanted to make. Another consequence of spreading commerce, then, was the increased pressure upon the political allies of the large merchant interests to make uniform the law applicable to trade, so that a formula intended to create a contract in Bruges would be held in Florence to have done so.

The movement toward objective evidence of an agreement led also to use of legal talent to break contracts which were technically defective. If a party did not wish to carry out a bargain, because it turned out to have been improvidently made or to be the product of a disparity of economic position, or simply because changed circumstances made it no longer advantageous, a lawyer could examine the contract to see whether it was enforceable. The writing, which was only the evidence of the agreement, began to take primacy over the substance.

The generalization of contract principles, and the growing pressure by the newer economic interests to secure recognition of the maxim that all contracts are to be kept, represented the bourgeoisie's effort to remove a significant set of social relations from the administration of governments. The idea of the contract as "private legislation" at the will of the parties ran counter to the ideology of feudal institutions. For some canonical theorists, moreover, such rigid rules detracted from the moral element of the promise and could be used to oppress the poor. Royal courts, too, resisted carrying the purely objective theory of contract, by which the written bargain was supreme irrespective of its fairness or the relative strengths of the parties, to its limits, which led the legal profession to protest the "equity" of *Parlement*. The theoretical underpinnings of bourgeois codes of laws begin to appear: the role of government is to provide a set of institutions which will force parties to keep their contracts or make them pay damages for not doing so.

Beaumanoir was not writing about the customs of such commercial centers as Bruges or Barcelona, but he nonetheless recognized the value of a written agreement as "a manner of proof" of contract. He cites three methods by which the parties to a written agreement may validate it: nobles may affix seals; commoners may bring their contracts before the seigneur where they reside, or before a royal officer (*bailli* or a notary authorized to practice) to be sealed; and ecclesiastical judicial officials may also affix seals, although their role is generally confined to matters within the Church's judicial jurisdiction, such as wills. Beaumanoir's suggested contract forms again reflect his legal training, as well as the forces pushing for the expansion of the domain of contract in economic life. He sets out detailed examples of contractual terms which renounce the benefits of various protections to minors, debtors, and so on, and gives forms for the renunciation of the benefits of "the law which says that a general renunciation is invalid." (He also points out that a plea of forced consent prevails against a renunciation, and that the king's court can overlook renunciations for "what pleases the king to do must be taken as law.")

LAWYERS AND LAWSUITS: THE JURISTS STEP IN

Technical words and technical devices began to contribute to a sense of popular alienation from legal institutions. The lawmaking role of the people began to be played down and then gradually eliminated in the urban settings where it had briefly flourished. The law itself, as a set of rules and maxims and complex procedures for applying them, became the occupation of a class of initiates. Beaumanoir tells us that fancy talk is the lawyer's *métier*. He describes a legal profession and court system which did not lack for business. We have already encountered the notaries who drafted contracts. The proliferation of *loiers*, also termed *avocats* or *procureurs*, marks a new stage in the evolution of the legal profession. (As feudal customs were displaced in the field of contracts and commercial law, they tended to survive only in the area of family relations. Even the communal municipal laws were, as we have seen, displaced by the new legal learning.)

The notary—who could represent both parties, enabling them to put their common accord in writing—differed from the advocate, who was a partisan adversary. The advocate was the agent of the litigant, empowered to act and speak on the latter's behalf, and to assist in the formulation of orders and judgments which act directly on the client. This notion of representation was a necessary step in the development of the legal system and of commerce itself. Prior to the thirteenth century, an agent could not act on behalf of a merchant without becoming personally liable. Beaumanoir, however, seems to recognize the newer principle that when an agent was appointed, the agent's signature on a contract created liability only for his principal.

The relation between the general principles of agency and those applicable to lawyers is shown by the use of the same term—*procureur*—to describe both sorts of representatives. The novelty of the concept of representation is seen in the elaborate and specific procuration which had to be executed and filed with the court in order to enable a lawyer to appear, as well as by Beaumanoir's statement that the lawyer must "present himself in the name of his client." As an aid to practice, Beaumanoir gives an example of a procuration:

> To all those seeing or hearing these present letters, the *bailli* of Clermont sends greetings. Be it known that in our presence to thus appoint, Pierres, of a certain place, has appointed Jehans, of a certain place, his general and special *procureur* on all causes moved and to be moved, for him as well as against him, against all persons whatever, ecclesiastical as well as secular, as plaintiff as well as defendant, before whatever ordinaries, legates, delegates, subdelegates, arbitrators, conservators, auditors, inquestors, *baillis*, provosts, mayors, *échevins*, and other judges whatever, ecclesiastical as well as secular, and their sheriffs and those who exercise their power. And gives to the said Jehans full power and special commission to replicate, to duplicate, to hear interlocutory and final judgments, to appeal, to pursue his appeal, to swear in the name of Pierres' soul all manner of oaths, to take positions, to receive that which is adjudged in his favor, to produce evidence or to call witnesses with solemnities of law and to make the said solemnities; and to do for him all the things which the said Pierres would do or would be able to do if he were present, and in cases of movables, real property, and in cases involving things which, though real property by their nature, are held in law to be movables. And gives also power to the said Jehans to subscribe in his place for all the times he pleads for him, that which he will subscribe to have the same effect as

> though Pierres himself were present. And promised him the said Pierres in our presence that all that will be said or done by the said Jehans or subscribed by the said Jehans, he will honor with all his property. In witness whereof, I have, at the request of the said *procureur*, sealed this procuration with the seal of the *bailli* of Clermont. This was done in the year of grace . . . .

The terms of this procuration reflect the influence of both canon and Roman law, and Beaumanoir may have copied it from an ecclesiastical source.

The profession of advocate, in the sense of a regulated group of practitioners with some formal training, emerged in the late 1200s. Both the English and the French sovereigns legislated with respect to the profession, limiting the practice of law to those who had been approved by judicial officers. This legislation—in England in 1292 and in France in 1274 and 1278—reflected a gradual development. Those landowners and businessmen regularly involved in litigation were probably the first to appoint someone to represent them, but others are reported to have appeared with friends and advisers.

The increasing currency of Roman law, the new royal legislation, and the growing complexity of commerce and commercial law all gave rise to the need for a trained lawyer. If our hypothetical Pierres, who hired Jehans the lawyer, had a case against Richard, he would face a tortuous path to judgment in his favor.

First, Jehans must choose a court in which to sue. If the defendant is a cleric Jehans must sue in the ecclesiastical court—"before the cleric's ordinary," or ecclesiastical superior. There he would face a fairly orderly, though complex, written proceeding. Pierres' contentions would be submitted in writing; Richard would respond in writing with "exceptions," legal points showing why the cause should be delayed (dilatory exceptions), or legal and factual points undercutting or denying the claim of Pierres (peremptory exceptions). Pierres would be entitled to file replications, attacking the defenses raised in the exceptions. The cleric could counterclaim against Pierres in the ecclesiastical court, and claim a setoff, or deduction, for some claim he had against Pierres. From there the proceeding moved by writing, the process of proof being in the form of written statements.

If Richard was not a cleric, Pierres' problem was more complex. If Richard was a bourgeois, he could be sued in the communal court, and probably only there. If Richard was a bourgeois of the king, and lived in a royal city, then the king's court might be competent. The concept of "privileged person"—one who could be sued only in the king's court and not in a seigneurial court—began to appear in the 1200s, and we see it creeping into the urban custumals, particularly in France. Bourgeois, students, royal officers, traveling merchants under special protection—all these might be answerable only before a royal officer. In Clermont that would be the *bailli*, Philippe de Beaumanoir himself.

If, however, Richard and Pierres were disputing about rural land that was not in the territory of any city or under the direct jurisdiction of the king, or if neither was a privileged person, Pierres could bring his case in the court of the appropriate seigneur. But which seigneur? Jurisdiction lay "before the seigneur of the place where the defendant goes to bed and arises," or, in the case of land, before the seigneur in whose domain the land lay, regardless of where the parties were from.

The lawsuit itself, before the *bailli* or a seigneurial court, could take a number of forms. Trial by battle was frequent in the 1200s; St. Louis attempted to stop it in 1260, at least in the royal domains, and substitute a system of inquests and testimonial proof: Beaumanoir states that the judicial duel is permitted only in cases of crime. But in the royal and feudal courts an ordinary case of contract might turn into a criminal matter if one party alleged that the other, or his witnesses, had lied. The trial could then be halted for a judicial duel over the issue of perjury.

If Pierres was willing to risk having to battle Richard, could find a court in which to sue him, and was confident that he could frame a demand that would be acceptable, he faced yet another obstacle. He could not get a judgment against Richard without forcing him to appear in court at a time when it was lawful for judgment to be pronounced against him. An astounding amount of medieval procedural law is devoted to the question by whom and how the defendant can be made to appear and defend a lawsuit. If Richard had a lawyer, summoning him might be easier since the procuration would be on file in the court. If the procuration was required for another court than that in which it was first filed, it had to be transcribed and a certified copy sent; the initial document itself served a notice-giving function which could be compromised by sending it out of the possession of the tribunal that first received it.

The notion of summons is allied to that of jurisdiction—Richard had to be sued where he resided because only his seigneur had the power to require him to attend court. The feudal idea that Richard is "the man" of his seigneur dictated judicial procedure. Beaumanoir even treats the judicial summons in the same chapter as the summons to fight in the lord's forces and to perform feudal services. Similarly, in principle all land is held of a seigneur, and that seigneur is uniquely competent to judge "concerning" the land.

An alternative means of summoning Richard was to arrest him, a measure available only for certain sorts of action and only against certain groups of people. The custumals of all the important commercial cities dealt with the right of arrest, generally limiting or abolishing the practice with respect to bourgeois of the city. In return, creditors were protected by municipal guarantees of the solvency of the bourgeois.

Once summoned, Richard was entitled to a certain number of delays for fixed periods, and perhaps to an indefinite delay which could require Pierres to summon him again. But the ritual for demanding these delays in court was so precisely defined that any slip could cost the right to delay. If Richard sent someone to court to answer the summons, and his representative tripped up on his demand, Richard was "in default" and lost the lawsuit. Practice books of the 1200s are full of hints for lawyers about how to prolong lawsuits without falling into default. Beaumanoir seems, however, to have the judge's and not the lawyer's view toward such tactics, for he not only declines to describe such techniques, but admonishes that "Sinful are the judges who haste not to judgment." This recalls St. Louis' directive that *baillis* "shall hear the matters brought before them . . . so that Our subjects may not be induced to forego their just rights for fear of trouble and expense."

We might ask the reasons for this extraordinarily complex procedure. For one thing, the judicial institutions Beaumanoir describes were built up over time, and there was clearly an initial reason for each new ritual or form of procedure added. For example, it seems likely that the delays in a feudal summoning procedure were originally designed to accommodate the needs of an agricultural society, at a time when a "summons" to the lord's "court" was a means to obtain the vassal's presence to plow, thresh, or fight, and delay was a concession to the vassal's own needs. As time passed, a procedural device became a form drained of content, usable for purposes other than those for which it was originally fashioned.

On the other hand, lawyers for the merchant class, anxious to do away with rituals that interfered with speedy and efficient disposition of mercantile disputes, were seeking and obtaining changes in the legal system as it dealt with their clients. In France, for instance, the rule that a litigant could not testify in his own case was relaxed in favor of the merchants. A food seller could testify as to debts owed by customers, for there was no other way to prove such obligations if the customer denied them. A creditor could testify to a written acknowledgment of the debt by the debtor. The rules, particularly the former, were preludes to the later shop-book principle, that a merchant's books of account are admissible to prove the sums owed by customers.

In England, in 1303, Edward I provided that if both plaintiff and defendant were merchants, and the God's penny had been given, wager of law was not permitted. The party with the right to "wage law" in an action for debt—usually the defendant and alleged debtor—gave a pledge that on a certain day he would make his law. On that day, he swore in open court that he did not owe the debt, and presented eleven neighbors who took an oath that they believed him to be telling the truth. As far as most merchants were concerned, wager of law was a kind of institutionalized mass perjury.

The lawyer was required to master the old ritual complexities, as well as being enlisted by the bourgeoisie to fashion new ones. In the 1200s, the dislocating influences of commerce had already led knights and clerics to define their status rigidly, to preserve their privileges, and to keep out usurpers and pretenders. A similar pattern of status definition marks the growth of the merchant group, and the lawyers responded in the same way. They were willing to allow trial by battle to give way to proof by witnesses, documents, official records, and presumptions. They welcomed the increasing use of written trial records, and approved Beaumanoir's advice that a judge ask for written briefs of legal points in the law court. But this rationalization of the law, coming through the mediation of the legal profession, had its price: to obtain the benefits of it, one had to pay for the services of a lawyer. Pierres could perhaps be confident that his lawsuit would win or lose according to written, or at least generally known, rules and according to the testimony of witnesses or documents that would re-create for the judge the circumstances that had led to the dispute. He could achieve this result, however, only through the intercession of an advocate who manipulated these legal and factual elements in a procedural system Pierres could not hope to master without lengthy study. This contradiction was often clearly perceived. One exceptional lawyer who served the poor in Brittany was made a saint in tribute to his uniqueness. A popular poem about him ran:

St. Yves is from Brittany
A lawyer but not a thief
Such a thing is beyond belief!

A revolutionary response to this procedural confusion would have leveled the judicial structure and erected a new one. The merchants, bourgeois, and maritime adventurers did not, however, consider that they had the power to do this. Instead, in certain disputes the established court system was simply bypassed, and parallel institutions erected alongside it, again with the help of lawyers. In Newcastle, for instance, a maritime court was approved by the king, and was required by its charter to judge all lawsuits before the third tide after the dispute was brought before it. The fair courts opened with the fair and closed with it; accounts had to be settled and disputes regulated within that time. (There is, however, evidence that disputes erupting at the fair might wind up in the royal courts. By merchant custom, an unpaid balance on goods sold gave the seller a lien—a nonpossessory property right—in the goods which could be enforced by seizure in case of default. And Beaumanoir noted that in the kingdom of France an oral pledge of suretyship was valid if it was made in the fairs of Champagne—that is, a third party could orally vouch for the buyer's credit and agree that if the debtor refused or failed to pay, he would be liable for the debt. These pledges were enforceable in the royal court, indicating that at least some disputes might survive the end of the fair.)

The bourgeois also turned to nonjudicial means of settlement. His lawyer might have authority to settle lawsuits out of court, or two parties to a dispute could agree to have it arbitrated. Arbitration was a normal commercial practice, but it might also be used as a means to avoid the rigors and uncertainty of a trial. The disputants could select arbitrators, giving pledges in the form of money or property that they would abide by the result. But contractual principles of good faith and the presumed intention of the parties, as well as the idea that the arbitrators must act reasonably and impartially—as judges were supposed to do—could be resorted to in the courts if the arbitration award was thought onerous by one of the disputants.

When, to take one example, a bourgeois injured another in a fight in Beauvais, the miscreant preferred to have the matter arbitrated by three persons chosen by the victim. The arbitrators ordered that the wrongdoer make three lengthy pilgrimages—to Italy, to Spain, and to Provence—that he go and live across the sea for three years, and that he sign a pledge that he would stand surety for the victim "as though he were a first cousin." The malefactor attacked the order and refused to abide by it, calling it a prearranged plan that was neither based on the seriousness of his wrong, nor rendered independently according to the evidence, nor within the intention of the agreement to arbitrate. Beaumanoir argued that the agreement need not be kept and that the order was void, and cited his judgment as showing that standards of justice and fairness could be imposed upon arbitral tribunals.

In brief compass, in the life and work of Beaumanoir can be seen the alliance in the thirteenth and fourteenth centuries between the large commercial interests, the newly powerful monarchs, and the legal profession. After the revolutionary period of the previous two hundred years, in which lawmaking was a popular activity carried on as an adjunct to, and in consolidation of, revolutionary strife, the emergence of the lawyer-civil servant betokens a new state of affairs. Law becomes the creature of the economically powerful, elaborated by a class hired by them and working in their interest. We will return to this theme again.

12.

THE MERCHANT CAPITAL OF GRASSE

The actions of individual men and women affected by legal rules do not appear clearly in the words of Beaumanoir and other jurists and civil servants. To measure the impact of the legal changes wrought by bourgeois insurgency and modified by seigneurial and royal action, we must examine at close range the life of one particular city. Grasse, a city in the south of France, twenty miles from the Mediterranean Sea and fifty miles from the Italian border, was a secondary manufacturing and commercial center which dominated and imposed the cash nexus upon the surrounding agricultural and pastoral regions, as well as upon lesser urban entities. Viewed close up, the rhythm of buying, selling, borrowing, and capital formation reveals the central place of bourgeois legal principles in the growth of commerce. While Grasse's archives offer us nothing akin to the work of Beaumanoir, we can nevertheless see the growing interpenetration of capitalist and feudal law, and get a sense of the latter's ability to regain the upper hand should economic growth falter. We are fortunate that Grasse, due to its mild climate and its relatively peaceful history, has managed to preserve extensive records of contracts, deeds, and official records dating back to the 1300s. And when we examine records in other cities, we can see that the economic and legal developments in Grasse closely paralleled those elsewhere.

While the progress of bourgeois legal theory in this period is best viewed through the eyes of the university-trained legalists who gained the confidence of monarchs, the daily life of Grasse is best seen through the eyes of someone like Leonet Dayot, a Jew whose name appears in an official roll in 1305 and in a notarial act in 1309 as the purchaser of a quantity of cloth, or through the eyes of the farmers for whom Grasse was the focus of economic life.

Grasse stands just where the slow rise from the Mediterranean gives way to the abrupt relief of the limestone pre-Alps. It was established in the tenth century under the suzerainty of a bishop and a noble family which took the name de Grasse. The commune was founded in 1155, electing two consuls who played the same role as the mayor in more northerly cities. Class wars within the city provided a justification for the suppression of the commune by the Count of Provence in 1227. Nonetheless, the city continued to enjoy its trading privileges, commercial freedom, and fairs and markets.

These commercial privileges were considerable, and Grasse was one of the Provençal cities allied by a treaty of commerce, friendship, and mutual protection with Genoa, depending on it to purchase its major products, tanned hides and agricultural goods. Furthermore, sitting on the main road across the Mediterranean littoral, linked to Aix-en-Provence, Marseille, and cities farther west, Grasse was the terminus of Provençal land trade. Less important roads linked it with the Provençal towns of Castellane and Digne, whose inhabitants looked to Grasse for their clothing, their farm implements, and for the sale of their produce.

The position of Jews in the 1300s reflects in equal amounts the bigotry, hypocrisy, and accommodating spirit of Christian capitalism. Jewish communities were tolerated in varying degrees in all the major cities of the Mediterranean littoral. We do not know where Leonet Dayot's family came from, but perhaps they came south from Paris in the late 1200s. In 1306, Philip IV of France banned Jews from the kingdom, making official and final a pogrom which had begun some years before. But the Jewish community of Paris had long since begun to clear out. In 1292, the tax rolls of the city of Paris contain the names of 125 Jews; there are only 86 on the rolls of 1296 and 1297. Both figures represent perhaps 10 percent of the Jewish population, as only a fraction had sufficient economic means to be subjected to taxation. From 1298 onward, however, there are no Jews on the tax rolls.

Under the protection of the Counts of Provence, the Jewish families who settled in Grasse found the place reasonably hospitable. In general, the Jewish community in feudal Europe was subject to shifting seigneurial protection.

Within feudal domains, the Jewish community lived apart, following the Mosaic law, the observance of which was tacitly guaranteed by each seigneur. In this state of semiprotection, or semibondage, as Jacques Ellul has written, "the seigneur considered himself more or less the owner of the Jews within his domain." Jews were forbidden to own serfs or to employ Christian workers in artisanal activities. They were driven, therefore, to professions such as tailoring or goldsmithing, and to money lending, an activity that was subject to churchly sanction if practiced by Christians. Jews thus lent money on their own account and as "fronts" for non-Jews who did not wish to acknowledge their activities. Periodical pogroms wiped out entire Jewish communities or forced the inhabitants to flee; one of the most vicious of these pogroms accompanied the beginning of the Crusades.

Despite their reputation as moneylenders, Jews did not prosper greatly. One indication of their relative financial position is that the 125 Jews on the Paris tax rolls in 1292 were taxed 126 livres; by contrast, the 200 Lombards, most of whom were involved in commerce and banking, were taxed 1,500 livres, reflecting much greater per-capita wealth. But in a secondary commercial center such as Grasse, we find few traces of economic activity requiring large amounts of capital in the 1300s, and the Jews of modest fortune were the economic equals to local merchants and artisans.

It was not until 1396 that the first official repressive measure was taken against the Jewish community by the rulers of Provence. At that time Jews were required to wear a distinctive badge and to live in a specific area of town. The Jewish business and professional community grouped itself near the synagogue in the center of the walled city; there Jews lived and worked as artisans, practiced as doctors, bought, sold, and lent. So important were their activities that the paschal lamb came to decorate Grasse's coat of arms.

Small loans fueled the local economy. The stock of capital from which these loans were made came from many sources, some of them rather surprising. In one case, a priest, acting for a bishop, placed the sum of fifty-eight florins (coins of 3.54 grams, fifty eight of which would contain about four ounces of pure gold) with Robin Mayr, Jaciel, and Jacob. In other contracts, Jews are named as receiving sums on loan from two Genoese merchants, and from a local noble. Taking into account the notarial acts of this period, which demonstrate a frequent use of "silent partner" *compania* arrangements, and the churchly prohibition against usury, we can conclude that the bishop, the merchants, and the nobles were placing their money where it would be lent out at interest. The loans, like virtually all such transactions at the time, were said in the recognizance of debt to be "for the causes of mutuality and friendship," without interest; no doubt the interest was somehow hidden in the transaction.

Grasse in the early 1300s represents another step in the breakdown of feudal relationships and their replacement by the bonds of a money economy. We begin to see the use of cash payments, whether on the spot or by means of credit, for even the basic necessities of rural life, as well as the accompanying erosion of seigneurial rights in the city, a development which we spoke of in the previous chapter.

In the larger cities—Paris, London, Genoa, or Bruges—or where the city, as in England, came early under the firm protection of a central monarch, the transition to a new form of economic life might only take two or three generations. In a city such as Grasse, as in countless other towns outside of England, the war between feudal and capitalist institutions went on longer and took on many forms. The bourgeoisie preferred to enlist existing state institutions to protect commerce, rather than attempting their destruction, and in Grasse this meant using its economic power to dissolve the traditional relationships in the countryside and city and replace them by bonds of supposedly neutral contract law, which confronted men and women with their own voluntary acts reduced to writing.

When we look at a second-class commercial city like Grasse, we therefore see the forging of thousands of small contractual links, a process that could take the economic life of the city and its dependent countryside out of the hands of the nobility, which continued to wield the dominant political power. In the early 1300s farmers came from some distance to do business in Grasse. On foot or on donkey, they came in the spring from as much as twenty-five miles away to buy farm implements. A typical contract in 1310 provided for payment on credit and for the regular repair and upkeep of iron parts for a period of three years. The ironworker was an independent artisan, working for cash, and situated in Grasse so that he could serve the entire region. If the harvest was bad, or its revenues exhausted before the year was up, the farmer could not, as his father had done, go to a lord for an advance of a little grain, dried meat, fish, and other necessities. The lord's son was as likely as he to be in need of cash, or if he had it, to be secretly investing it in Grasse.

The typical rural tenancy of 1310 was not feudal, but a variation of one of two essentially contractual devices, the *acapt* and *metayage*. In a tenancy by accept, also termed *emphytéose* (in Latin *emphyteusis*), the property right of the lord was divided into two parts, the *domaine direct* and the *domaine utile*. The latter, the right to use the land, was given to the farmer in perpetuity in exchange for a one-time payment (*acapt*) when he took possession and a cash rent (*cens*). The *acapt* varied between a substantial amount of money in prosperous times and a purely symbolic "pair of partridges" when times were bad, workers in short supply, and there was a need to find someone to cultivate the ground. The lord or other owner retained only the right to enter and retake the property if the annual rent was not paid, to take it back if the tenant died without heirs or abandoned the tenancy, or to declare the contract void if the land was not well cared for. (The duration of the *acapt* was generally perpetual; hence, it was somewhat inaccurate to use the word *emphytéose* to describe it, since the Roman law *emphyteusis* was for a limited period.)

Thus the lord opted out of the manorial system for a fixed cash payment four times a year and a one-time payment which might be in cash or kind. The spread of knowledge about the Roman *emphyteusis*, and its conversion into the *acapt* of southern France, was no doubt fostered by the realization that feudal services could be bought just as well as exacted as the price of tenure, and perhaps at a saving. There are records of such cost comparisons in the custumals of manors.

The *acapt* was, however, a double-edged device. If the perpetual tenant—and his heirs—really remained on the land perpetually, the annual rent would soon become insignificantly small, as would the fixed house rents in the charters to the city dwellers, as inflation was brought about by the increased money supply and the brisker circulation of commodities. The noble whose only income was ground-rent was condemned to penury if economic growth continued; the bourgeoisie had only to wait for economic factors to take their toll and then buy up the estates of the impoverished gentry. This happened in many cases, but not easily and certainly not peaceably.

When merchants and other non-nobles had land to let, or when nobles defied tradition and entered into the spirit of enterprise in imitation of the Italians, they avoided the disadvantages of *acapt* through use of an agreement known as *metayage* or *facheria*. This entirely contractual means of assuring cultivation spread north from Italy and Provence. Contractually, the *metayage* was similar to the *société* or *commenda* of French and Italian commercial life. The proprietor of the ground would sign a contract—for three, four, or more years—with a farmer who agreed to assure its exploitation. The farmer would keep two-thirds or even three-quarters of the harvest (in the first year he might keep all of it) for his own consumption or to sell. In the same contract, he might receive a loan from the owner to set up the farming operation, or the owner might agree to provide certain equipment or take care of certain farming tasks. A *notaire* in Grasse who had a vineyard on the plain below the town let it out to a farmer but provided that once a year he would take off his robes, leave his law books and study, and personally prune the vines back to encourage the proper growth of the next year's crop. This clause should not surprise us; the act of pruning the vines back to improve both yield and quality was a technical advancement of considerable importance, and the *notaire* would logically want to see it well done.

A related device used by the merchants of Grasse was to sublet their pasture land. Many contracts reveal a bourgeois of the city signing an *acapt* for a quantity of pasture held by a noble, then turning around and subleasing portions of it for short periods for the raising of sheep, cattle, or goats. This variation of *metayage* was known in the notarial practice as *mègerie*, and was characterized by an equal sharing of the profits between the merchant and his subtenant, the merchant using a part of his share to pay the *cens* due under his *acapt*. (Though the *metayage* permitted the landowner to hedge against inflation, nobles did not in great numbers attempt to convert their *baux à acapt* into *metayage* holdings. Their reasons were doubtless ideological: the tradition of devices like *acapt* and the repugnance at commercialism triumphed over economic self-interest.)

The tenant who held in *acapt* or *metayage* financed his purchase of necessities with small loans. To buy seed, tools, or household goods, he would go to Grasse with an heirloom silver goblet, a length of cloth, or a robe, to use as a pledge. Were he too poor to possess such a treasure, he might pledge a portion of the next year's harvest. The contracts show the lender requiring that the farmer's family or friends come to the city and sign the contract as surety for the debt. If the debt was not repaid, the lender had the contractual right to seize the farmer's goods, or to require him (or the other sureties) to come to Grasse and work off the balance. Money lending was not too risky: the contracts show that many people with a little spare cash were directly or indirectly involved in it.

The contract of debt would be drafted by a *notaire*. This legal scrivener might be summoned to the lender's house, or to the city gate, to take notes on the agreed bargain; he then drafted a formal document in Latin for both parties to sign under oath. No doubt for a small loan given to a bad credit risk, the lender would exact a high rate of interest, but the interest would be hidden in some way and never stated. The simplest procedure was to have the debtor sign a document admitting that he had received a certain sum, when in fact he had received much less. The *notaire* would carefully insert a clause waiving the objection that the amount stipulated was not received.

Desultory attempts were made to combat the practice of disguised interest, but they amounted to little. Later, the *Parlements* insisted that debt instruments state the sum due in round numbers, a reaction to the frequency of contracts setting out the debt as, for example, 952 livres, when in fact only 900 had been borrowed. The *notaires* promptly shifted over to using round numbers to mask interest on a loan of a lesser amount. Thenceforth, a debt instrument for 1,000 livres would be drafted, though the borrower received only, for example, 941.

The prohibition on usury was enforced fairly late in Provence. Had our farmer come to town, as his father perhaps had done, in 1295, a contract of debt would have stated the principal and interest separately. After about 1300, the results of a Church-led antiusury campaign can be seen in the notarial practice. Thenceforth, all loans were said in the contracts to be "friendly," "for the sake of love," and surely without interest.

Repayments were to be made on the religious feast days set to celebrate the completion of one or another aspect of rural work. When the harvest was complete, the farmer would carry his produce to market and bring in the share for his silent partner if the land were held in *metayage*. From his profit, he would pay off the small loans he had made. He would then return to his land to start again on the annual cycle of debt and repayment.

The farmer could not read even the notes of the *notaire*'s brief summary in Provencal let alone the lengthy Latin of the formal document. His recourse to the law was the product of necessity, and the law of his contracts could not have been more alien to him. We are not looking here at contracts destined to be the basis of contested lawsuits; the contractual agreement to submit any dispute to a variety of jurisdiction, lay and ecclesiastical, is a clause of style, a notarial flourish. The central importance of the contract lay in the fact that guarantees of payment were enforceable without any judicial intervention—seizure of goods, sureties, hostages. For the farmer, the contract, like the promise of homage his grandfather had made, was the acknowledgment that another controlled his and his family's life. His freedom—to buy and sell, to pledge his assets, to make contracts without the approval of any seigneur—was illusory.

In other realms of life, however, the contract was a genuine consensual lawmaking device and contractual relations played a genuine role in the affairs of drapers, tailors, tanners, soapmakers, and other artisanal bourgeois. For them, it was an instrument of credit, a way of ordering goods and regulating work. It betokened a free movement of goods.

The bonds of bargain placed the bourgeois who knew the legal devices offered by contract law in the center of a network of profitable social relations. The *mègerie* form of *metayage* is the most striking illustration. The merchant, armed with capital which he in many cases borrowed from Lombard bankers, leases for a small sum a great tract of ground from a noble needing cash but himself unwilling to soil his hands in commerce or unschooled in the legal possibilities. This tract of land, held at a modest *cens*, then becomes a staging ground for raising animals on a commercially profitable basis. The bourgeois is profiting both from his manipulation of the land—still "owned" ostensibly by the seigneur—and from his realization of profit from the work of the rural laborer who actually raises the beasts. Such a contractual incursion on feudal authority could be substantial, but it relied upon the farmer being able to come to Grasse to sell his harvest or deliver the animals to the *abattoir*, upon his being able to till his fields peaceably, and upon the bourgeois in Grasse being free to travel between Italy and western Provence to make his arrangements with the Lombard banking interests.

The peace and order necessary to protect this nascent commerce were guaranteed by the rulers of Provence, as part of the domain of the Kingdom of Naples. The reigns of Charles I and Robert (1309–1343) saw the establishment of such new judicial machinery to aid the development of commerce as the *Chambre des Comptes* at Aix-en-Provence.

When, in 1350, the political collapse of the house of the King of Naples coincided with economic recession, the spread of the Black Death, and the ravages of bands of unemployed knights and impoverished lesser nobles, Provence entered one hundred years of economic regression. The farmers could no longer safely travel to Grasse, and could hardly continue to till their fields. Farms were abandoned. Cities pulled back behind their walls. The rural area around Grasse, for example, was apparently largely abandoned in the late 1300s and not resettled until 1496.

The pattern was similar in most of the cities that were not major industrial centers. Feudal institutions were strengthened as the lords took the abandoned land back and sought people to till it. The money economy paled somewhat in importance, for it was not strong or well-established enough to survive the political collapse. The necessities of military defense and/or assuring basic economic needs struck at the infant bourgeois industries.

The story of the demise of Grasse's commercialization, and the weakness of bourgeois institutions in the face of the violence generated by feudal civil war and the ravages of dispossessed feudal functionaries, points a lesson about the legal system as confronted by a revolutionary class. The violence across the face of Provence was both a tribute to bourgeois economic success and a reproach to its political weakness. The ravagers were those whose social function had disappeared or become attenuated by the growth of the new network of contract relations and by the extension of sovereign power to assure both public order and military defense. Concessions wrung from the rulers permitted the growth of bourgeois institutions in the midst of a feudal system. But those concessions, even given the best of faith on both sides, were tentative and partial; they were not accompanied by a seizure of state power over the whole territory in which the new class could foresee conducting economic activity, and the deployment of enough force to destroy internal and external enemies of the new order.

13.

PEASANT REBELLION *AND* LAND *LAW*

The plague and the economic crisis of the late 1300s had profound impact in England as well. There the years after 1260 had seen the gradual abandonment of knight-service as a means of raising a military force in favor of a standing army maintained by the crown. The lord of the fief was transformed from an active fighting agent into a passive recipient of feudal services. The lords whose great-grandfathers had, in order to provide ten knights at the king's behest, enfeoffed ten men and given them small domains sufficient for their maintenance, were now anxious to take back these fiefs and have the revenues and feudal services of a larger area for themselves. The financial pressures on the smaller domains led many such knights to take up arms as brigands. The late 1200s and early 1300s saw many legislative efforts to curb their armed attacks on merchants. Civil wars (1307–1327) and fighting in Scotland added to the number of armed men roving the countryside.

The plague brought on a crisis by depleting the labor supply and intensifying the difficulty of making the land produce enough to keep its proprietors. Government reaction to the economic dislocation was swift, and a series of statutes enacted in 1349 and 1351 set maximum wages, required all able-bodied persons to work, and forbade workers to leave the employ of their masters except under exceptional circumstances. In a frontal attack on migration to the cities, the statute of 1388 provided that "Any male or female person who works steadily as a Carter or at the plough or at some other agricultural labor or service until he or she is twelve years of age shall work only in this employment from that time forward, and shall not be put to a trade or craft. . . . "

All the king's men could not, however, contain the forces which had been set at work in the countryside. The liberation of serfs had begun in good times, and the landowners themselves preferred to put matters on a more commercial basis. The explosion came in the Peasant Rebellion of 1381.

Serfs and men bound to the soil by feudal ties burned the manorial records and hanged the lawyers and stewards who kept them. Many of them exacted from their lords the right to occupy their lands and till them at a reasonable rent. These grants were confirmed by charters often written out under duress by the lord, and in many areas of England created a new form of customary-law tenancy—the copyhold, which parceled out land into an individual plot for each family and a common area of woods and pasture, a cooperative, not to say communal, idea.

With the records of their bondage to the manor reduced to ashes, and the lord's steward strung up in the courtyard, the villeins may have felt confident they had won a measurable victory. Those who ran away, and became "seised of their liberty," had won. Those who stayed to till their land often found their tenure challenged after the rebellion was put down and the reaction set in. The struggle in the courts over copyhold persisted for more than two hundred years, and—as we shall see in a later chapter—was not finally resolved in the tenants' favor until the urban bourgeoisie and royal power united behind the ideal of free trade in land. By then, the beneficiaries were not the tenants but the landowners. (The lords' concession of the copyhold by charter was in fact a forcible creation of a written customary right, enforceable by the manorial court. But the lord was the judge in that court; hence the struggle in later years to invoke royal judicial power to force him and his heirs to honor the charters.)

The peasant struggle in the countryside was also directed against the "justices of laborers" (later justices of the peace) who were charged with enforcing the various wage-freeze statutes, and against royal tax-gatherers. The latter had been sent out in 1380 to collect a "capitation tax" enacted not only to gain revenue but to force men and women to work. As tradition has it, a tax-collector's affront to the daughter of Wat Tyler sparked a march on London in which 100,000 peasants and lower-class city dwellers captured and beheaded the Lord Chancellor, the Chief Justice of the King's Bench, and the Lord Treasurer. Again, because they were said to have been instrumental in proposing and enforcing the tax, lawyers were special targets of the revolutionary violence.

As Shakespeare put it, writing of a somewhat later tenants' struggle:

> DICK: The first thing we do, let's kill all the lawyers.
> CADE: Nay, that I mean to do. Is not this a lamentable thing, that of the skin of an innocent lamb should be made parchment? That parchment, being scribbl'd o'er, should undo a man? Some say the bee stings; but I say, 'tis the bee's wax; for I did but seal once to a thing, and I was never mine own man since.

The revolt was suppressed, and the strict terms of the statute of 1388 added restrictions on arms-bearing to its provisions on the duty to work at low wages.

In the English countryside, noble landholders (and non-noble buyers of great holdings) received rents from tenants who continued the pattern of family farming and employed labor to till the remainder of their lands. The decisive fact of English legal history is not, therefore, the reassertion of feudal power in the face of adversity, but the assertion of royal police power to maintain the economic security of the landed class. From their strengthened base in the countryside, this class built a system of political power whose last vestiges survived into the 1830s.

Two economic consequences of the troubles were, however, to lay the basis for England's precocious passage from mercantile to industrial capitalism. The first was the creation of a great pool of wage-labor in the countryside, impeded from moving to the towns by a lack of economic opportunity there and by the legislative inhibitions on leaving their rural work. When the economic picture changed, and the capitalists were able to muster the political power to change the statute of 1388, the important element of wage-labor was ready to be brought into the process of industrialization.

A second important element were the copyhold tenants. Serfdom was greatly weakened: a step had been taken toward the universal holding of all land free of feudal services—the "free and common socage" subsequently ratified by Parliament in 1660. But the presence of small-plot village farming and the great spaces given over to common land were to prove barriers to economically advantageous exploitation of the land by a class of rentiers. Within less than two hundred years, the descendants of the tenants who had burned the manor records, killed the lawyers, and won the right to occupy the land would again rise up to defend what their forebears had won. At great cost, the tenants had loosened the structure of feudal landholding. But the ultimate beneficiaries of their sacrifice would be the new men of property who swept to power 150 years later.

PART FOUR

THE BOURGEOIS ASCENDANCY

(1400--1600)

14.

INTRODUCTION

Between 1400 and 1600, influenced by the influx of gold, silver, and primary products from the New World and by what R. H. Tawney has called "the mastery of man over his environment," the economies of Western Europe were profoundly altered. No matter what this period is called—Renaissance, Reformation, Age of Discovery, Price Revolution of the sixteenth century, Age of Humanism—by 1600 the main principles of bourgeois private law, that law regarding interpersonal dealings in contract, property, and so on, had in theory though not everywhere in practice replaced personal feudal relationships.

In the field of commerce, a new structure of economic relationships came into being. In 1400, there was no banker who was not a member of the banking or money changing guild. There was no weaver who was not in the weavers' guild. There was no merchant who did not hold membership in the bourgeoisie of one, or even several, cities. Though the formal legal equality of "membership" had no direct bearing on the very real differences in wealth, power, and influence among different members, the status of membership defined the capacity in which a person acted and the legal consequences of his or her acts. By 1500, changes in economic relationships had taken a heavy toll, and this legal system began to fall apart in earnest, to be replaced by one more nearly reflecting the true allocation of power.

On a broader scale, certain basic institutional assumptions collapsed. On one hand, individual cities, and even leagues of cities, found they could not survive; military defense, and the generation of sufficient capital to participate in expanding commerce and nascent industrial capitalism, dictated that only the nation-state was an appropriate economic, legal, and political form for the next historical period. On the other hand, the Catholic Church's illusion of a single unified Christendom was dispelled by the Reformation, as well as, in a more literal way, by the discovery of the New World.

To see the essential validity of these assertions, one need only recall the central historical elements of this period. The Hanseatic League was in decline, having failed to attain the unity necessary to compete for the spoils of the New World and enter the new age of mercantile capitalism. With the fall of Constantinople, Italy lost its sources of goods in the East. The Medici Bank collapsed in 1494, and with it a large part of Medici power. Meanwhile, the Italian bourgeoisie and wealthy nobility were unable to achieve the political unity necessary to form a national bourgeoisie and a national marketplace of goods and labor. Machiavelli's *The Prince*, essentially a call for Italian unity under the Medicis, was written about 1500 in the vain hope of a Medici restoration. Though Spain and Portugal were the first to tap the resources of the New World, neither achieved a form of social organization permitting systematic investment of the capital they obtained there. The French and the English won a disproportionate share through trade, privateering, and piracy.

The bourgeoisie's creation of a *legal* order suited to its own development from 1500 onward took place almost entirely in France and England. By different means, and at markedly different tempos, these two nations created the legal models that were to be borrowed by other states which entered upon the capitalist road once they had achieved political unity.

Before 1400, the merchant was either a locally based artisan or an international adventurer. Trade was at first isolated and noncontinuous, developing, as the growth of towns and of networks of communication permitted, into commerce—the systematic pursuit of gain through exchange. In the period between 1400 and 1600 we see a new phenomenon: the growth and eventual dominance of manufacture, which involves the coordination and systematization of artisanal production.

The early merchant had a purely "external" relationship to the mode of production, buying from the producer and moving the goods to the point at which they would fetch the highest price. Gradually merchants began directly investing in production, integrating the separate processes which led to creation of a finished product; at the same time, a section of the producers accumulated capital and began to organize production on a capitalist basis free from the restrictions of the guilds.

One political form was especially suited to this development, the nation-state, and by the fifteenth century we begin to see the emergence of this peculiarly bourgeois institution, in which within the political boundaries of a territory dominated by a single sovereign all internal impediments to free movement of goods were removed. As Maurice Dobb has written:

> The rapid rise of manufactures, particularly in England, gradually absorbed the vagrants and dispossessed. With the advent of manufacture, the various nations entered into a competitive relationship. The struggle for trade was fought by war, protective duties and prohibitions, whereas earlier the nations, in so far as they were connected at all, had carried on an inoffensive exchange with each other. Trade from now on had a political significance.

To begin the march to industrial capitalism, to impose new economic forms, to share by right or conquest or theft in the wealth of the New World, to maintain a balance of trade such that more wealth flowed into a country than left it—all of these things were accomplished at a great price. There was earnest dispute, and sharp struggle, over each of them. If in retrospect these things seem inevitable steps on the road to modernity, they did not seem so in 1500. Many were opposed to, even shocked by, the destruction of old values and institutions which accompanied these political and economic developments. The life and work of Thomas More, who opposed the Tudor economic and social policies with his satire, his counsel, and finally his life, provides us with a view of these events.

15.

THOMAS MORE AND THE DESTRUCTION OF THE MEDIEVAL VISION

Thomas More (1478–1535) was among the most accomplished people of his age. A superb lawyer who commanded the highest fees in the common-law courts, he was also a brilliant social critic whose major work, *Utopia*, published in 1516, presents a vision of an ideal society couched in fine prose and full of mordant social criticism. His epigrams, poems, and jokes, his denunciations of heresy, his lifelong friendship with Erasmus, his constant study of the Scripture, his concern to educate his daughter in Latin and Greek, his lectures on St. Augustine's *City of God*—all confirm him as recognized leader of the European humanist philosophical movement. In sum, More combined the best qualities of the medieval common lawyer with the qualities we have come to associate with "Renaissance man."

If More represents a medieval tradition, it is nonetheless one informed not only by a humanist spirit but also by considerable experience in practical affairs. The conflict between medieval traditions and the rising bourgeois ideology was not simply between enforced uniformity of belief and freedom of conscience, nor between a catholic corporatism and an abstract idea of individuality. The roots of the conflict lay deep within his society and can be illustrated to some degree at least by examining the choices More himself made—choices that were to lead to direct conflict with Henry VIII and, ultimately, to his execution as a traitor.

The choices seemed to be between real economic and human consequences, chosen in the light of a pervasive, compelling belief in a real God who, in the medieval conception, exacted compliance with his wishes upon pain of damnation, and, in the emerging view, looked for good works as confirmation of salvation.

A brief sketch of More's life also shows him to be a product of a decisive period in bourgeois legal history. Son of a judge of the King's Bench, one of the two principal common-law courts, More was trained in the common law of England, although he studied Continental civil law and had some acquaintance with canon law. He also evidently knew merchant law, or at any rate merchant practices, for he was given the "freedom" of the Mercers' Company, the most important association of the new generation of the English merchant bourgeoisie, and was selected by various merchant groups for a number of diplomatic missions to Flanders, the manufacturing center closely connected with England's growing cloth trade. More was a member of Parliament for some time, and was Speaker of the House of Commons at a time when both its independence and financial role were beginning to be defined. After holding several offices of trust under Henry VIII, he was appointed Lord Chancellor, a post that had generally been held only by clerics; the selection of More was an extraordinary tribute to his knowledge of the law. In this capacity, More exercised a judicial jurisdiction to revise and correct, according to principles of equity, judgments of the common-law courts and to provide a remedy when the latter would not. We do not single out More as the primary mover of English society at this point; rather, in his life and death one can see at work the contradictions which were rending the feudal order.

The year More was called to the bar—that is, after he had spent enough time at Lincoln's Inn, the professional training ground of lawyers, to be qualified to plead—he also lectured on St. Augustine's *City of God*. At the time, medieval cosmology survived in the belief in the unity of the One True Church. St. Augustine, to name only the most prominent of the early visionaries, had preached that unity of belief was the only means to a godly society on this earth. The persistence of his ideal was repeatedly attested to in the struggles accompanying the Reformation. Even Calvin paid a backhanded compliment to this medieval ideal, for he no more tolerated heresy from the one true—Protestant—faith than did the Inquisition.

But this unity did not exist, and had never existed, except perhaps in the early communities of persecuted Christians; Luther and Calvin were right in finding its spiritual component rotting and infested. The vision nevertheless persisted as a goal toward which human society ought to strive. The basic virtues to be striven for were clear: the just price, the true religion, a place for everyone, distrust of gain for its own sake. And it seemed to those holding this vision that those who would discard it for a society built upon the more concrete elements of manufacture, trade, and bullion were leading their countries to moral and human disaster.

For More, the social costs of economic expansion in England were too high, the more so because this expansion meant the end of the medieval humanist ideal. *Utopia* is a re-creation of the spiritual universality of the early Church's vision, informed by the rationality which in the 1500s had begun to characterize the study of philosophy and of technology. *Utopia* depicts a communal society which does not compel conformity but achieves it through the evident justice of its institutions. There is work for everyone, though not of an organized industrial kind. There is no need for large-scale production. "You'll be surprised to find," More writes, "how few people actually produce what the human race consumes." Correspondingly, there is no encouragement of the entrepreneurial spirit or the profit motive. There is no greed in *Utopia*, for humans are not naturally greedy; there are no lawyers, and no nobles. More's religion was intertwined with a practical view of English society, forcefully criticized in the introductory section of *Utopia* by the character Raphael.

> There are lots of noblemen who live like drones on the labor of other people, in other words, of their tenants. . . . Not content with remaining idle themselves, they take round with them vast numbers of equally idle retainers. . . .
>
> Thieves do make quite efficient soldiers, and soldiers make quite enterprising thieves . . . . It [warfare, standing armies] is practically a worldwide epidemic. France, for instance, is suffering from an even more virulent form of it.
>
> Sheep . . . , those placid creatures, which used to require so little food, have now apparently developed a raging appetite, and turned into man-eaters. Fields, houses, towns, everything goes down their throats. . . . Nobles and gentlemen, not to mention several saintly abbots, [are] no longer content to lead lazy, comfortable lives, which do no good to society—they must actively do it harm, by enclosing all the land they can for pasture, and leaving none for cultivation. Each greedy individual preys on his native land like a malig-

> nant growth, absorbing field after field, and enclosing thousands of acres with a single fence. Result—hundreds of farmers are evicted. . . . By the time they've been wandering around for a bit, . . . then what can they do but steal—and be very properly hanged for it?

The speaker goes on to note that many poor weavers have been priced out of the market by the inflation in the price of raw wool, the sale of which is controlled by a few rich men.

Compressed in these few lines is the economic history of the hundred preceding years, as well as the consequences of Tudor economic policy under Henry VIII and his successors. One wonders what Henry VIII must have been thinking when, though he had read the copy of *Utopia* given to him by More, he nonetheless appointed More to his service and continually advanced him until he held the second-highest post in the realm.

But what of this history? For centuries English wool had been exported to the woolshops of Flanders or northern Italy. The records of bankers and merchants give a clear picture of this trade, from the viewpoint of Flemish and Italian purchasers, Lombard bankers, and merchants of the Staple. The Staple was the name given to the body with a royal monopoly of primary products which, for the greater part of the 1400s, had headquarters at Calais (which was in English hands until 1558) and exercised authority granted to it by the Crown. The officially established monopoly of the Staple was a typically medieval means of trading in an important national commodity. (A great deal of the wool shipped through the Staple was apparently carried in Italian ships, though in earlier years Hanseatic merchants had taken part in shipment to the manufacturing centers at Bruges.)

There were, however, ways to circumvent the Staple's monopoly. For instance, Scottish wool could be shipped directly to Flanders or, more important, a merchant could apply for a special royal license to export wool independently. Between 1455 and 1485, during the Wars of the Roses, the British Crown granted a number of such licenses to Italian bankers in exchange for ready cash or to pay off loans already made. Heavy speculation in such loans was a principal cause of the financial ruin of the London branch of the Medici Bank.

Around 1400 trade in finished cloth became sufficiently important to have a separate organizational basis, and the "merchant adventurers" in cloth—a name given to those who journeyed abroad to sell goods—began to organize a corporation to carry on and regulate this trade. England had traditionally had a negative trade balance with Italy, due to heavy imports of the luxury goods of the East. Exports of finished cloth helped trade balances. In addition, when the fall of Constantinople to the Turks in 1453 ended Italian domination of trade with the Levant, England and the other countries of Western Europe began to develop their internal markets. The influx of gold and silver from the New World provided capital for this expansion, while rising prices, particularly after 1550, led to the ruin of small farmers and great nobles alike. The manufacture of cloth, formerly divided among a number of different crafts—washers, spinners, weavers, fullers, dyers, and so on—came increasingly under the control of an entrepreneur who purchased the raw wool and controlled the process of production. The guilds lost practical significance.

We have seen some of the human costs of this development. As the common land of villages was fenced in and production was organized to assure a supply of wool, pastoral village life became impossible. A potential working class came into being, made up of the vagrants More referred to, those who had no livelihood until they could be absorbed into the process of production. A different social perspective on the same events is found in a poem circulated in Cambridge in the mid-1500s to justify pulling down the sheep enclosures:

Syr I thinke that this wyrke
Is as good as to byld a kyrke
For Cambridge bayles truly
Give yll example to the cowntrye
Ther comones lykewises for to engrose
And from poor men it to enclose . . .
Therefore it is goud consciens I wene
To make that common that ever hathe bene

The action of the city officials against which the verse complains is recorded in the annals of the Town of Cambridge in the mid-1500s:

> A piece of noysom ground is taken in owte of the common and enclosed with a middle wall at the end of Jesus lane, for the wyche the incorporation of the towne is recompensed, but not the whole inhabytantes of the towne, which find themselves injured.

In other words, the medieval ideal of a town as the common possession of the inhabitants, descendants of those who had united upon their solemn oaths, was giving way. The "corporation" came to mean the town officials, the wealthiest and most powerful of the inhabitants, who treated the town's property as their own, selling it and pocketing the proceeds.

In order to accommodate the rationalization of production, fields had to be enclosed, guild privileges overriden in charters to companies of entrepreneurs and exporters, and land laws rewritten; the task required a powerful, centralized authority, and the bourgeoisie were early champions of a powerful state apparatus. Nation-states like England and France, which managed to unite around a strong central power, survived and were strengthened by the economic turmoil.

Against these developments, men like More inveighed. In *Utopia*, if we take More to mean what he says, we find the keys to his own life and death. He died for a principle: "The King's good servant, but God's first." He had consistently opposed Henry VIII's divorce from Catherine of Aragon, advising the king that it was contrary to canon and divine law. When, in the wake of his divorce, Henry secured from Parliament recognition that he was Supreme Head of the Church of England, More declined to take the test oath acknowledging that Henry might bear that title. His position was that which he had maintained in his own attacks on heresy: one might believe what one wished, and so long as one did not publicly give "occasion of slander, of tumult, of sedition against his prince," then no liability for punishment ought ensue.

More was tried for treason, the "desire to deprive the King of his dignity, title, or name of his royal estates." While the issue upon which his trial turned was thus the narrow one of his refusal to take the oath, it had a far broader basis: More held that Parliament could not declare a layman supreme in matters of faith, because such a pretension moved in the direction of fractioning the fragile unity of Christian belief commanded by the Gospels. Such a step would increase warfare and destruction, and irremediably impede the creation of a cooperative commonwealth. More and Erasmus were at one in seeing the boundaries of states as "a pattern scrawled to amuse the childish malice of princes." More the Catholic devout could no more assent to Henry's religious claims than More the humanist could contemplate the sacrifice of all personal ties to the bonds of cash and contract. Nor could he agree that principles ought to be flexible enough to accommodate any reason of state or economic advantage which might plausibly be argued. We have seen from *Utopia* that More had held these views for some time. He had also, in an unfinished history of Richard III, described Richard's character in terms which reject "nonmoral statecraft." More wrote that "the gathering of money" is "the only thing that withdraweth the hearts of Englishmen from the Prince."

More's was not a mystic vision, nor was he an apologist for feudal savagery or for the politics of an incumbent Pope. As a lawyer, he saw clearly the institutional consequences of the decisions and forces he opposed. When Thomas Cromwell, who was to be his principal interrogator, came to see him after his resignation as Chancellor, according to More's son-in-law More advised him:

> Master Cromwell, you are now entered into the service of a most noble, wise and liberal prince; if you will follow my poor advice, in your counsel-giving unto his Grace, ever tell him what he ought to do, but never what he is able to do. . . . For if a lion knew his own strength, hard were it for any man to rule him.

Cromwell did not follow More's advice. Machiavelli had written in *The Prince* that "the man who leaves what is done, for what ought to be done, learns sooner his ruin than his preservation." Cromwell had perhaps not read Machiavelli, but he respected the fundamental ideals of Tudor statecraft. His speech on the scaffold, when he in his turn displeased Henry, shows his respect: "I am by the law condemned to die; I have offended my Prince. . . . "

More was wrong in believing that reason, discourse, or faith could greatly change the course of events set in motion by the Tudor sovereigns. But his clear vision of the forces at work has made his life and work a subject of study by writers as diverse as G. K. Chesterton and Karl Kautsky. The latter wrote: "The aims More set before himself are not the fancies of an idle hour, but the result of a deep insight into the actual economic tendencies of his age." In our own study, we can see these tendencies reflected in the bourgeois law of land.

16.

RECASTING THE *LAW* OF REAL PROPERTY

Tenure is the decisive characteristic of feudal land law. The grantee takes the land and holds it "of" the grantor; it may be inherited by the grantee's children, a right that was established early. The lord was nevertheless entitled to certain services and benefits: originally the services were military, but later principally labor, a portion of the harvest, a payment on entry of the heir (relief), and wardship of a minor heir. One task of the law was, therefore, to ensure that there was someone at each level of the feudal order whose goods and person could be seized to guarantee that feudal services were rendered. Under the earliest English common-law proceedings—the so-called real actions—a judicial judgment could be obtained, enforceable by the armed power of the Crown, as to which services were due, from whom, and on what occasions; further, a grantee might be restored to an estate—a "tenement"—from which he claimed to have been dispossessed. Hence the maxim, *nulle terre sans seigneur*, no land without a lord.

The feudal notion of property also regarded landholding as carrying certain responsibilities. In Tawney's words:

> Property is not a mere aggregate of economic privileges, but a responsible office. Its *raison d'être* is not only income, but service. It is to secure its owner such means, and no more than such means, as may enable him to perform those duties, whether labor on the land, or labor in government, which are involved in particular status which he holds in the system. He who seeks more robs his superiors, or his dependents, or both. He who exploits his property

> with a single eye to its economic possibilities at once perverts its very essence and destroys his own moral title, for he has "every man's living and does no man's duty."

With this notion went that of nonexclusivity—land might be held in common, or a piece of land might be used at different seasons by different persons for the benefit of the community.

The view of the modern bourgeoisie toward land presents a remarkable contrast. As expressed by Karl Renner, author of a basic treatise on bourgeois law:

> The right of ownership, *dominium*, is a person's all-embracing legal power over a tangible object. As far as the object is concerned, ownership is a universal institution: all corporeal things, even land, can be objects of ownership if they are recognized as such by the law and are not by special provision put *extra commercium*. Ownership is equally universal with regard to the subject. Everybody has an equal capacity for ownership, and he may own property of every description. These are the norms which are characteristic of this institution.

Thus, the institution of property in the sense it came to have in bourgeois law posits a person (*persona*) and a thing (*res*), joined by the legal norm called property or ownership. Human society is dissolved into isolated individuals, and the world of goods split up into discrete items. One can no longer speak of a duty to use property or behave toward others in a certain way: all such duties as may be imposed by law are *prima facie* derogations from the fundamental "right of property."

These two opposing versions of land law—for we do not yet speak of movable property—represent tendencies rather than actual states. They began to be formulated into specific legal rules as the struggle over who was to own the land intensified in the 1400s and 1500s. By 1500 we can speak of feudalist and bourgeois interests on a national scale within both England and France.

The feudalists had the initial advantage. The common-law courts had jurisdiction over the majority of real property questions and were firmly tied to the Crown. By "common law" we mean here the law applied by the royal tribunals, as distinguished from the local law of the remaining manorial courts, the law merchant and admiralty law applied by bourgeois tribunals, the ecclesiastical law and the equity power of the Chancellor—of which we shall speak presently. The House of Commons may have had borough representation, but during this period it was in the hands of rural property holders whose interest was not in refashioning the land law. Until direct taxation achieved decisive importance much later, much of the Crown's revenue was derived from feudal services. In sixteenth-century England and France, the bourgeoisie—which controlled the movable wealth (cash and assets easily convertible to cash) that could be used to pay direct taxes in money—agreed to direct taxation in exchange for increased participation in government and royal concessions in refashioning land law as applied by the royal courts; law in the royal boroughs of England was already made by the borough courts, and the land held in "burgage" came the closest to expressing the bourgeois ideal. Not until 1660, in a legislative ratification of the English Revolution, was all the land in England to achieve a similar degree of transmissibility by will and purchase.

The complexities of the land law, outside of the cities, were the principal source of revenue for the common-law lawyers. Thus, a career as an advocate in the common-law courts was not necessarily the preferred occupation of the son of a merchant, for the bourgeoisie was not, in 1500, the preferred client group of the common lawyers. The bourgeoisie, as we have seen, had its own courts, both borough and merchant tribunals; it was not until the early 1600s that the common-law courts developed a system of legal rules that worked favorably to trade.

All legal rules tend to outlive their reason for being; that is why lawyers are sometimes driven to countenance revolution, and have at all times had a reputation for twisting old rules into new shapes. The form taken by land law tended to persist long after the social relations which gave rise to it passed away, partly because the acquisition of an interest in real property, unless the land is left fallow or in its natural state, necessarily involved investments and actions which were not easy to undo, and created interests that were not easily unraveled.

The tension between feudalist and bourgeois forces appears repeatedly as the common-law courts fashioned the land law. Attempts to avoid payment of feudal dues were often litigated. For example, as late as 1581, the Court of King's Bench announced as law, in what is known as the Rule in Shelley's Case, a principle which had the declared purpose of preserving the lord's right of wardship and relief. Imagine a situation in which A conveys to B a certain parcel of land. Were the bourgeois property norm to be fully honored, this would be the end of it; B would acquire the land and the sole legal relationship would be between B, *persona*, and Freeacres, the *res*. The tableau was not so simple in 1500. A might convey land to B, but by doing so he only substituted B in the feudal hierarchy, requiring B to perform feudal services to some lord, L. Among the lord's rights, and a very important one to increasingly hard-pressed seigneurs, was a payment to be received when B died and his heir (usually, in England, the eldest son) succeeded to B's interest.

This anachronism invited evasion, and some lawyers accepted the invitation. Relief was due when someone took by inheritance, but not when he took by deed (by "purchase," as the technical phrase had it). When B took the land from A, in our example, he entered by purchase and therefore paid no relief. But if A conveyed "to B for life, and then on B's death, to C and his heirs," C would pay no relief because he was named in the deed and took by virtue of it. In the parlance of the real-property law, B had a life estate and C had a remainder in fee simple absolute.

How easy, then, to substitute for C an outsider, the heirs of B. The conveyance would read: to B for life, remainder to the heirs of B. In that case, B's heir would take under the deed (by purchase) and not as B's successor in law. B's heir, then, would pay no relief. The common-law courts rejected this stratagem, and held the grant was in effect to B in fee simple.

The common-law lawyers then tried an elaboration of the scheme, whereby A conveyed to B for life, then to D for life, then to the heirs of B in fee simple. The judges were not always deceived, however, as can be seen in a case that pitted the lord's lawyer Cavendish against the heir's lawyer Finchden:

> CAVENDISH: If the lease was made to your father for life with remainder to his right heirs then the father had the fee . . . and if you were under age the lord would have wardship and consequently relief.
>
> FINCHDEN: He cannot avow upon us for relief as heir . . . because we are not in as his heir.
>
> CHIEF JUSTICE THORPE: I know very well what you want to say. You have pleaded that you ought not to have to pay relief since you are in as purchaser, being the first in whom the remainder takes effect according to the words of the deed; but you are in as heir to your father . . . and the remainder was not [given] . . . to you by your proper name but under the description of heir;

> and so it was awarded by all the justices that the lord should have return of the distress. . . .

That is, the lord could keep what he had grabbed as security for the relief he claimed.

Strenuous insistence upon feudal dues continued and even intensified through the 1500s, as lords and knights with incomes limited by the land and by custom faced mounting inflation. Need, if not penury, pushed seigneurs in all of Western Europe to a harsh insistence upon their rights, and they found support at hands of the monarchs, themselves dependent upon feudal revenues. Attempts at evasion by various legislative devices were equally widespread. The bourgeoisie in the countryside waged a seesaw battle on the issue with varying success.

In France, for example, in the early 1500s, sovereigns once again put lawyers to the task of reducing customs in each locality to writing. Once approved by the representatives of the three estates—clergy, nobles, and commoners—these were then ratified by the *Parlement* and the King. Each of these custumals clearly reflects the royal will to unify and extend royal judicial power, as well as whatever local interests were powerful enough to demand recognition. In the cities, these urban custumals are the law codes of the bourgeoisie, and to a great extent they deny or sharply limit seigneurial rights in the land. Outside the cities, where the third estate—the bourgeoisie, workers, and peasantry—surely existed, its voice does not appear in the custumals. Seigneurial rights are recognized even where the relationship between lord and man has been emptied of its earlier content of military service and reciprocal personal duties.

The custumals do indicate, however, a growing consciousness of the distinction between those lords actively engaged in the running of their estates and those whom the bourgeoisie would term parasites, living off feudal dues but providing nothing in return. The 1567 custumal of Amiens, for instance, distinguishes between what it terms the working fief and the fief in simple homage. The former conserves much of the substance of feudalism, though not with respect to military duties. The latter does not, but the lord exacts feudal dues in any case. This distinction does not appear in the Amiens custumal of 1507, indicating the growing awareness that in the purely technical fief, the lord was a passive collector of tributes which he claimed by immemorial usage, not in recognition of any social function.

Recognition that some feudal relationships served no social function required rethinking the separation, in French land law, of the *domaine direct*—the grantor's superior right to services or other payment, and the rights of all those above him in the feudal pyramid—from the *domaine utile*—the right to work the land under any form of ownership. If the custumals are any guide, the amount of land still subject to feudal services was extensive in the 1400s and early 1500s. The payments, services, and reliefs due the holder of the *domaine direct* are repeatedly spelled out in great detail. In the region around Amiens, the holder of the *domaine utile* could sell it, but one-fifth of the price went to the lord. A relief was payable on entry of the heir. In either case, the lord could sue for payment in the royal court, which was an increase in royal jurisdiction at the expense of the seigneurial courts. (Many of the custumals indicate that the Church and its agencies were among the most important holders of land and hence exactors of a full measure of feudal dues.)

Bourgeois purchases of noble land in the countryside, which accelerated throughout the 1500s, were of two types, one which struck directly at the division between *domaine direct* and *domaine utile*, and the other which tended to preserve it as a charge on the land which burdened the peasantry. In the former case, the bourgeois purchaser would buy both *domaines*, either for cash or a perpetual ground rent; by this means, formerly seigneurial land was taken outside the feudal system. In the latter case, the bourgeois bought only the *domaine direct* for cash or a perpetual rent, and sometimes even purchased the lord's title as well; such a purchase put the bourgeois in the lord's place in the feudal system. This latter form of purchase suited the aspirations of those bourgeois whose class consciousness was rooted in feudal social relations, and who regarded their material success as simply a means to acquire by money that which their nonnoble origins denied them as birthright. By 1600, three-fourths of France's noble families had acquired their titles in this way.

Thus the flow of bourgeoisie into the countryside did not, to the extent the newcomers stepped into the shoes of their grantors, greatly modify the system of legal relations on the land. The tenacity of these feudal elements in French property law, not to mention their cost to the more productive orders of society, was formidable. They were not scourged from the law books until the French Revolution.

In England, the change in legal relations on the land was more dramatic, and is one important key to an understanding of why industrial capitalism developed earlier in England than in France. While French legal writers elaborated the theory of absolute monarchy, the Tudor princes really were such monarchs. Henry VIII wielded the power of the state to stamp out all threats to his rule. Being Supreme Head of the Church certainly helped, for heresy automatically became treason and the inquisitorial powers formerly used by Church tribunals to root out heresy were taken over by secular authorities as well.

Under the Tudors, the unification of the country was accomplished at the expense of local suzerainties of the kind that continued to plague French kings. The destruction of the power of the local feudal rulers necessarily involved changes in the law of the land, the principal element of feudal power. The event which had the greatest effect on a new law of real property was Henry's seizure of the monastic lands. To see the impact of this move more clearly, one might draw the following parallel: if there is a small center of artisanal production bound by guild rules, and someone wants to challenge its position in the law and in the market, the new capitalism showed the way. A new enterprise, organized along entrepreneurial lines, might start up and ruin its older, less efficient competitor. Royal blessing, and a royal monopoly on distribution of a product, would help accelerate the process but would not be indispensable. Land, however, does not by its nature lend itself to such a process. First of all, land is a commodity in limited supply. In order to change established patterns of trading it, one has to wait for new social relations to penetrate old patterns of distribution and exchange. The only way to get around this limitation is to engage in wholesale seizure and redistribution. By a large enough confiscation the market in land may be so affected that the whole system of real-property relations is changed. Henry's seizure initiated such a change.

The quarrel with the monasteries has been too frequently described to require retelling here. Suffice it to say that within the space of three years Henry managed to bring into his hands about one-sixth of the land in England, with an annual revenue equal to or greater than that which he already had. Henry did not act in anger at the Pope over his divorce from Catherine of Aragon and the settlement of the succession. Nor did he act in haste. Nor was he alone. There was popular sentiment against the monasteries.

Henry first obtained from Parliament a bill giving him 10 percent of the yearly revenues of the Church's land. Then, in 1535, under the direction of Lord Chancellor Thomas Audley (who had been More's prosecutor), a commission of investigation went out to value the ecclesiastical property. It reported not only the income of the religious houses—about £200,000 annually—but also scandals in the administration of some of them.

These scandals provided the ostensible basis for the 1536 Act of Parliament confiscating the lesser houses (those with under twelve clerics in residence). They were depicted as centers of "manifest sin, vicious, carnal, and abominable living," wherein the residents "spoil, destroy, consume, and utterly waste." It was difficult not to be against sin of this sort. Farmers and clothworkers took up arms against the confiscation of Church properties in the north of England, but were put down; their anger focused upon the confiscation, but had been fed by enclosures and the systematic destruction of artisanal independence in the cloth industry. The Church was regarded by the rebels as protector of village life against the incursions of the bourgeoisie.

The confiscation of the remaining monastic lands took place in 1539. Other Church lands—of guilds and chantries—were taken in 1547.

Over the remainder of his reign, Henry sold off much of this land to Court favorites to finance wars in Scotland and France. Courtiers and friends who purchased these desirable properties formed a core of political support. When the abbots and other clerics left the House of Lords, the basis of their feudal power and titles destroyed, new peerages were created from this new group of supporters. Some were able to exploit their new wealth; others resold their properties, principally to financial interests in London and other major cities. Tawney notes that the largest single grantee was Sir Richard Gresham, a theorist of monetary and trade policy.

These lands were mostly outside the cities. They had been farmed not by the clerics who held them, but by tenants who lived in villages and grazed their few beasts on common land. But the efficient exploitation of these properties for mercantile purposes meant drawing together the production of raw wool and the manufacture of cloth; this is turn entailed the enclosure of the commons and the conversion of the villagers to wage-laborers. If the poem of the Cambridge fence-destroyer that we cited earlier seems harsh, listen to the words of one grantee of monastic lands, speaking to his tenants:

> Do ye not know that the King's Grace has put down all the houses of monks, friars, and nuns? Therefore, now is the time come that we gentlemen will pull down the houses of such poor knaves as ye be.

The tenants who remained on the land had their copyholds declared tenancies at will—that is, for no definite term—by the new landlords, who claimed the right to put up rents as they would: some were increased two and threefold. Those who could afford it went to court, and many of the copyholders' claims were found to have been meritorious. In the main though, the bourgeois idea of land law—the relation between *persona* and *res*, with no obligation other than to hold and use for personal profit—began to be applied with a vengeance.

The poor had their champions, who succeeded in passing laws setting up parliamentary inquiries and even pardoning those who pulled down enclosures. After all, the law as declared in Parliament quite clearly provided that arable land was not to be converted to pasture. But this limitation upon the absolute character of the property relationship was seldom observed, as a succession of commissions of inquiry found. Tawney quotes a churchman:

> In suppressing of abbies, cloisters, colleges, and chantries, the intent of the King's Majesty that dead is, was, and of this our King now is, very godly, and the purpose, or else the pretence, of other wondrous goodly: that thereby such abundance of goods as was superstitiously spent upon vain ceremonies, or voluptuously upon idle bellies, might come to the King's hands to bear his great charges, necessarily bestowed on the common wealth, or partly unto other men's hands, for the better relief of the poor, the maintenance of learning, and the setting forth of God's word. Howbeit, covetous officers have so used this matter, that even those goods which did serve to the relief of the poor, the maintenance of learning, and to comfortable necessity hospitality in the common wealth, be now turned to maintain worldly, wicked, covetous ambition. . . . You which have gotten these goods into your own hands, to turn them from evil to worse, and other goods more from good unto evil, be ye sure that it is even you that have offended God, beguiled the king, robbed the rich, spoiled the poor, and brought a common wealth into a common misery.

More died in 1535. But years before he had polemicized against Simon Fish, who had urged seizure of all Church properties in a pamphlet of 1529 entitled *A Supplication for the Beggars*. Though More's condemnation in *Utopia* of idle spoliators had extended to "fat abbots," he wrote this in answer to Fish's observation that the Church held a third of the kingdom's wealth:

> But now to the poor beggars: what remedy findeth their proctor for them? To make hospitals? Nay, ware of that! Thereof he will none in no wise. For thereof, he saith, the more the worse, because they be profitable to priests. What remedy then? Give them any money? Nay, nay, not a groat. What other thing then? . . . [L]et him give nothing to them, but look what the clergy hath, and take all that from them. Is not here a goodly mischief for a remedy? Is not this a royal feast, to leave these beggars meatless, and then send more to dinner to them?

As the consequences of seizure became clearer, More's sentiment began to be echoed by erstwhile adherents of Fish's view. The radical anti-Catholics had assumed that the Church-maintained hospitals, schools, and other charitable institutions would continue under royal auspices and that the Church lands would be redistributed or let at reasonable rents. They misjudged either the intentions or the powers of their allies in the City of London. The lands, as we have seen, passed into the hands of the bourgeoisie. The hospitals and other institutions were replaced by jails and workhouses designed to encourage the peasantry, driven off the land, to enter the force of wage-laborers.

There is in this recounting an answer for those who find Renner's formulation, quoted earlier, of the bourgeois property norm too bald, unencumbered as it is by the ideology of natural right and liberty with which the seventeenth- and eighteenth-century commentators were to clothe it. Henry VIII's expropriatory legislation had its justifications: putting down sedition and heresy, protecting the Crown, purifying the profession of the faith by separating it from the pursuit of wealth. But it was nonetheless an expropriation, followed by a redistribution. The eighteenth-century bourgeois notion of the laissez-faire state as neutral arbiter was nowhere in evidence in Tudor England; the state was concededly an instrument, shared by the Crown and its powerful allies, to smash resistance to a new system of social relations. The later legal ideology of property as a natural right was an ideology for those who already owned land or were in the process of acquiring it in the normal course of trade; it was another way of saying that whoever had managed to capture a portion of the earth in the previous hundred years' troubles ought to be able to keep it.

The public-law consequences of this revolution in the private law were formidable. The mechanism for change was the statute, and Henry only briefly experimented with the idea of passing laws himself without calling a Parliament. Henry was in continual need of both the political support and the financial resources of the bourgeoisie. At each crucial juncture in Henry's policies, the bourgeoisie insisted that the dual goals of Tudor statecraft and its own advantage be served. Control by Parliament over royal revenues raised through direct taxation, and the requirement that Parliament alone could legislate, were two principal concessions Henry was forced to make. The near absolute sovereign thereby created the device that would be captured by the bourgeoisie and turned against experiments in absolutism.

In the House of Lords, Henry had created enough new peerages to be sure of success. His battles with the Commons were more difficult, for the lower house consisted mainly of landed gentry, knights who held lands in feudal tenure, and representatives of the cities. The Commons was a forum of bourgeois struggle, and the balance of political power there had an impact upon the conflict between feudal and bourgeois notions of land law. The Statute of Uses and Statute of Wills provide two striking examples.

The conveyance to use provided a means of evading wardship and relief. A conveys to B and his heirs. B reconveys to a group of people, as joint tenants, with a provision in the deed that they are to hold the land for a specific purpose declared in the deed, in a separate contract, or in B's will. Such joint tenancies were exempt from requirements of wardship and relief. The instructions in the deed, contract, or will might be to hold the land on B's death to the use of his heir—that is for the heir's benefit: such a provision to hold to the use of another on B's death operated as a bequest of real property, not otherwise possible except for a limited class of estates, mainly those held in burgage, that is, in the cities; in general, land descended to the eldest son. Further, B's creditors might be misled, for B, on the face of things, had no title to land which could be seized to pay his debts.

Both creditors and lords complained about this situation, and the creditors' complaints received attention in the courts and in Parliament. Most lords, however, were content to let things be, for they could employ the conveyance to use against their superiors, including the Crown. Henry considered the revenues being lost to him under such arrangements and in 1529 proposed to compel registration of all uses and to abolish a number of complicated rules of land law. As some consolation to the lords, Henry's proposal permitted them to continue to make special and rather complex settlements of their estates; under Henry's proposal, however, peers could not sell their land without the express consent of the Crown. This proposal guaranteed rights to the peers and revenues to the king; it also risked putting numberless lawyers out of business by abolishing the lucrative practice in conveyancing, while depriving property holders who were not peers—the gentry—of the right to make secret arrangements concerning their land, and making them responsible for unaccustomed levies on behalf of the king.

The combined power of the gentry and the common lawyers in the House of Commons put an end to the proposal and exacted concessions as the price for conceding taxation authority. Henry then found another way to tighten his grip on feudal revenues, but it entailed guaranteeing the free transmissibility of property. By the Statute of Uses, all uses were "executed," and the person entitled to the benefit of the land (*cestui qui use*) became the legal owner. Only uses which were "active," rather than merely fictitious, remained valid. A related statute required registration of conveyances involving a use.

The Statute of Uses preserved to the common lawyers their mystic domain of real-property estates in land as well as the technical and profitable delights of conveyancing. It did not require land transactions to be made public. It virtually ended, however, the transmissibility of land by will, which had been a major advantage of the conveyance to use. In 1540, therefore, as a concession to the gentry, sections of which had united with the peasantry in open rebellion against the consequences of the seizure of Church lands, Henry gave his support to the Statute of Wills, which made the greater part of English land transmissible by will. This was another victory for the bourgeois property norm.

17.

CONTRACT:
A STUDY OF LAW AND SOCIAL REALITY

The development of the contract law in England and on the Continent reveals the limitations of legal reform as a means of achieving fundamental social change. Bourgeois legal writers were fond of writing that the movement from feudalism to capitalism was achieved through the device of contract. As Sir Henry Maine wrote in the nineteenth century, the history of human progress is one of liberation from obligations based upon status and of their replacement by those based upon contract, or free bargain. In other words, the legal institution of contract was the motive force of the bourgeois revolution.

This statement, found in the writings of every bourgeois legal philosopher of that period, contains an important historical truth and a serious analytical falsehood. The historical truth is that a developed system of bourgeois social relations, such as came to maturity by 1800 in both England and France, had a well-developed theory of contract. The bonds uniting the different elements of such a society are almost exclusively bilateral and nominally consensual—that is to say, contractual. No longer, as in the feudal period, could landed property, its exploitation and defense, mediate the legal relations between people. Property became the relationship of *persona* and *res*. The contract—to work, to sell, even to live in marriage—took pride of place.

The analytical falsehood is the assertion that bourgeois social relations will come into being, regardless of material conditions, whenever the legal idea of free bargain is sufficiently developed. The law of contract did not burst into existence and become established on the basis of the self-evident justice of its principles. The field in which contracts operate is limited by the system of economic relations and this system is in turn determined by the level of technology, the strength of the opposing classes, and, in general, the state of development of the forces of production. Having access to a sophisticated theory of contract is no guarantee of the presence of the ensemble of forces needed to put it to work.

A high level of scholarship and legal science, therefore, was of no particular use to the bourgeoisie, for there was no way to create a unified national "common market" regulated by consistent principles of commercial law. Possession of a sophisticated theory of contract could not itself transform social relations. Transformation is a question of power, of appropriating and running a system of production.

In examining life in southern France in the 1200s and the 1300s, we saw how depopulation and economic stagnation led nascent bourgeois institutions to wither and die. Between 1400 and 1600, in the move toward a society dominated by the bourgeois class and governed in its interest, France and the Italian city-states, with their highly developed and sophisticated law of contract, were outdistanced by England, which began the period with a relatively backward system of contract law.

A glance at the records of the Medici Bank during the time of its greatest financial success—around 1450—reveals a sophisticated appreciation of all the contractual techniques that were to concern the draftsmen of the Code Napoléon 350 years later. Yet the Medici family banking empire was to collapse by the end of the century. The Medici wrote contracts to set up branch offices—agreements that were in the form of partnership arrangements for a certain period of time, specifying the partners' shares of capital, the remuneration due the branch manager, the sphere of permissible operations, and the courts that would have competence to deal with any dispute. Medici loan contracts, and disguised loans designed to evade the prohibition on usury, also show a considerable level of technical competence in drafting.

Where, as in Florence, the Medici family had interests other than banking, the form of social relationship was also contractual. The Medici would buy raw wool and use agents to coordinate the process of its being worked into cloth by a number of artisans. Although some of the initial operations of cloth making were carried out in the Medici woolshops, weaving, spinning, dyeing, and finishing were accomplished on the putting-out system common to many European areas at this time. Individual spinners and weavers, whose services were contracted for by a labor contractor, worked at home on their own machines. The elements of their labor relation with the Medici proprietor of the woolshop were in the main contractual, with only a few overtones of feudal, or status-based, social relations. (We might take as a point of contrast the industrial labor relations of the 1800s. The industrial worker hired out his labor by the day, week, or month. The contract was, in the terms used by civil-law lawyers drawing on the Roman law tradition and terminology, *locatio conductio operarum: locatio conductio* was the general name of a bilateral contract of hiring, just as *emptio venditio*—literally, buy-sell—was the general designation of a contract of sale. The coupling of terms signified the bilateral nature of the agreement. The term *operarum* means "of labor." The industrial worker of the 1800s had no tools, only his labor, which he "rented" at an agreed price and according to agreed terms of work. He gave up, to the rules of the factory, his freedom for the period for which his work was hired.)

Payment under contract in the Medici operation was not for "hours of work," but for each piece of wool woven or quantity of thread spun. At the same time, woolbeaters and corders might work for a daily wage, or be paid, at least in part, in food or other goods. Medici entrepreneurs might make loans to a worker to buy a loom, which would remain the property of the Medici until paid for in full.

Although some historians have described France of the 1400s and 1500s as in a state of relative stagnation, the theory of contract was undergoing considerable study on a sophisticated level. The Roman-law tradition, divided among those who took their lead from the canonists and those who looked to secular civil law, was used in the writing of custumals under royal supervision. To minimize and harmonize the differences between written-law and customary-law regions, scholars and lawyers began writing commentaries and comparisons. In 1608, Antoine Loisel drew this material together in *Les Institutes Coutumières*, a title designed to indicate the equality of customary and Roman-based law in France. Among the writers of such commentaries and comparisons, the most eminent is clearly Charles Dumoulin (1500–66), also known as Molinaeus. His views on the custumal of Paris and his comparisons of civil law and customary law were still being cited as authoritative in the great rebirth of legal writing in the early 1700s—for example, in Claude Ferrière's authoritative commentary on the customs of Paris in 1714. Dumoulin's style was orotund, combative, discursive, and exhaustive; his impressive scholarly analysis always came back to concrete contemporary problems. In taking the side of the merchants on an issue of contract law, he contrasted canon, Roman, and customary doctrine and insisted that French customary law had endorsed the canon-law rule that an oral promise was binding, concluding that the freedom of contract permitted by Roman-law principles should not be constrained by rules relating to the *form* of the bargain, rules which he claimed had not survived the Roman period.

The wealth derived by the French Crown and bourgeoisie from trade with Spain, following the opening of the New World, permitted expenditures on the arts and sciences and in universities. At the University of Bourges, Jacques Cujas and his pupils began the systematic restudy of Roman law from a humanist or Renaissance perspective. Returning to the Roman texts disputed and distorted by the glossators and by generations of practicing lawyers, Cujas represents one school of scientific textual study. But his pure Roman-law solutions made no further contribution toward uniformity of practice than the consultative work of Dumoulin and the other advisers to the profession.

The reduction of the customs to writing permitted Dumoulin and his contemporaries to note the adoption of Roman-law-based rules conducive to commerce (including a sophisticated law of contract); and local customs, in being written down, were subject to royal pressures toward uniformity and Romanization. At the same time, the very reduction to writing tended to ossify those archaic legal principles that the customary law continued to rely upon. To codify is to ossify, for analysis and judgments are thereafter limited by meanings which may logically, permissibly, or plausibly be assigned to the newly written words.

The urban custumals greatly resemble those of other areas directly under royal control. They owe an obvious debt to the Custom of Paris, and contain impressive borrowings from Roman law in the fields of contract, property, and procedural law. The custumals of areas where royal power was more attenuated are either silent about the legal principles which might favor commerce, or reject outright particular Roman law-based rules. This distinction could not be eroded unless the intellectual resources represented by the commentators were harnessed to a state apparatus strong enough to put their proposed solutions into effect. And neither the bourgeoisie as a class nor its allies in the royal establishment had such power. Even though the competence of the royal tribunals increased to the detriment of seigneurial courts, and even though seigneurs were forbidden beginning in the 1500s to hold court themselves and were obliged to recruit professional judges, the procedure followed, and the law applied, remained to a great extent locked in the rules of the custumals.

The tenacity of localism and archaism was both symptom and cause of stagnation. The exaction of tolls and the creation of barriers to the internal flow of goods bespoke seigneurial power in the face of royal authority and provided the means for its continued existence. The seigneurs would not voluntarily give up their feudal exactions while sections of the bourgeoisie either bought the right to receive such payments—and hence could not countenance their abolition—or made loans to seigneurs which would become worthless if their debtors had no means to earn or extort the means of repayment. In England, the increasing number of royal officers was a means to centralization; in France, it was not. Royal office was attractive to the young bourgeois, as it continued to be for the reasons discussed in the previous chapter, but the French Crown could not be sure of the loyalty of these officials.

Charles Loyseau's *Treatise on Offices*, published in 1610, documented the difficulties of the royal bureaucracy. He noted that from at least the 1300s, judicial offices—and many others in the royal service—had been sold by the crown. Prohibitions against the practice had been enacted by the Estates-General in the 1400s, but without effect. Charles VIII issued an *ordonnance* in 1493 that required each magistrate to swear before taking office "that he had not given, nor promised to give, by himself, or any other, of gold, silver or other equivalent thing" for his office. Remarked Loyseau: "It was scandalous that the judges of France should enter upon their duties by a solemn act of perjury, that in taking office they should commit a public falsehood." But the need for money was so pressing that in 1522 François I actually established a special bureau for selling offices—in Loyseau's words, "a boutique for this new merchandise." In 1567, the Crown recognized and approved the transfer of offices between living persons, provided a tax was paid on transfer. The attractions of judicial office for those with the money to buy them was great indeed; one could expect to cap a career with a royal bestowal of the *noblesse de robe*, a new brand of nobility reserved for jurists. The cost of the judgeship could be exacted from litigants over the years. In Montpellier, between 1547 and 1577, the nobles of the robe were outdistanced only by the financiers in buying up land around the city that had been in the hands of small proprietors.

Not surprisingly, the creation of a royal administrative apparatus with no measurable loyalty to the Crown, and with a property right to remain in office, at times caused "the throne to tremble." And when these nonloyal judges sat in provincial royal courts—the *Parlements*—their effect could be greater still, and by 1550 these had become centers for anticentralist agitation.

In sum, the presence in France and Italy of substantial groups of law-trained men and women in the service of the bourgeoisie was of no avail without a unified national marker and a strong state apparatus wedded to bourgeois interests. These conditions existed in England: the legal ideology of the bourgeoisie there became the expressed justification for the exercise of state power on its behalf. King Henry's confiscation of Church land gave legal rights to a new group of landowners, reinforcing the position they already had by virtue of their entrepreneurship and mercantile activity. Here the law could be a battering ram, to take down the houses of "poor wretches." But law—those principles which made up the legal ideology of the old nobility—was also a shield for that class and for those who, owning property outside the cities, shared its problems. They too had to be brought into the system of bourgeois legal relations. At least those relations had to be integrated into the old common law and applied by the King's courts, which had been established to serve essentially feudal interests.

The common law, we have seen, was in its origins the law of "the land"—that is, of realty. Between approximately 1400 and 1600, it became the law of "the Land," of the country, and it incorporated principles developed in the merchant and maritime jurisdictions. In 1400, King's Bench and Common Pleas grudgingly admitted to only the most limited and rudimentary ideas of contract. Just after 1600, Sir Edward Coke—who became Attorney General in 1594 and Chief Justice of the Court of Common Pleas in 1606 and who was a prolific commentator on the law—declared the law merchant to be part of the common law, by which he meant that the common lawyers and common-law courts would thenceforth serve the interests of merchants.

This process is worth describing, for it was accomplished without overt violence to the landed class, whose interests were nominally protected, left to be dealt with more harshly at some future date. The fiction of uninterrupted tradition could, with some recasting of history, be maintained. "Let us now peruse our ancient authors," Coke wrote, "for out of the old fields must come the new corne."

Coke was not the first to venture the opinion that the common law had to be expanded. Thomas More, as Chancellor, had sought to coerce the common-law courts into changing by the liberal use of his power to issue injunctions directed to them. When the complaints of the common-law judges reached him, More invited all of them to dinner in the Council Chamber at Westminster. His son-in-law, William Roper, recounts that

> after dinner, when he had broken with them what complaints he had heard of his injunctions and moreover showed them both the number of causes of every one of them, in order, so plainly that, upon full debating of those matters, they were all forced to confess that they, in like case, could have done no otherwise themselves. Then offered he this unto them, that if the justices of every court (unto whom the reformation of the rigor of the law, by reason of their office, most especially appertained) would, upon reasonable considerations, by their own discretions (as they were, he thought, in conscience bound), mitigate and reform the rigor of the law themselves, there should from thenceforth by him no more injunctions be granted. Whereunto when they refused to condescend, then said he unto them, "Forasmuch as yourselves, my lords, drive me to that necessity for awarding out injunctions to relieve the people's injury, you cannot hereafter any more justly blame me."

It is a great pity that we do not know the precise terrain over which the argument between More and the common lawyers was waged. But we can surmise what at least some of the questions must have been.

To do this, we must first recall something of the setting within which the dispute took place. More, having been trained as a common lawyer at Lincoln's Inn and spent time at the bar, knew his opponents well. At that time a lawyer was trained not in university, but in the Inns of Court, lodging there for three years to receive formal training from the younger members of the bar and to learn by example and discussion from the older members. Judges of the common-law courts were drawn from the ranks of practicing lawyers. Sir John Fortescue's *De Laudibus Legum Anglie* (In Praise of the Laws of England), written about 1470, gives us a glimpse of the process. At the Inns, he wrote:

> there is in addition to the study of law a kind of academy of all the manners that the nobles learn. There they learn to sing and to practice all kinds of harmony. They are also taught there to dance and engage in pastimes that are proper for nobles.

Fortescue's picture is a bit idyllic, but certainly the Inns welcomed many sons of noble families who were not seeking to enter legal practice.

Legal education consisted of reading judges' opinions and reports of argued cases and participating in mock legal battles. But the most important subject of study was procedure and pleading: Thomas Littleton, author of a leading treatise on land law, *Of Tenures*, said to his son:

> It is one of the most honorable, laudable and profitable things in our law to have the science of well pleading in actions real and personal; and therefore I counsel thee especially to employ thy courage and care to learn this.

It was good advice. One could not proceed in the common-law courts without mastering a bewildering array of procedural devices, each of which required a written pleading in a precise form. Every common-law lawsuit was initiated with a writ. The only suits permitted were those in which the facts alleged could be fitted to the requirements of one of the available writs. The first writs were authorized soon after the Norman Conquest, as directions to a royal officer to bring in the defendant so that inquiry could be made about the right to possess a given piece of land. The writ system was elaborated to provide remedies in a broader range of actions, but it also retained a rigid format which required a prospective plaintiff to fit his case within a standard form. The development of the law was thus linked to the interpretation of the words of standard forms of initial pleading. If none of the authorized forms fit the facts of one's case, there was no remedy in the common-law courts. To abate the rigors of this system, lawyers pressed for creation of new writs—new "forms of action"—and indulged in sometimes spectacular feats of casuistry to adapt the facts to one of the available forms.

If the plaintiff of 1500 consulted a common lawyer complaining that a contract had been breached, the lawyer first turned to the writ of covenant. To sustain an action of covenant one had to allege and prove that there had been a formal contract reduced to writing and sealed. A simple, unsealed written agreement, much less an oral one, could not be enforced. To surmount this difficulty, many contracts were written in the form of bonds. One party would say that he owed the other a sum of money, but it would be stipulated that the bond was void upon the performance of certain conditions. If the conditions were not performed, the injured party could bring a writ of debt to collect.

Such roundabout ways of making and enforcing bargains did not appeal to merchants who had a large volume of business to transact and relied upon simple forms of contract. At first the merchants turned away from the common-law courts for the bulk of their legal business and sought royal assistance in creating parallel institutions which would fashion and apply a more hospitable law of contract. For example, they had recourse to the judicial jurisdiction of the Lord Chancellor—to More and his predecessors and successors—who had from about 1350 exercised judicial powers, based in theory upon the obligation of the Crown to administer "justice," irrespective of the rules of the common law. By 1500 there was a clearly defined core of such "equity" doctrine, grounded in the notion that the Chancellor would provide a remedy for injustice when the common law would not.

What were the sources of this doctrine? From its beginnings, equity jurisdiction was meant by the Crown to be used for mercantile causes, such as when the sovereign was bound by treaty to see that foreign merchants had an efficacious tribunal. It is likely indeed that the mercantile courts of the City of London, which also had cognizance of merchant matters, were responsible for much of the legal learning put into practice by the Chancellors. One detects also, in the Chancellors' jurisprudence, a continual absorption of canon-law and Roman-law principles. Notions of "justice" and "conscience," watchwords of basic equity theory, sound both of canonist concern with souls and of Roman-law ideas of contractual good faith. Under the Tudors this reception of Roman-canon principles was accelerated. In this respect, Thomas More was an ideal Chancellor, for he was probably unique in combining common-law experience, and knowledge of canon and

Roman law, with a deep personal sense of justice and extensive familiarity with merchant affairs.

In theory, equity power was purely personal, in the sense that the litigant was commanded to do or refrain from doing a certain thing on pain of losing his soul. Should that not be enough, the Chancellor could lock up his body. A defendant brought before the court of equity might be ordered to carry out a contract for which the common-law courts provided no remedy; or he might be ordered to abandon a suit he had brought in the common-law courts if the Chancellor was convinced that the suit would result in a judgment which, though "lawful," would offend mercantile-law principles that had been basic to the original bargain between the parties. Such decisions created both the hostility More confronted at dinner in Westminster Hall and some unsubtle pressure for the common-law courts to modify the doctrine they applied.

Merchants also had tribunals specially created for their needs by treaty, by royal charter, by virtue of municipal privileges, or otherwise. Merchant and admiralty courts continued to function through the 1500s. Indeed, as the royal navy became more important to trade and war making, the admiralty jurisdiction was increased. A number of special courts were created to administer specific aspects of economic and land policy, and judges trained in civil law were appointed to them. (It has even been contended, with some justice, that England came close to adopting the Roman law as the basis of jurisprudence, as a kind of final ornament to the changes being wrought by the Tudor monarchs.)

Merchant causes could also be heard in courts established by royally chartered corporations of merchants, the corporation having a partial or total monopoly on a particular branch of trade. The Mercers are the most notable example, and in the 1400s a branch of the fellowship—those interested in exporting cloth, particularly to the Low Countries—began to meet separately, as indicated by a 1443 mention in a royal charter of "des Aventurers del Mercery." From 1486 onward, the Merchant Adventurers among the Mercers took the lead among all exporters in organizing and controlling English trade to the Low Countries.

In form the Adventurers were a corporation under royal charter. They were presided over by a governor, apparently named by the king on nomination of the group. Henry VII sent John Pykering to be governor over "oure trusty and welbeloved subiettes the marchauntes adventerers" in the Low Countries, "at the desyre and nomination of the most partie of you resident in our said citie of London." The Adventurers had the right to hold their own courts and to impose sanctions on all those carrying on overseas trade in the region assigned to them. Their courts applied mercantile law. Their jurisdiction was assured in London by royal grant, and in other lands by treaty confirming their power over all English traders in a particular sovereignty. Thus, the royal chartered company with a monopoly, a model for later colonial enterprises, was combined with the earlier model of the consular court, which had existed since the Crusades. The importance attached to encouraging and protecting the Merchant Adventurers' trade is apparent in the obvious diplomatic effort expended on their behalf. It is likely that More's being given the "freedom" of the Mercers in 1509 was a reward for some of his efforts.

In sum, the wealthy bourgeois in the middle of the 1500s confronted great opportunities in trade and enterprise, provided he was willing to submit to the rules of a financial system run from London—a domination which caused some distress to Merchant Adventurers in the North. Contracts drawn under merchant law were enforceable in merchant courts, in chancery, and in admiralty. More and more, the principles of this Continental import were being applied and studied. The common lawyers, from whose ranks the judges of the King's Bench and the Court of Common Pleas were drawn, knew that the portion of the legal system they administered was in danger of being reduced to insignificance as their clientele, the landed nobles or the gentry, declined in relative financial power. For its part, the bourgeoisie welcomed the opportunity to have access to the common-law courts, which were more independent of the Crown than some of the special tribunals established by the Tudor monarchs; alliance with the Crown was one thing; dependence on it quite another.

There was room, therefore, for an alliance of the common lawyers and the bourgeoisie, if only the lawyers could convince the forums where they practiced to be receptive to bourgeois legal principles. The closing years of the century saw the alliance begin to take shape, as the common-law courts moved toward a bourgeois theory of contract. In 1602, in *Slade's Case*, all the common-law judges, meeting in Exchequer Chamber, ruled that a contract for the sale of goods, though not under seal, could be sued upon in the common-law courts. It would have been simpler for the judges to adopt the merchant rule, but their respect for tradition required taking a different route.

The action of covenant, which could be brought only on a contract under seal, was clearly unsuited to merchant contracts. There was also the action of debt, for a written promise to pay money, but this had its own limitations. *Slade's Case* turns, therefore, on the reinterpretation of a third writ, that of *assumpsit*, and the judges were ratifying and making express a process of development in the use of this writ which had begun decades earlier. The common lawyers had begun to argue: suppose I agree with a contractor that he shall make me a house, and this agreement is under seal; if he does not make the house at all ("nonfeasance"), I have an action in covenant. If he makes it badly, and he has promised, even orally, to make it well, I am cheated because he has defaulted on an undertaking (an *assumpsit* which is dishonored by his "misfeasance"). The argument that violation of an undertaking to use care and skill, even one not under seal, could give rise to an action in *assumpsit* began to be used around 1400 in actions against carpenters, against veterinarians who agreed to cure animals, and in other similar circumstances. Rather than simply adopt the mercantile principle that a bargain must be kept, the common lawyers began to reinterpret the notions of fraud and deceit. Default on an *assumpsit* was cheating; once that notion was established, the road was open to adopting the essential elements of contract law.

In the 1500s the action in *assumpsit* was extended to cover certain debts. If there was a debt owing, and the debtor said he would pay it by a certain date, the creditor, according to developing doctrine, could sue on the debt or on the promise (*assumpsit*) to pay the pre-existing obligation. Hence, *indebitatus assumpsit*.

Slade's Case united and refined the doctrine. If A agrees to sell corn to B on a future day, and B to pay for it, this is an executory contract, i.e., one to be performed in the future. If A does not deliver, or if B does not pay, the defaulting party has violated his *assumpsit*. That is, as the judges declared, "every contract executory imports in itself an *assumpsit*." From old fields had come new corn.

Once the principle had been accepted, it became easier to admit the mercantile notion of contract through the front door. The King's Bench reaffirmed and expanded its custom of admitting evidence of merchant customs and empaneled a jury of merchants to establish them if necessary. To accommodate the claims of international traders, the common-law courts expanded their geographical jurisdiction: they permitted the plaintiff to plead that Amsterdam, or some other foreign city where a dispute had arisen, was "in the parish of St. Mary-le-Bow, in the Ward of Cheap" in the City of London, and then declined to permit the opposing party to deny the allegation.

The struggle of the common lawyers and judges to attract the business of the newly powerful merchants intensified in the late 1500s and persisted into the 1600s. The common-law judges, at the behest of the defendants who appeared before them, began to issue writs prohibiting the merchant or admiralty court from proceeding, or ordering the plaintiff to desist and come to them. The merchant jurisdictions, and especially admiralty—which enjoyed royal support—responded with writs and injunctions of their own. This struggle within the legal profession, at the expense of the litigants whose business was at stake, persisted into the 1600s.

The common lawyers' gradual assimilation of bourgeois law was one necessary condition of their alliance with the bourgeoisie which came to full fruition in the English Revolution of the mid-1600s. That alliance could not succeed unless the paper war of writs and injunctions could be settled to the advantage of the common lawyers, either through royal intervention or, as proved necessary, by some more violent means.

The alliance of the bourgeoisie and the common lawyers had a constitutional dimension as well, for the common-law courts were not the creatures of royal prerogative as were the merchant and admiralty tribunals and the other "special" jurisdictions. As we explain more fully in our discussion of the English Revolution, Sir Edward Coke was a major architect of the alliance's ideology. Magisterially, not to say outrageously, he recast English history and precedent. The old fields were the common-law reports, and perhaps Magna Carta, seen not as concessions extracted by some barons but as a charter of liberty. From Magna Carta could be deduced the notion that the King was limited by the "law of the land," a phrase used in that document most probably to refer to protection of baronial privilege, but capable of wider interpretation. From the old common-law reports came a recast legal system accepting of new principles, but resting on old traditions. This rewritten history of royal concession and judicial decision, as T. F. T. Plucknett has remarked, "limited Crown and Parliament indifferently."

The bourgeoisie bore no small responsibility for the creation of a monarchy with claims to absolute power, for its interests had been served by forceful Tudor policies. But having achieved a redistribution of land, and having profited from the breakup of village life, the bourgeoisie sought allies in a new struggle to restrain the power of the Crown to interfere with trade. The common lawyers proved ready to join such an alliance.

PART FIVE

BOURGEOIS VICTORY

(1600--1804)

18.

FRANCE: THE TRIUMPH OF THE THIRD ESTATE

The Code Napoléon was enacted on the 29th of Ventose, in the twelfth year of the Republic—March 20, 1804. More than a year earlier, the major outlines had been presented to the Conseil d'Etat by Member Jean Portalis and his principal collaborators, Bigot-Preméneu, Treilhard, and Tronchet. An earlier draft, from which these four worked, had been prepared by Jean-Jacques Cambacères, Second Consul under Napoléon.

In a speech before the Conseil, Portalis reflected on the work that had gone into preparing the Code and putting its provisions into law, a few at a time, over the course of a year. With Napoleon's authorization, this speech became the official version of the Code's history. Beginning with references to Charlemagne's first legislation, Portalis went on to consider Louis XI's *établissemens* and *ordonnances*, then made reference to the studies of Roman law, and remarked on the lack of success of all attempts to unify and simplify the law of France. (In an earlier report, one year before, he had also paid homage to those who reduced the customary law to writing so that it could be studied.)

In peroration, he set out the official version of the French bourgeoisie's struggle for power:

> "It was our discoveries in the arts, our first success in navigation, and the ferment happily born of our successes and discoveries of every sort that produced, under Louis XIV, Colbert's rules on manufactures, the law of

waterways and forests, the regulation of commerce, and that of the maritime trade.

"Good was born of good. When the legislator has focused his concern and attention on a few important matters, he feels the necessity and has the desire to encompass all. There were judicial reforms, civil procedure was corrected, a new order was established in criminal justice, and the vast project of giving a uniform code to France was conceived.

"[Those who attempted the Code] met insurmountable obstacles, in public opinion which was not sufficiently prepared, in the rivalries of power, in the attachment of people to customs the conservation of which they regarded as a hereditary right, in the resistance of the sovereign courts which continued to fear that their power would be diminished, and in the superstitious disbelief of lawyers in the utility of any change which would affect that which they had laboriously learned and practiced for all their lives.

"Nonetheless, the ideals of reform and uniformity had been liberated in the world. Savants and *philosophes* seized hold of them, evaluating legislative proposals in the light of reason and experience. Laws were compared with one another, studied in their relationship to the rights of man and to the needs of society. The judicious Domat and several of his contemporaries began to doubt whether legislation was a true science. I call science a series of truths or rules united one to another, derived from first principles and brought together in a body of systematic doctrine touching one of the principal branches of knowledge. . . .

"In the sciences, as in letters and the arts, even while ordinary talents struggle with difficulties and exhaust themselves with vain efforts, there appears suddenly a man of genius who springs forth and moves our thought beyond its accustomed frontiers.

"The celebrated author of *L'Esprit des Lois* [Montesquieu] did just that in the last century; he left far behind him all others who had written of jurisprudence; he went to the source of all legislation; he divined the motive force of each law; he taught us never to separate the details from the whole system, always to study laws in the light of history, which is the physical laboratory of legislative science. He brought us into contact with the legislators of all epochs and in all parts of the world.

"Thus was the spirit that moved among us, thus our knowledge and resources, when suddenly a great revolution erupted.

"All abuses were attacked at once, all institutions questioned. At the voice of the orator, institutions seemingly unshakeable crumbled; they were without roots in the sentiments of the people. Power found itself quickly conquered by opinion.

"It was, one must admit, one of those decisive times which occur sometimes in the history of nations, and which alter the position and the fortune of a people. . . .

"Among all the reforms proposed, the idea of uniform legislation particularly occupied the attention of our deliberative assemblies.

"But how to prepare a code of civil laws in the midst of the political troubles agitating our country?

"The hatred of the past, the impatient desire to live for the present, the fear of the future led to the adoption of the most exaggerated and violent measures. Caution and prudence, the attitudes of conservatism, were replaced by the desire to destroy everything.

"Certain unjust and oppressive privileges, which were but the property of a few men, had weighed on the heads of all. To recover the advantages of liberty, the country fell for a brief moment into license. To suppress the odious system of privilege and preference and to prevent its rebirth, some sought to level all fortunes after having leveled all social ranks. . . .

"But more moderate ideas came back to the fore; the first laws were corrected, new plans demanded: it was understood that a civil code must be prepared with wisdom, and not imposed with furor and haste."

There is a great distance between the measured conservative tones of Portalis and the enthusiastic iconoclasm of the revolutionary decrees that preceded it, such as the 1789 decree of the National Assembly abolishing feudalism and promising redistribution of the land. The Code is revolutionary, to be sure, for it enacts the bourgeois ideals of contract and property and recognizes them as generally applicable. As a code of private law, however, it is uniquely in the service of the bourgeoisie, and is a clear betrayal of the aspirations and interests of the workers and peasants who were shock troops of the Revolution.

Portalis' statement makes clear that earlier thrusts toward disorder, destruction, and leveling had been firmly shoved aside. The Revolution was "sudden," "power" was "conquered" not by arms but "by opinion"; "exaggerated and violent measures" had been taken. Now that power had been won, this sudden revolution was to be regarded as a discontinuous, almost chance, event, rather than as the capstone of eight hundred years of bourgeois struggle. The new Code would acknowledge as parents no bandits or levelers and scarcely any armed rebels; instead Montesquieu, Colbert, Domat—even Louis XIV—were claimed as ancestors of the document Portalis extolled.

THE LEGAL AND HISTORICAL BACKGROUND OF THE REVOLUTION

The French nation was formed in 1600. For purposes of representation in the infrequent Estates-General called by the Crown to approve taxes and give advice, the nation consisted of three estates: clergy, nobility, and commoners (roturiers). The latter included the wealthy bourgeois, lawyers, professors, master craftsmen, artisans, wage laborers, and agricultural small holders—in short, a disparate collection of persons and interests gathered into one group.

The bourgeoisie in 1800—as it had for eight hundred years—openly recognized the class conflicts within itself. The earliest urban rebels sought recognition of their unique position in the feudal system, filling a different function from that of other free non-nobles such as lesser vassals, small freeholders, and the few agricultural day-laborers. As distinctions between masters and workers sharpened, the wealthy bourgeoisie began to insist upon its separate status. In France, it is clear that insisting on this separate status did not necessitate remaining within it—as evidenced by the bourgeois tendency to acquire nobility whenever possible. Only later did the bourgeoisie perceive the advantages of uniting and leading the Third Estate to overthrow feudal institutions.

Abbé Sieyès, in his 1789 pamphlet *What Is the Third Estate?*, declared frankly that the term designated alternatively the bourgeoisie and the mass of the people. Including the latter was useful for rallying the majority against the nobility, "This class . . . assuredly foreign to the nation because of its do-nothing idleness." The former referred to that small part of the Third Estate which occupied leadership positions.

In the early 1600s, Loyseau denied that the entire Third Estate could be termed the "bourgeoisie," insisting on etymological grounds that a bourgeois was one who lived in a city. He divided the Third Estate into men of letters (theology, law, medicine, the arts); those who held offices giving them the right to a share in the royal finances (including many who would in modern parlance be financiers or bankers); judges, lawyers, and court personnel; and merchants. And the great majority? Those who worked with their hands he termed "vile," "bumpkins," "dolts," and "dishonest and sordid." Even artisans, he wrote, were vile and abject; he protested against the recognition by royal patent of master craftsmen, for it only led the bumpkins to put on airs, "as though they were officers of the prince." But Loyseau knew his history, and he was aware that many merchant fortunes had begun in artisanal workshops under the aegis of the communal societies. Therefore, he stated, "There are occupations that are artisanal and commercial at the same time . . . ; to the extent one in such a position participates in commerce, his calling is honorable."

As for the countryside, "today we term the laborers and villagers whom we call peasants vile persons." And then, more cautiously, "They are particularly oppressed by taxation, so much that one wonders how they survive and how we will continue to find laborers to feed us." (So frank and arrogant an indictment of the "vile" classes does not appear in the volumes of debate on the Napoleonic Code; there these sentiments are masked behind fears of disorder, rebellion, and threat to property.)

The main lines of French bourgeois ideology leading to 1789—from Loyseau's pungent word to Sieyès' pamphlet to Portalis' closing strophe—were thoughtfully prepared. The differentiation of the bourgeoisie from the mass of the Third Estate, and the careful justification of its right to lead first the insurgents and then the nation, was a common theme of these works. Each element of the *ancien régime* was analyzed, scandalized, satirized, and classified. Voltaire, Diderot, Montesquieu, and others pointed the way. From the reign of Louis XIV, or more accurately during the time of his minister Colbert, the ideological outlines of the impending revolution became clearer. Its architects were lawyers.

Joseph-Robert Pothier and Jean Domat, in the practical tradition of Dumoulin, wrote copiously of the bourgeois law of the 1600s and 1700s, still hemmed about with feudal limitations, churchly dogmas, and the principle of royal supremacy. Meantime, in France and elsewhere in Europe, representatives of the great trading and manufacturing interests—such as Montesquieu in France or Grotius in Holland—confronted feudal, canonical, and popular objections to a legal system constructed on principles of free contract and freedom of property.

Moreover, as we shall see, leadership of the forces which successively seized control of the National Assembly after 1789 was principally in the hands of lawyers, their radicalization measured by the extent to which they believed that the newly won bourgeois victory could be contained within the old institutions, or, on the contrary, that these institutions would inevitably betray the Revolution and had therefore to be crushed. This chapter traces the growing self-awareness of the bourgeoisie as a *class*, rather than as simply one group among many which opposed and were separate from the temporal and spiritual overlords whose social function was increasingly attenuated and whose financial demands were, therefore, increasingly perceived as predatory.

Jean Baptiste Colbert, Louis XIV's Minister of Finance from 1661 to 1683, played an important role in these events. Son of a relatively wealthy merchant family, Colbert entered the service of Louis' adviser Mazarin, who until his death in 1661 was the most powerful man in the realm. Pierre Goubert says of Colbert:

> Singled out by Mazarin at an early age, he stuck to him as Mazarin had done to Richelieu and served him indefatigably, even in such menial tasks as supervising his dinner. He was in an admirable position to know all the affairs of Mazarin and the state, and to further his own. He had great perseverance, an immense capacity for work, a liking for order, administrative experience, some clear, if occasionally wrong-headed ideas, and inordinate greed. Only this last trait was at all typical of his time.

Colbert did not need to be an innovator; he had only to look to England and Holland for models of economic progress and to try to understand why France lagged behind. His solution, designed to serve the Crown's fiscal, political, and foreign-exchange position while benefitting the bourgeoisie, was state-sponsored mercantile capitalism on the English model. In order to develop an internal system of production and establish an export trade in both domestic manufactures and in products developed from colonial exploitation of sugar and coffee plantations, Colbert saw to the creation of corporations which had royal charters and a guaranteed monopoly—for both of which the Crown exacted a heavy tribute—over some branch of trade. Royal subsidy and innovations in the law favorable to the new modes of trade and manufacture combined to draw financiers and wealthy bourgeois into these fields. The old pattern of bourgeois fortune-building—from commerce to landholding to the nobility in three generations—began to change. Those financiers who preferred not to invest but rather to advance money to the Crown in exchange for the right to "farm" a portion of the national taxes were induced to change their preferences. The merchant and manufacturing bourgeoisie favored in the years of Colbert's ministry continued to prosper in the 1700s, becoming powerful forces in French political life. Montesquieu came from their midst, and Voltaire was greatly influenced by them. From a position of financial power, these financiers of domestic manufacture and colonial trade moved, with sporadic royal help, to attack the guilds of artisans and master craftsmen, which in the context of feudal society had been formed as bourgeois enclaves.

The enclosure movement in France, and the struggle to establish bourgeois property rights in the countryside, took place one hundred years later than the same events in England and without a wholesale confiscation. Rather, those bourgeois financiers who had purchased feudal estates were permitted to establish manufacturing enterprises on them, to the detriment both of the guilds in the towns and of the common use of grazing, farming, and wooded land.

We can trace these events in the writings of lawyers, who shaped the old institutional forms to accommodate change. Louis XIV, taking Colbert's advice, ordered a number of merchant customs codified, promulgating a code of civil procedure and a code relating to waterways and forests. Between 1689 and 1697, portions of Jean Domat's *Les Loix civiles dans leur ordre naturel* appeared. Though published privately, Domat's work had the approval of Louis XIV and was an authoritative summary of the existing law. It is an odd mixture of bourgeois legal principle supported by natural law along with an express recognition of feudal prerogative.

Domat divided laws into those which are God-given and therefore immutable, and those which are manmade and therefore "arbitrary."

> Immutable laws are called thus because they are natural and therefore just always and everywhere, laws which no authority may change or abolish. Arbitrary laws are those which a legitimate authority can establish, change, and abolish according to need.

And what are some of these immutable laws? Property rights, for one: "The master of a thing remains master of it until he parts with it voluntarily or has it taken from him by just and legitimate means." Though he recognized sovereign legislative prerogative, Domat believed contract to be the foundation of society, in the sense that the contract as private legislation ought principally to govern reciprocal rights and obligations between subjects. Mutual needs ought mainly to be satisfied by free bargain.

With respect to women, Domat took up a Roman-law theme that was to reappear with vigor in the Code Napoléon:

> The "sexual characteristics" which distinguish man and woman make between them this difference in regard to their status, that men are capable of all sorts of engagements and functions if not excluded by particular obstacles, and that women are incapable by sole reason of their sex of many sorts of engagements and functions. . . . By our usage, married women are under the power of their husbands. This is natural law and divine law.

The persistence of feudal forms of property and status is apparent in *Les Loix civiles*, and is indicative of Domat's effort to accommodate old rules to new systems of ownership and trade. For example, even though lending at interest had been recognized by the English parliament for more than one hundred years and was permitted on at least a limited basis in almost every custumal and legislative system in Western Europe, Domat attacked the practice with ecclesiastical fervor. *Les Loix civiles* describes in detail, however, each of the classical devices for evading the prohibition: the creditor not paid at term has the right to interest; in the context of a partnership—*société en commandité*—the partner providing the capital can expect a share of the profits; and so on through a list known for seven hundred years.

Joseph-Robert Pothier, a professor at Orléans, published a lengthy commentary on Justinian's Digest and a series of works on aspects of private law—obligations (contracts and torts), decedents' estates, property law, family law. Pothier's work was not original; it survives because his *Traité des obligations* was adopted by the draftsmen of the Code Napoléon as one of their technical guides (along with the work of Domat, or Bourjon, author of *Droit commun de le France*, and of Loisel, who wrote *Les Institutes Coutumières*). The *Traité* was translated into English and was briefly popular in the United States in the early 1800s, and no doubt helped by the efforts of American judges, lawyers, and law reformers—Justice Joseph Story, Chancellor Kent of New York, David Dudley Field—to bring civil-law concepts of mercantile practice, and perhaps the law merchant itself, into American law.

THE ALLIANCE OF PHILOSOPHY AND FINANCE

It was one thing to restudy the legal writing of the old regime, tracing elements derived from royal *ordonnances*, customary law, Roman law, canon law, and the law merchant. Another sort of spirit moved in the loftier arenas of the law. Charles de Secondat Montesquieu (1689–1755), whose book *The Spirit of the Laws* was widely read by those who led the American Revolution, was a lawyer and publicist. President of the *parlement* at Bordeaux, Montesquieu was also a stockholder in the Compagnie des Indes, the royal monopoly which exploited the sugar and coffee plantations of the French Caribbean and carried on the slave trade to provide them with a work force.

Montesquieu wrote extravagantly of the ancient nobility which, he said, had liberated France from barbarism. In the modern world, however, he found that a different motive force prevailed:

> The natural effect of commerce is to bring peace. . . . The spirit of commerce brings with it that of frugality, economy, moderation, work, wisdom, tranquility, law, and order. . . . In order to maintain the spirit of commerce, it is necessary that the principal citizens engage in it themselves, and that its spirit rule alone, unhindered by any other, and that all the laws favor it.

Just what was this natural effect of commerce which opposed feudal privilege and guild restrictions? We know some of the effects of free commerce at the time Montesquieu wrote. One iron forge established in the countryside consumed enough wood to heat the city of Châlons; who, a contemporary wondered, is taking account "that these factories leave nothing behind when they cut timber to heat their furnaces" A bishop filed a complaint with the controller-general in 1769 on the depopulation of his bishopric, complaining of proposals to introduce new industry:

> Agriculture requires livestock to richen the earth and strong arms to cultivate it. The changes proposed will diminish both considerably. It is to be noted that perhaps one-quarter of the people of the region have not enough pasture for the livestock they raise, and some have none at all. . . . If the commons are denied to them, these families, reduced to the most dire poverty, will be obliged either to leave the province to search employment in manufacturing of the kind not found in our region, or if they continue to live here, they will raise only the sickliest of children. . . .

The official response was that forcing cultivators off the land to work in manufacture was not a bad thing at all. The demand for grazing rights on common land, wrote the subdelegate of the region, "is the desire to be free, putting up a hut anyplace at all, in order to profit from the pastures of others, something which is contrary to natural law."

The natural law which defended, indeed required, this form of free commerce was not the rigorous, structured law of which St. Thomas Aquinas had spoken. It was rather the law of what the American revolutionaries later called "Nature and Nature's God." The "natural" economy was that which ran without official interference, in accord with its own inner dynamic, it was the meeting ground of philosophers and financiers. The Crown needed the financiers and aided them with legislation; the financiers patronized the ideologists of natural law and right reason. In the 1700s, it seemed possible to fashion an entente of royal and financial power, on terms sketched by jurists and extolled by philosophers. As late as 1790, such an accommodation, conditioned on a scaled-down royal establishment, was seriously discussed as a means of heading off the social revolution which was already underway.

WHOSE REVOLUTION?

The French Revolution can for our purposes be traced from the first decrees of the National Assembly to the promulgation of the Code Napoléon by examining proposals for legal change. In the lawmaking and law-enforcing of the Revolution we begin to discover who directed its policies and in whose interests French citizens fought and died.

In 1789, facing bankruptcy after years of bad harvests and agricultural crises, Louis XVI summoned the Estates general for the purpose of raising new taxes. There is every indication that the bourgeois deputies elected in the countryside—where 89 percent of the population lived—were prepared, based on the sentiment in their districts, to use this opportunity to curtail noble prerogatives, particularly those relating to taxation and manorial rights. On July 12, 1789, a poor woman encountered by a British traveler told him: "Something was to be done by the great folk for such poor ones, though I know not who or how, but God send us better, for taxes and feudal services are crushing us."

What was done is familiar history. Within the context of the Estates-General, the Third Estate and elements of the nobility transformed themselves into a National Assembly with the declared task of formulating a constitution. On the night of August 4, 1789, in a decree finally promulgated—after extensive debate and the addition of clarifying amendments and commentary—the following November 3, the Assembly expressed itself on the issue of property law:

> The National Assembly destroys entirely the feudal regime, and decrees that all rights and liabilities, feudal and personal, tending . . . to servitude . . . are abolished without indemnity, and all others are declared repurchasable, and that the price and means of repurchase will be fixed by the National Assembly. The rights not abrogated by this decree will continue nonetheless to be enforceable until they are compensated for.

Succeeding articles abolished the noble right to fish and hunt in streams and woods and the right to hold court.

The opening sentence of the decree assured the peasantry that the "feudal system" was abolished. The very word "feudal" was apparently coined by the revolutionaries. But what was this feudal system, and for whose benefit was it to be dismantled? Personal servitude hardly existed in 1789; here the decree only confirmed a state of fact. The lords' rights of fishing, hunting, and justice were an anachronistic nuisance; their final abolition simply made it easier to reorganize the theory of land law. The feudal dues which weighed so heavily on the peasants—their rent, the portion of the harvest due the seigneur, the money payments due on sale of the land—were declared purchasable, not abolished. The National Assembly promised at some future time to set fair prices so that with a single payment a peasant might become a proprietor of the land he and his family had farmed for generations. When the committee on feudal rights finally reported on September 4, the intent of the decree became clearer. The Assembly, the committee recommended, ought to make clear that it was abolishing the illegitimate prerogatives of the nobility and creating a uniform, indivisible "right of property"—the right to use and to abuse what one owned. The right of property was to be a relation between a person and a thing—*persona* and *res*; all personal obligations associated with ownership or with an estate in land were but deformations of this legal idea.

Had this view, which animated the subsequent legislation of the Assembly, been preceded or followed by a distribution of land to the peasantry in full ownership—as was demanded at various times in the streets and in the Assembly itself—the impact would have been profound. But this was never the intention of a majority of the Assembly. Two years after the decree, a village in the south complained that there had been no change in actual conditions. The villagers expressed their fear that there would be no liberation from the "odious regime" of feudal rights "for a thousand years."

The reasons for the limited impact of the August 4 decree must be sought in the structure of landholding and finance. Those seigneurs who held parcels of land and exercised feudal rights over them were ruinously and inescapably in debt to the financiers of the rising bourgeoisie. These financiers were clients both of the lawyers in the National Assembly and of the nobility who were "of the robe" and allied with the Third Estate. They cared little for the right to hunt, fish, and dispense justice, but they insisted that the dues that were exacted from the tillers of the land and that secured the debts owed them be redeemable in cash.

The questions posed—redeemability, repurchase, terms, and conditions—continued to be debated. In Portalis' discourse on the eve of adoption of the Code Napoléon, he referred to them as being of current importance. And although the Code ratified the law of August 4 and made all ground rents redeemable, in practice few tillers could afford to pay off the capitalized value of their formerly feudal dues; they left the land, became day-laborers, or took up leaseholds at an annual rent. This solution satisfied the codifiers of 1804 as it had the revolutionaries of 1789. Portalis thought that in a developed country agriculture should be another branch of commerce.

The National Assembly's confiscation of Church and royal land provided another opportunity for redistribution to the peasantry, and there was earnest discussion of such a prospect among the members of the Assembly. Little was done along such lines, however, and the major part of this land was put up for public auction, to be purchased by the only group with the money to buy—the bourgeoisie. It is difficult to estimate the extent to which this happened in the years between 1789 and 1800. On the eve of the Revolution, the nobility owned about 25 percent of the arable land of France. As the nobles were foreclosed on, exiled, or dispossessed, most of this land passed to the bourgeoisie, which already held 30 percent. Bourgeois holdings were further increased at the auctions of Church and royal lands. On the other hand, in some areas the peasantry seized land that it has never given up. We have walked in hill villages in the south of France and seen a series of tiny plots—often as small as 100 square feet—held by families since 1790.

In July 1789, thinking that the power had already passed as far toward the people as the bourgeoisie could stand, Abbé Sieyès wrote:

> All can enjoy the advantages of society, but only those who contribute to the public establishment are the important shareholders of the great social enterprise. They only are the active citizens, the true members of the Association.

Or, as another deputy put it, "There are no true citizens except owners." Other voices, like that of Jean Marat, were only heard briefly: "What will we have gained, to have destroyed the aristocracy of the nobles to replace it with that of the rich?"

By abolishing feudal interests in landed property, the bourgeoisie made good its loans to the old nobility and the Crown and established the basis of its future power. Looking back, the bourgeois economist Jean-Baptiste Say concluded that the intervention of the financiers in the Estates-General to force creation of the National Assembly was motivated solely by such considerations:

> The decisive impulse was given the revolutionary movement from the moment the moneyed powers, normally so conservative, rose up against the old order; the fear of bankruptcy stirred up the financiers, the bankers, the businessmen, and made them champions of the cause of the Third Estate. As Mirabeau said, "the deficit is the treasure of the nation."

There still remained, however, the question of social relationships, of contract. As Domat had noted a hundred years earlier, contract was a sort of private law. Two persons agreed to do or not, to buy or sell, and the public power stood ready to enforce their bargain. The liberty of contract was legitimately limited by the status of those contracting, by public-law provisions such as the prohibition on usury, and by privileges such as those held by the guilds and societies. But the decree of August 4 sanctioned the gradual stripping away of limitations upon the contractual freedom of peasants and landholders. The owner now met the peasant relatively unhindered by any consideration except his absolute right to do with his land what he wished. The natural-law ideal was, to this extent, realized.

The position of the guilds remained to be settled. The debate surrounding this question, which had begun under the *ancien régime*, put Voltaire and the financiers on the side against guild privilege, and Marat and great sections of the working population on the other side.

To become a master ironworker or weaver required a long apprenticeship. The masterwork required as a final qualification might take two years to produce. Production dominated by these masters was inspected to ensure product quality and conditions of work. (In some fields, such as that of bread baking, the guild system persisted in modified form until 1863, for a number of reasons that had more to do with social factors than with the nature of the work: the tax paid by master bakers for the privilege of being licensed was a source of government revenue; there was no economic incentive to industrialize the baking process; bread was, and is, a major item in the French diet and controls on quality and price were necessary to stave off violent popular reaction.)

In all fields of endeavor which were to acquire importance in an industrial capitalist society—such as ironworking and weaving—there were financial incentives to rationalize production and to do away with these controls. This process had begun under Colbert, and during the 1700s the King's Councils virtually halted creation of new categories of guilds. At the same time, limitations on the number of workers a master could employ were suspended in such occupations. As in England, authorizations to construct forges and factories outside the cities, where guild privilege had existed by historic grant, multiplied. In these new factories, worker and owner encountered each other directly rather than through the mediation of a guild and struck bargains that in theory reflected their mutual needs, free of any limitations concerning hours or conditions of work. Laws fixing maximum wages and requiring everyone to work helped induce those displaced from pastoral and agricultural pursuits to move into manufacturing. For the financiers, the establishment of these factories had evident advantages. This was a perfect example of the use of commerce, as Montesquieu had written, to create a social order based on natural law.

Voltaire characterized the guilds as a conspiracy to oppress the workers: "All these guilds of masters, all these oathbound societies were devised only to take money from the poor workers, to enrich the members, and to crush the nation." Spokesmen for the guilds, like Marat, were somewhat ambiguous:

> Nothing is better than to free all citizens from the fetters which prevent the development of talent and leave the unfortunate in their misery. But I do not know if this plenary liberty, this abolition of all apprenticeship, or of any period of training for all occupations, is wise. . . . If, to get rich quick, one casts aside the desire to make a reputation, then farewell good faith; soon every professional trade degenerates into intrigue and knavery. As all that is necessary to sell one's work is to give it a certain allure to the eye and the

> lowest price, without any concern for solidity and workmanship, all craftsmanship will descend to the level of junk. . . . It will be the ruin of the poor consumer.

Marat was writing in response to the National Assembly's adoption in March 1791 of a law that provided that "All privileges of professions are suppressed. From next April 1, every citizen will be free to exercise any profession or occupation he wishes, after obtaining and paying for an authorization." The guilds were thereby destroyed. Only money counted—enough to buy the authorization from the state and set up shop.

This move was favored by many workers, who saw it as a blow to the masters against whom they had risen on a number of occasions. But the natural-law theory of liberty of contract, which was reflected in the abolition of the guilds, allied with a firm faith in the primacy of commerce, led to more than the end of the masters' privileges.

No social legislation touched, let alone regulated, the terms of the contract *locatio conductio operarum*—literally, the hiring of labor-time. A law drafted in June 1791 by Le Chapelier, a lawyer for the great colonial sugar and coffee interests, took up the theme of the March legislation. The law first confirmed that all regulations of child and female labor, and of the hours of work and rates of pay, were to be swept away. It then reaffirmed in the revolutionary context what a series of royal enactments had provided on the ground of public need and order: workers were forbidden to organize. Individual workers were to confront their employers and bargain on their own account:

> The elimination of all sorts of corporate organizations of the same class or profession being one of the bases of the Constitution, it is prohibited to reestablish them under any pretext whatever. . . . The citizens of the same status or profession, the assistants or workers in any craft whatever, may not, when they find themselves assembled together, name a president or secretary, or bargaining agent, keep records or membership lists, enact rules, or formulate demands concerning their supposed common interests.

What had begun as the abolition of guild and small employers' privilege took its final form as an expression of pure bourgeois contract theory: let the individual enterprise bargain with the individual worker.

THE CODE NAPOLEON

The ideals of contract and property run in myriad ways through the legislation of the National Assembly and the preparatory work of what was to become the Code Napoléon. Successive drafts of a Civil Code were presented to the Assembly throughout the 1790s, then put aside or sent back to committee for redrafting. The earliest draft was too cumbersome, laden with remnants of the old law. The second, a scant 297 articles, seemed too brief, a mere statement of principle. These first efforts demonstrated, in effect, that the events of the Revolution had not yet bestowed victory firmly upon the bourgeoisie.

The actual work—the discussions, speeches, and written reports—on the final draft of the Code Napoléon are recorded in volumes of reports. Here it is clear that the bourgeoisie has been victorious. The old regime, too costly to bear, was swept away. The excesses of the 1790s were corrected. Portalis' comments on the background of the Code and the aspirations of the codifiers, cited earlier, are echoed in almost every speech on the Revolution, including the preliminary report of the drafting committee:

> Institutions succeeded one another with rapidity, and without the possibility of settling upon any one of them. The revolutionary spirit penetrated everywhere. We term "revolutionary spirit" the exalted desire to sacrifice violently all rights for a political goal, and not to admit any consideration but a mysterious and changeable interest of the State.

The speaker was tracing out the patterns ordained by God and natural reason. "Law cannot replace natural reason in the affairs of life," remarked the preliminary report, and the committee that drafted the provisions on contract and conventional obligations emphasized that its task was not to make law, but simply to restate self-evident principle:

> In the parts of the Code already promulgated, the legislator was able to work his will, and his will—which might have been different—has become general law. . . . [In the field of contract, however,] all he puts forth must be the expression of the eternal truths on which rests the moral law of all people. The book from which he draws his laws must be that of conscience, where all men find the same words when passion does not blind them.

The notion of free contract pervades the Code. Marriage is a civil contract, founded by natural law and sanctified by religion:

> The mutual respect, the mutual duties and obligations born of the union once it is formed, and which establish themselves between rational, sensitive beings, all this is a part of the natural law. From then on, it is not simply an encounter of which we speak; it is a true contract.

As one speaker remarked during the debates on the Code, the subject matter of contracts touches every family, every individual: "Thus is marriage, considered by itself, and in its natural effects, independent of any positive law. It offers us the fundamental idea of a contract properly speaking, and a contract perpetual by its form." The parties to this contract called marriage could, after the state had ratified their bargain, seek the Church's blessing. But it was, and remains to this day, a crime for any priest or minister to perform or bless a marriage until the state has declared the couple united, the bargain ratified.

Freedom of contract was carried into other domains, sometimes with odd results. If marriage is a contract, it is dissolved by the death of one of the parties, and this implies that the family dissolves as well. The Code did not recognize the concept of a patrimony that could be passed on undivided. On the death of one parent, family property is divided among the children, the surviving parent taking a share according to the matrimonial property arrangement agreed to at the time of marriage. This legislation had serious consequences for peasant families, who found it impossible to keep their land together in economically profitable portions. The impact could be avoided, then as now, only by various rather costly legal devices, or by having enough property to ensure that the required partition created no difficulty.

Although the Code left work conditions as a matter for bargaining, it did make clear that it was dealing with the rights of *men* and not of humans. The authority of husbands and fathers must be maintained. Napoléon, who participated extensively in the discussions on the Code, showed himself well-informed on the Roman law's rigor in this regard. The Code extends the liberty of contract only to those with the "capacity" to contract. We have determined, a committee informed the deliberating body, to follow Pothier and to classify married women with minors and fools. They do not have the capacity to contract without the authority of their husbands.

This "salutary incapacity," to quote a phrase from Bourjon, carried forward and strengthened a rule of the *ancien régime*. There was a moment, Regine Pernoud relates, when women radicals united to call for the expulsion of the conservative forces in the National Assembly, and on May 10, 1793, a Society of Revolutionary Republican Women was formed. An influential male, Fabre d'Eglantine, wrote:

> I have well and truly observed that these societies are not composed of mothers, of girls of breeding, of sisters occupied with their younger siblings, but rather of a sort of adventurer, of lady knights-errant, emancipated girls, and female bombthrowers.

The society was outlawed in November 1793, with the following justification:

> Since when has it been permissible for women to abandon their sex, and to make themselves into men? Since when is it seemly to see women abandon the pious cares of housekeeping, the cradle of their children, to come into the public square, to ascend the platform and harangue passers by, to take up the duties which nature has confided to men only?

This attitude was not surprising. When Mirabeau, the most baroque orator of the Assembly, wished to bestow a high compliment upon Marie-Antoinette for her courage and ability, he said, "She is the only man at the court."

THE ISSUE OF SLAVERY: PROPERTY TRIUMPHS OVER CONTRACT

There is further evidence in the legislative work which preceded the Code that the more radical ideas and the intent of the armed movements battling outside always succumbed to the will of those who wished to express, codify, and extend the bourgeois vision. The treatment of slavery is but one example. On August 29, 1793, following slave uprisings at Santo Domingo, a radical National Assembly abolished slavery and the slave trade. The decree was never enforced.

Montesquieu, in an attempt to harmonize his vision of natural rights with the observed success of the India Company of which he was shareholder, had written:

> It must be said that slavery is against nature, though in certain countries it is founded upon natural reason. One must distinguish between such countries and those in which natural reasons reject it. One must therefore limit slavery to certain portions of the earth.

He added: "Sugar would be too expensive if one did not use slave labor."

Voltaire heaped praise upon a book entitled *Essai politique sur la commerce*, which defended the slave trade, although in his biography of Louis XIV he praised that sovereign for having introduced the Black Code, thereby improving the conditions of slaves. In Diderot's *Encyclopédie*, "colony" is defined as "the transport of a people, or part of a people from one country to another. . . . From thence it has been necessary to conquer certain territories and chase out the former inhabitants in order to bring in others." One slave-trader, Pernoud reports, named his ships *Voltaire*, *Rousseau*, and *Social Contract*. The English hostility to slavery in the nineteenth century was based to a large extent on the presence in the English colonies of an indigenous work force which could be utilized for the same purposes as slaves in the French possessions.

Prior to abolition—on paper—in 1793, the Assembly (again Le Chapelier had a role in the drafting) adopted the following policy statement:

> Considering the colonies as a part of the French empire, and wishing to make them part of the salutary work of national renewal, the Assembly had nonetheless never thought to include them in the constitution which it has decreed for the kingdom, thereby to subject them to laws which could be incompatible with their special needs. . . . The National Assembly declares that it does not intend any innovation in any branch of commerce . . . with the colonies. It places the colonial subjects and their property under the safeguard of the nation, and declares criminal anyone who seeks to incite uprising against them.

The Assembly had listened to the requests of the bourgeoisie, such as a supplication from Rouen:

> Listen to the voices of three million Frenchmen who tremble for their properties, their subsistence, their lives. . . . From the noble desire to pay honor to philosophy, do not in any way undo the happiness of the fatherland.

Napoleon saw to the enactment, in 1802, of a thirty-four word statute restoring all laws relating to the slave trade "in conformity with the laws . . . existing prior to 1789."

THE CODE AS CAPSTONE OF THE REVOLUTION

The French Revolution left laws and legal theory, particularly in the field of public law, which indisputably advanced the cause of human liberty. Its legislative work, enforced by the armed power of a newly organized state apparatus, represented a formidable effort to restate some main themes of the Revolution. But its principal directors (and beneficiaries) never lost sight of the system of social relations which, at bottom, all legislation had to protect. Advancement and justification of this goal was even more important than an accurate rendering of the bourgeoisie's own history. In the words of the Preliminary Discourse of the Code's draftsmen:

> You must agree that formerly the divers people of the world communicated very little among themselves, that there were no relations between states, that people came together only to make war, that is, to exterminate one another. It is to those past times that the author of *The Spirit of the Laws* traces "the mindless rights of escheat and shipwreck." "Men," he wrote, "thought that foreigners were not united to them by any bond of civil law; they owed them, on the one hand, nothing by way of justice; and, on the other, nothing by way of mercy." But commerce, in its development, has cured us of those barbaric and destructive prejudices. It has united and brought together men of all countries. The compass opened the universe. Commerce civilized it.

The Code Napoléon crowned the National Assembly's work, reflecting the spirit which had moved the bourgeoisie from the time of the first urban uprisings. The dominant ideas of the Code were adopted—often verbatim—in a score of countries which had their own bourgeois revolutions in the 1800s. The Code reflected the judgment that old institutions could no longer be accommodated. Its fundamental notions were simple—deceptively so for the workers and peasants who had been the shock troops of the Revolution. As Karl Renner phrased it: "Fundamentally [the Code] proclaimed only two commandments: a material one, that everyone should keep what he had, and a personal one, that everyone should mind his own business."

19.

ENGLAND: THE TECHNIQUES OF THE COMMON LAW

The Cromwellian revolution left no monument of bourgeois legislation in any way comparable to that of the more self-conscious French bourgeoisie 150 years later. The legislation of the Cromwell Protectorate, although a step forward for the bourgeoisie, was not even assembled into one volume until the twentieth century, and even today it is hardly recognized as such.

The draftsmen of the Code Napoléon insisted that they had inherited the Roman-law notions of freedom of contract and property. They were less than honest, for they wanted to stress that feudalism—the revolutionaries of 1789 invented the word—was an aberrant, discontinuous episode in the law and life of French society. Not only did such an attitude lend weight to the claims that feudal privilege should be destroyed, but it also discredited the compromises made with the feudal order by an earlier, weaker, less developed artisanal and merchant bourgeoisie. These compromises remained—until they were swept away in 1789—in the form of guild privileges and city charters and custumals which bestowed the formal status of bourgeois upon the inhabitants. They also remained in the persons of older bourgeois who had struggled against the feudal system in order to gain a place within it: the more conservative nobles of the robe (not the newer jurists like Montesquieu), and the bourgeois installed in the chateaux bought from ruined noblefolk. At the same time, many rules that were not of Roman provenance also found their way into the Code; family law and the law of succession to property, for instance, owe as much to customary law as to anything else.

The striking contrast between the English and French bourgeois revolutions—leaving aside the signal fact that the English bourgeoisie was able for a variety of reasons to begin its industrial revolution a century earlier—is one of ideological method. The bourgeois legal revolution in England, which took place in the 1600s and 1700s, claimed the parentage of that most feudal of documents, the Magna Carta. Roman institutions and concepts in the realm of commerce may have been adopted, but they were cleansed of most Latin appellations and referred to as the "law merchant," while other Roman- or canon-law institutions were eradicated as being conducive either to absolutism or to the denial of fundamental liberties.

English law, the "common law of England," exhibited at that time as it does today a steadfast devotion to continuity, or at least to the illusion of continuity. In the eighteenth century Jonathan Swift wrote:

> It is a maxim among these lawyers that whatever has been done before may legally be done again; and therefore they take special care to record all the decisions formerly made against common justice and the general reason of mankind. These, under the name of precedents, they produce as authorities.

More recently, Eric Hobsbawm has commented: "This evasion of drastic confrontations, this preference for sticking old labels on new bottles, should not be confused with the absence of change."

Certainly, Jonathan Swift was right in exclaiming at the English common lawyers' passion for precedent. But if the uncritical recital of history may be, as Swift believed, a kind of silence about present injustice, it may also serve to legitimize new institutions as the natural children of ancient ones.

The goal of refashioning English legal ideology was the curtailment of sovereign prerogative, to confine government to the role of protector of economic and political liberty. Under Cromwell, the bourgeoisie, which owed to Tudor absolutism its interests in land and a measure of its economic power, dismantled the Tudor apparatus of monarchical power. When, at the Restoration, the Stuart kings sought to reintroduce the public law of the earlier period, the great financial powers procured the swift intervention of William of Orange, who took the throne on the basis of his wife's dynastic claim and with the real assistance of his own army.

We can see most clearly the use of precedent and the conscious fashioning of legal ideology in the light of three principles developed during the 1600s and 1700s: the privilege against self-incrimination, the right to confront and cross-examine those with evidence against one, and the right to trial by jury.

In its modern form the privilege against self-incrimination is the most discussed element of common-law criminal procedure. Its fundamental tenet is that no one may be compelled to be a witness against himself or herself. This principle ramifies into others. Summoned by the authorities or interrogated by the police, a person has the right to remain silent in the face of questioning. In a criminal trial, the privilege serves as the basis of a particular kind of adversary procedure: the government must prove the guilt of the accused by relying on the testimony of others, and the accused need not provide any evidence from his own mouth that can be used against him, or even testify at all.

The struggle to establish this principle in English law goes back to the ancient law codes. Compulsion to testify—on the threat of sanctions—and the obligation to inform police and judicial authorities is a major feature of Continental systems of criminal procedure even today. The origins of such "inquisitorial" systems lay, as we saw in Part Three, in late Roman and canonist graftings on earlier Roman procedure. The "inquest," with examination of the possibly guilty party, was a mainstay of criminal procedure in France from the 1200s, as well as of canonical inquisitions into suspected heresy.

English inquisitions were conducted according to canonical procedure beginning in the 1300s, and included the use of torture to compel the testimony of the suspected. In 1401, in response to the Lollard heresies of John Wycliff, Parliament put the inquisition under official auspices with the statute *de Haeretico Comburendo*. Thenceforth, secular justice would burn the body to help the Church purify the soul. Those suspected of heresy were to take the oath *de veritate dicenda*, to tell the truth in answer to all questions put by the inquirer concerning matters of faith. The oath was *ex officio mero*—of the inquirer's office. Should a person not respond, he or she was assumed to have confessed to the offense.

The heresy procedure of the statute *de Haeretico Comburendo* was abolished under Henry VIII, but in name only. Installation of the king as head of the Church of England, and therefore of the English church, put heresy and treason on the same footing. The two offenses were similar in concept, particularly in the tendency of both to equate the idea with the act, the desire with its accomplishment. The special jurisdiction of the High Commission (principally ecclesiastical) and of the Court of the Star Chamber (principally political) extended to mental transgressions against both the spiritual and the secular integrity of the state.

The High Commission owes its name to the special royal "commissions" which, at various periods beginning in the reign of Henry VIII, ratified its powers. Following the Act of Supremacy, Henry directed the Commission to inquire by canonical methods into offenses against the faith. In line with English history and the canonical reinterpretation of Roman tradition, the content of the mind was extracted by compulsion of the body.

The Star Chamber was a special instance of the King's Council exercising judicial power. Its organization and jurisdiction were confirmed by a statute of 1487, and it had an extensive judicial business. In the 1500s and early 1600s, however, the Star Chamber's increasing workload of political cases came to characterize it in the eyes of its detractors. It was certainly true that the Star Chamber claimed the right to proceed along Roman-canonical procedural lines to root out sedition, just as the High Commission was moving against heresy.

During the 1400s and 1500s there were fitful protests against these procedures, predictably from those who were at a particular moment resisting the authority of Crown or Church. In 1563, John Foxe's *Book of Martyrs* collected tales of people who had refused the oath *ex officio*. Foxe's martyrs, in their own words or as reported by anonymous observers, justified their resistance by reference to Magna Carta's guarantee that

> No man shall be taken or imprisoned or dispossessed or outlawed, or banished, or in any way destroyed, nor will we go upon him, nor send upon him, except by the legal judgment of his peers or by the law of the land.

That "law of the land," it was argued, forbade the oath and required that the public authority proceed against crime by indictment of a grand jury, and that conviction take place before a jury drawn from the vicinage—that is, where the alleged offense took place. "Law of the land" had no such precise meaning in 1215, but "from the old fields must come the new corne."

Not until the early 1600s did the question of High Commission and Star Chamber procedure bring together a body of opponents—mostly from the bourgeoisie—strong enough to mount a frontal attack on it. While they believed that the Tudor state ought to be strong enough to protect and extend the realm's trade, and to destroy feudal patterns of landholding and privilege, the rising commercial interests had no interest in either ideological conformity or in maintaining monarchical power once feudal institutions were smashed. As common lawyers struggled to attract merchant clients, they mounted a campaign against not only the Commission and Star Chamber, but against all judicial institutions other than the common-law courts.

The common-law courts' hospitable attitude toward a law favorable to merchants, the common lawyers' economic self-interest, and political hostility to Crown prerogative were the principal ideological bases of this alliance between lawyers and the bourgeoisie.

As a first step, the common-law courts claimed the power to halt proceedings in the ecclesiastical and prerogative tribunals. Lord Coke developed the notion of the "law of the land" as binding upon King, parliament, and judges. In a series of opinions, the King's Bench, as a common-law court, issued writs of prohibition and writs of habeas corpus to this end. These writs were directed not only at the courts for special business created in the wake of the dissolution of the monasteries, but also at such tribunals as the High Commission and the Star Chamber. The prohibition and habeas corpus writs multiplied in the early 1600s, abated somewhat after 1610, and increased again. Since both Star Chamber and the Commission were used as instruments of personal monarchy by James I and Charles I, each monarch at various times directed judges to disregard the writs issued by the common-law courts. As a show of determination, James I presided personally in the Star Chamber on at least one occasion—a case of alleged seditious libel.

The example of Star Chamber–High Commission jurisdiction most often cited as having mobilized popular opinion is the case of John Lilburn, a leader of the Leveler movement. Summoned by the Attorney General in 1637 for questioning concerning the alleged importation of seditious books into England, as a preliminary to a Star Chamber examination, Lilburn declined to answer. Brought before the Court of Star Chamber, he refused the oath *ex officio*: "Another fundamental right I then contended for, was, that no man's conscience ought to be racked by oaths imposed, to answer questions concerning himself in matters criminal, or pretended to be so."

Lilburn's Case is described by Sir James Stephen:

> The extreme unpopularity of the officio oath is set in a clear light by the case of John Lilburn. . . . He was committed to the Gatehouse "for sending of factious and seditious libels out of Holland into England." He was afterwards ordered by the Privy Council to be examined before the Attorney-General, Sir John Banks. He was accordingly taken to the Attorney-General's chambers, "and was referred to be examined by Mr. Cockshey his chief clerk; and at our first meeting together he . . . began with me after this manner. "Mr. Lilburn, what is your Christian name?" A number of questions followed, gradually leading up to the matter complained of. Lilburn answered a good many of them, but at last refused to go further, saying, " I know it is warrantable by the law of God, and I think by the law of the land, that I may stand on my just defense, and not answer your interrogatories, and that my accusers ought to be brought face to face, to justify what they accuse me of." . . . Some days after he was taken to the Star Chamber office that he might enter his appearance. . . . Lilburn thought the object of the examination was to get materials for a bill, and accordingly when the head of the office tendered him the oath "that you shall make true answer to all things that are asked you," he refused to do so, saying, first, " I am but a young man and do not well know what belongs to the nature of an oath." Afterwards he said he was not satisfied of the lawfulness of that oath, and after much dispute absolutely refused to take it. After about a fortnight's delay he was brought before the Star Chamber, where the oath was again tendered to him and he again refused it on the ground that it was an oath of inquiry for the lawfulness of which he had no warrant. . . . On the following day they [Lilburn and a fellow prisoner, Wharton] were brought up again. Lilburn declared, on his word and at length, that the charges against him were entirely false, and that the books objected to were imported by another person with whom he had no connection. "'Then,' said the Lord Keeper, 'thou wilt not take the oath and answer truly.'" Lilburn repeated that it was an oath of inquiry and that he found no warrant in the word of God for an oath of inquiry. . . . As both absolutely refused to take the oath they were each sentenced to stand in the pillory, and to pay a fine of £500, and Lilburn to be whipped from the Fleet to the pillory, which stood between Westminster Hall Gate and the Star Chamber. Lilburn was whipped accordingly, receiving, it was said, upwards of 500 lashes, and was made to stand in the pillory for two hours after his whipping. In May, 1641, the House of Commons resolved "that the sentence of the Star Chamber given against John Lilburn is illegal, and against the liberty of the subject: and also bloody, cruel, barbarous, and tyrannical."

But *Lilburn's Case* was only one among many. Demand was growing for a Parliament to be summoned to end Charles I's autocratic rule.

Christopher Hill has summarized the opinions of those who called for a Parliament, and the motivations of the members of the Long Parliament that finally assembled in November 1640:

> It was, as the Duke of Newcastle put it, "neither the church nor the laws that kept up the King so long, but part of the nobility and the gentry." "The strength of our party," wrote a Parliamentarian pamphleteer, "consists mainly in honest tradesmen; the gentry are naught and the country people are for the most part blinded and misled by their malevolent hedge-priests." In Somerset "all the prime gentry" were for the King; only clothiers and freeholders for Parliament. In Essex the cloth workers, "being poor and populous," were "naturally mutinous and bold." Their employers were "sordid men," who equally naturally supported Parliament, "whose constant style was tenderness of commerce. . . . The clothiers through the whole kingdom were rebels by their trade." "For 'tis notorious," said a bishop after 1660, "that there is not any sort of people so inclinable to seditious practices as the trading part of a nation."

The Long Parliament enacted its right to be summoned frequently and to control taxation, and in 1641 abolished the Court of Star Chamber and the High Commission, as well as a series of lesser courts of the same provenance and with similar procedure.

The statute of abolition is a remarkable document, as much a brief as a piece of legislation. It contains a historical argument going back to Magna Carta, that charter of guarantees for the greater nobles which was an accepted ascription of fictitious historical authenticity to quite modern ideas of due process of law, and running through the history of English opposition to the special jurisdiction of the King's Council and to the intrusion of Romanist rules and procedures. But while it was indisputably true that Parliament and the common-law courts had on a number of occasions protested royally sponsored innovations, much of the common lawyers' protest, at least before the 1500s, was in the name of their erstwhile clients, the nobility and gentry, and against the use of special jurisdictions and special rules to foster commerce at the behest of the rising bourgeoisie. Further, while it was true that resistance to Romanisms had a lengthy history, the merchants had been mostly on the other side of that battle, supporting the creation, by means of royal power, of courts that would apply civil-law-based rules relating to mercantile and shipping practice.

The dubiousness of Parliament's historical reasoning should not, however, mask the importance of the statute. Abolition of the oath *ex officio* and the procedure against sedition and heresy by means of inquisition was a most important affirmation of human liberty. The privilege against self-incrimination remains, in the Anglo-American system, a salutary guarantee against governmental power, at least where the institutions established to protect it function as they were designed to.

Further, the privilege was established in a true contest between a newly powerful class and an older order. It was not simply that one principle was established in place of another. Abolition of the prerogative courts was one long step toward sweeping away the apparatus of the Tudor state, which in the hands of the Stuarts was both expensive and wrongheaded about the growth of trade. The Tudor institutions had served as the bourgeoisie's hammer against feudal resistance, but the spread of economic relations based upon contract, and the protection of the property relations in the Reformation settlement, meant that there was no need for Tudorism after 1600. As in France at a later date, the bourgeoisie felt that government could retire, in the name of freedom, from all functions save military defense, the maintenance of systems of internal and external communication, and the internal policing of the country.

The abolition of the prerogative courts represented a victory for the new alliance of common lawyers and traders, supported by the "mutinous and bold" workers, but it was not a complete victory. The way was opened, however, to fashion a new procedure for criminal cases which would institutionalize popular control of the charging and guilt-finding process and rationalize modes of proof. Institutionalizing the grand jury, reaffirming the independence of the trial jury, and rigorous insistence on the right of cross-examination were three important reforms.

If criminal procedure were to be refashioned, corollaries of the procedure *ex officio* had to be abolished as well. The first was that the accused could be examined and then convicted solely on his or her own words and by a panel of royal judges; there was neither need nor occasion to bring in those who might have reported the misconduct, or to examine them under oath to determine if they spoke truly or not. Another was that the examining court charged the accused, and then tried and convicted him or her without further formality. The procedure in all courts deriving their rules from the civil law was by deposition, with the written records of answers providing the necessary proof.

There was no grand jury of citizens to determine if an indictment should be brought, or a trial (petit) jury to pronounce guilt or innocence by its unanimous voice. We have seen that the grand jury in criminal cases indicted on its own local knowledge; it was a means to ferret out crime and bring it to the attention of the King's justices. The petit jury had various beginnings, tracing back at least five hundred years: it was in some cases a group of citizens brought in by a party who had the right to make his proof of a disputed proposition of fact. If he or she could round up twelve people to swear to the fact, he or she carried the day. This system, called compurgation, has been termed by Professor Riesenfeld a form of institutionalized perjury. The notion of the jury as a body drawn from a given community to decide the facts based upon their own knowledge persisted into the 1500s. Thus the report of a case in 1550 contains the observation: "Some of the jurors knew this to be true."

The destruction of the village communities and the forcible breakup of older patterns of life made it less and less likely that the facts of a dispute would be common knowledge. If only "some," or even "one," of the jurors knew the facts, what then? As a law report stated in 1650:

> In a tryall at Bar between the inhabitants of Hartford and Bennet a caryer upon an action brought against them upon the Statute of Winchester, for a robbery committed within that hundred upon his servant, it was said by the Court that if either of the parties to a tryall desire that a juror may give evidence of something of his own knowledge, to the rest of the jurors, that the Court will examine him openly in Court upon his oath, and he ought not be examined in private by his companions.

So the jury became not the friends of one party engaged in a bit of group oath-taking, but a supposedly neutral body called to decide the facts. In the next stage of this process, reached by 1650, the jury no longer *knows* the facts, but rather *finds* them. Coke had said that from old fields new corn must come. From Fortescue, who had written in the 1400s, came a description of the procedure to be followed:

> If before a judge the parties to a suit come to a controversy on a matter of fact, which those learned in the law of England call the issue of a plea, the truth as to such issue by the civil laws must be proved by the deposition of witnesses, for which two suitable witnesses suffice. But by the laws of England

> the truth cannot be clear to the judge except by the oath of twelve men of the neighborhood where the fact is supposed. We may ask, therefore, which of these two procedures, so different, should be thought more reasonable and effective. . . .
>
> By the civil laws, the party in the contested suit who alleges the affirmative must produce witnesses whom he shall name at his own will. . . . He must be thought poor indeed in power, and of little diligence, who from all the men he knows cannot find two so devoid of conscience and truth that they will go against all truth for fear, love, or profit. Such then can he produce in his behalf. And if the other party wants to contradict them or their testimony, it does not always happen that their character and deeds are known to the one wanting to contradict them so the witnesses could be impeached for the baseness and vices. . . . Who then can live in security for himself and his goods under such a law since the law furnishes such help to anyone who wishes to be his enemy? . . . Thus the wicked Jezebel produced two witnesses, sons of Belial, against Naboth at a trial by which he lost his life and King Ahab possessed his vineyard.

Thomas Smith, a minister under Elizabeth, described the jury trial this way:

> An enquest or quest is called this lawefull kind of tryall by xii men. . . . When the quest is ful, they be sworne to declare the truth of that issue according to the evidence and their conscience. Then the Sergeantes of either side declare the issue, and each for his client sayth as much as he can. Evidences of writings be showed, witnesses be sworne, and heard before them, not after the fashion of the civil law but openly, that not only the xii, but the judges, the parties and as many as be present may heare what each witness doeth say: The adverse partie or his advocates which we call counsellers and sergeantes interrogateth sometime the witnesses, and driveth them out of countenance. . . . When it is thought that it is enough pleaded before them, and the witnesses have saide what they can, one of the judges with a briefe and pithie recapitulation reciteth to the xii in summe the argumentes of the sergeantes of either side, that which the witnesses have declared, and the chiefe points of the evidence showed in writing, and once againe putteth them in minde of the issue, and sometime givethe it them in writing, delivering to them the evidence which is showed on either part, if any be . . . and biddeth them goe together. Then there is a baylife charged with them to keepe them in a chamber not farre off without bread, drinke, light or fire untill they be agreed . . . for it goeth not by the most part, but each man must agree.

What proof would these twelve jurors hear? Coke had spoken of "the strange conceit that one may be an accuser by hearsay," and instances of fraud or mistake in the use of depositions were cited with increasing frequency.

The rule against hearsay evidence began as a caution against listening to "a tale of a tale," and finished the 1600s as an accepted element of common-law procedure. The witness was to tell, in court, in the open, and under oath, what he or she knew. He or she was not, except under certain circumstances—the "exceptions to the hearsay rule"—to repeat the out-of-court declarations of others. With this protection against mendacity and incorrectness went the right to confront and to cross-examine, in order to uncover gaps or mistakes. The jury sat and listened and decided the issue. If it was to decide based on testimony in open court, prior familiarity with facts was disqualification; it might indicate prejudgment. This system was the basis of a new and rational court procedure.

In criminal cases, the requirement that action by a grand jury and the unanimous verdict of a pent jury was necessary to convict was also a salutary reform, though it was always stated as a reaffirmation of centuries-old rights. But if the jury refused to convict, despite the evidence, what measures could the Crown take? This question was put to the test in the case of William Penn in 1670.

Penn and other Quakers had assembled in Gracechurch Street in London, and the Crown prosecutor insisted that they had rioted in breach of the peace. At his trial, Penn was indignant, outraged, and rowdy. He maintained his innocence and complained repeatedly that he could neither understand the charge against him, nor intelligently plead to it. (Counsel was not provided, even in felony cases, until the 1800s in England.) A jury acquitted him and his companion, William Mead, whereupon the jurors were locked up for having given a verdict against full and manifest evidence. Bushel, foreman of the jury, obtained a writ of habeas corpus requiring his jailer to justify the detention. Chief Justice Vaughan, after hearing of the jury's conduct and the reasons for its detention, ordered the jurors released, holding that a jury, no matter how motivated, could acquit a defendant upon virtually any ground it saw fit. *Bushel's Case* thus ratified a further dismantling of Tudor institutions—one of the frequent uses of Star Chamber had been to punish jurors in political cases who returned verdicts displeasing to the Crown. As a 1594 treatise reported:

> Note that the London jury which acquitted Sir Nicholas Throckmorton [a plotter against Queen Mary] . . . of high treason, was called into the Star Chamber . . . forasmuch as the matter was held to have been sufficiently

> proved against him; and eight of them were there fined in great sums, at least five hundred pounds each, and remanded back to prison to dwell there until further orders were taken for their punishment. The other four were released, because they submitted and confessed that they had offended in not considering the truth of the matter.
>
> See also eleven jurymen who acquitted one Hodie of felony before Sir Roger Manwood . . . against obvious evidence, were fined in the Star Chamber and made to wear papers in Westminster Hall about 1580; and I saw them.

Bushel's Case thus wrote a formal end to a little-used practice that the Crown had tried to revive at the Restoration in 1660. Vaughan's opinion also was a step toward clarifying the use of the writ of habeas corpus to obtain judicial review of any sort of detention.

Amidst the procedural innovations, reaffirmations, and protections of the 1600s and 1700s, the private law of the bourgeoisie developed as well. In 1660 the last feudal elements were purged by statute from the law of real property. The common-law courts moved from a sporadic willingness to hear evidence on merchant custom to an outright incorporation of the law merchant. "The law merchant," Lord Mansfield was able to write by the late 1700s, "is the law of the land." Joint-stock companies and other capital-pooling devices flourished. Enterprises began to grow outside the traditional towns, away from local bourgeois privilege and near coal, running water, ports, or the new system of canals. The techniques applied by the bourgeoisie, the common lawyers, and Parliament in the field of private law were the same as those applied to procedural reform.

Looking back from the vantage point of 1750, the date conventionally ascribed to the beginning of the industrial revolution in England, one is struck by the extent to which the common law was reconstituted in just two hundred years—doubtless with as much bloodshed and violence as there was to be in the achievement of bourgeois victory in France. And although the bourgeois revolution was not complete—as a concession to the gentry and the common lawyers some archaic rules concerning real property and a cumbersome judicial machinery remained until the nineteenth century—the fundamental changes in social structure, and new laws to define these changes, had been accomplished to the extent that the English bourgeoisie could take advantage of the innovations in technique and revolutionize the process of manufacture.

So it would be wrong to say, as do some modern historians, that the distinctive feature of English law is its gradual, peaceable development in an unbroken line since Magna Carta, or even since 1066. There were, on the contrary, revolutionary changes between 1600 and 1800. If obstacles remained that could not be knocked over with a law, or surmounted with a writ, the English bourgeoisie was not unwilling to turn to overtly revolutionary tactics. There was at least an implicit connection between reason and violence. "I pray thee, in the bowels of Christ, think that ye may be mistaken," Cromwell implored. But, on that occasion, he had his army with him.

Similar to the myth of English continuity, and equally false, is the insistence on the part of some French scholars that there is a fundamental discontinuity between French legal history before and after 1789—as though the Revolution destroyed the past and everything since then has been newly constructed. In fact, in both England and France a victorious class imposed a new legal ideology by force, and because the interest of the bourgeoisie in both countries was virtually identical, the systems of private law in both turned out to be remarkably similar. Yet the bourgeois revolutions in these two countries had rather different histories and one can detect a difference in innovative technique and in the rhetoric by which social change was advocated. There is a profound difference between Diderot's image of old idols crashing and Coke's metaphor of a new harvest from old fields. The common-law judges and writers in England and America have preserved Coke's approach. "In order to know what it [the law] is," wrote Mr. Justice Holmes in the last century, "we must know what it has been and what it tends to become." The image is not of the legislator changing and building, but of judges and lawyers fashioning out of historic usage new institutions to meet new needs.

We are not advocating the myth that changes in legal rules are the result of impersonal reason, nature, God, or a tendency of things to get better. We are addressing ourselves to the means by which such a myth is created. The system which develops, in the context of an unbroken continuity of usage, new rules for deciding the disputes of private persons with one another and with the state seems credible and legitimate because of its claim to have a logical link to the past. Such a system makes it possible to conciliate, to reform, and to adapt. The existence of such a system of resolving disputes has had a great impact on the strategies of reformist groups in common-law countries, as compared with those in territories governed by civil-law institutions. The most obvious examples in the twentieth century are the repeated use of judicial proceedings in the United States to protect and extend the popular rights that were at the heart of the public-law revolution of the 1600s and were later embodied in the American Constitution.

We have focused here upon the victories of the bourgeoisie in England and France, as the two countries whose legal ideologies have had the most direct impact on our own lives. Every subsequent bourgeois revolution has borrowed from the experience of these two. And the fact that lawyers trained in the civil-law tradition, and believing in the self-evident rightness of codification, were authors of the civil codes of the Eastern European socialist countries has left a noticeable bourgeois imprint upon these countries' institutions of private law.

From the revolutions in England and France, and the earlier bourgeois uprisings all across Europe, comes the legal system under which we now live. In our last chapters we will attempt to draw some general conclusions about the relationship between legal ideology and social change in the West.

PART SIX

INSURGENCY AND JURISPRUDENCE

20.

THE DEVELOPMENT OF LEGAL IDEOLOGY

In the foregoing chapters we have traced eight hundred years of Western European legal history in order to show the role played by law and legal ideology in the rise to power of the bourgeoisie, and we have seen that social relations as expressed in formal legal rules and systems of law played—and continue to play—a central role in all movements which aspire to take and hold state power.

Here we want to restate these assertions about law in a systematic way, to dispute some current explanations of the reasons for making laws, and to reflect on the attitude toward law of movements for social change in the West today. In discussing these questions, we will stress the pronounced tendency of ideologists—at least in Europe and America—to express ideas of social and political theory as edicts, as proclamations, and as formal systems of laws. This tendency is reflected in the importance accorded to lawyers and to legal training in all Western governmental structures and in all movements for social change which aim at seizing state power.

Legal rules are, of necessity, time-bound; they are the constructions of a group of people at a given stage of society's development. Particular legal forms are not "natural" or "basic" conditions of human existence. Indeed, "law," in the sense of rules drawn upon the basis of an agreed set of normative judgments about conduct, is—in Western societies—a relatively recent phenomenon. This concept of law, as George Thomson has shown, came into being along with other abstract concepts when the ancient

Mediterranean civilizations had advanced to the point that money was used as a medium of exchange, and was therefore an abstraction of commodities. Before that time societies certainly agreed upon socially necessary principles of conduct whose violation would result in punishment. This kind of "law" is an illustration of the principle expressed by Cicero as *ubi societas, ibi jus*—wherever there is community, there is law; it is merely descriptive of real social relationships of ownership and nonownership. But law conceived of as such comes later, at the point when advances in technology point up the distinction between concrete and abstract, nature and norm, *physis* and *nomos*. With the distinction between "nature" and "norm" comes the development of justifications of conduct other than that it is the "will of the gods." The "will of the gods" justification precludes any distinction between what happens and what ought to happen.

Unpredictable, vengeful, and sanguinary godly justice is characteristic of the didactic works of the early Greek dramatists. The shift to a more judgmental stance, in which even god-given rules and edicts are subjected to a critical evaluation from "outside," is illustrated in Sophocles' *Oedipus* cycle. In *Oedipus Rex*, the first play, the king is blinded and cast out for acts the significance of which he was not aware. In the second play, *Antigone*, rationality is introduced in the rebellious impiety of Creon, who is subsequently destroyed. Finally, in *Oedipus* at *Colonnus*, written much later, the old, blind Oedipus declares, "I did not sin," and re-enters human society.

This distinction between nature as coming from the gods and norm as the product of rational considerations, which may judge the former, or at least modify its human consequences, is the basis for the existence of law as we understand the term today, and with it comes not only the possibility of a critical stance toward events and institutions, but also the possibility of contradictions between rules of law and the system of social control or allocation of power which gives rise to them. Criticism of the rules may be extended to criticism of the social relations they uphold.

Since the late Athenian age, laws have been crystallizations of power relationships in a given group or society. Laws lock into words, expressed as commands, the rights or duties which a particular group will use its power to protect or enforce, and provide predictable modes of settling disputes which arise within this context. Law is a superstructure erected upon the base of power relationships. The extent to which such time-bound superstructures are regarded as important varies from society to society. René David has written with respect to the Chinese:

> Marxist-Leninist philosophy contains elements which accord with this traditional [Chinese] philosophy. Positive law has never appeared to the Chinese as being a necessary condition or even a normal condition of a well-ordered society. Positive law, is, on the contrary, a sign of an imperfect society, and a connection exists between the idea of positive law and that of coercion. Communism, presaged in Marxist thought, is nearly an ideal society as such a society is envisaged by the Chinese.

As we have seen, positive law is regarded quite differently in the West. Evidences of the centrality of legal ideology can be seen in every period we have examined.

This is not to say that revolutionary groups either refrained from the use of violence to achieve their aims, or lost sight of the central fact that laws in a system of state power ultimately rest on force. This theme that power, as exercised in the form of state-controlled violence, must be justifiable by reference to some commonly credited system of authority is as central to the argument of those whom the bourgeoisie overthrew as it is to the bourgeoisie itself. They only used an old practice of erecting, recording, and endowing with authority systems of legitimation for the exercise of violence.

In the bourgeoisie's rise to power we see a recurring concern with the problem of legitimacy. The Church tried to trace its antecedents in texts whose indisputable authenticity rested upon the supposed words of Christ. Soon after the collapse of the Roman Empire, feudal lords continued token obeisance to the symbols of Empire in order to justify their own power. Libraries and manor houses full of charters attesting to the voluntary entry into conditions of servitude of the tillers' forebears are a reflection of this concern. Challenges to the legitimacy of the actions of particular sovereigns were couched in terms drawn from existing systems of authority—the Church, Roman law, or biblical texts.

One important constituent of legitimacy is that power must be exercised in a predictable way. This predictability comes about by building up a structure of formal legal rules and procedures that will be used before violence is invoked. Such predictability is not self-evidently necessary or wise: a group holding state power in a given country might have only one law, a "rule of recognition." For example, if a band of brigands took over a valley of peaceful folk, the brigand chief might proclaim that whatever he said on a particular day would be enforced as law during that twenty-four-hour period. Such a system would eliminate gaps between the actual system of social relations existing in the valley and the rules which people were obliged, on pain of having violence visited upon them, to follow. The annual redrafting of the praetorian edict in early Rome, before it became regularized and fairly permanent, resembled such a situation.

It is possible to escape from a system of rules through a conscious decision to repose great discretion in lower levels of administration, or even in relatively autonomous local groups who devise both the substance and means of application of the detailed rules governing conduct on the basis of very general principles. This seems to be the case in present-day China and Cuba.

The pattern in the West, even in times of great social upheaval, has been very different. During the French Revolution the legislation of the National Assembly was chaotic and changed often, but the number of decrees it issued indicates its wish that as the Revolution progressed the system of social relations at each particular moment be crystallized into a formal system of constitutional and legal rules defining the appropriate means by which the organs of state power should act. It was not content merely to watch the Revolution, or even to issue decrees justifying or authorizing the dismantling of the old order, but wanted to build a logical system of rules.

A similar process of crystallization, though spread over a much longer period of time, occurred in seventeenth-century England, beginning with Lord Coke's battle on behalf of the common law, continuing through the legislation of the Protectorate to the proclamations, law cases, and legislation which surrounded the Glorious Revolution of 1689.

Somewhat closer to American sensibilities are the Constitution of 1789 and the Bill of Rights of 1791. The basic social theory of the Constitution, rooted in Locke and Montesquieu, was based on the protection of private property, the establishment of a representative federal form of government, and the institution of a set of prohibitions upon the national government designed to preserve substantive and procedural guarantees of freedom. These guarantees were justified in terms of "natural justice," but their origin was less recondite; they grew out of specific revolutionary and pre-revolutionary events. The guarantee against arbitrary search echoed the colonists' experience with the writs of assistance, which empowered British officers to search from house to house to uncover tea and other goods upon which the tax had not been paid, and with the English case of *Entick v. Carrington*, in which judgment was given against Lord Halifax for authorizing the seizure of a subversive newspaper. The assurance of fairness in criminal proceedings was born of social struggles that had taken place in England more than a century earlier, in which the treatment accorded political criminals was a major focus of concern. The judgment that freedom of speech should be protected was similarly informed by knowledge of the utility of free speech and a free press in bringing about social change.

Earlier we saw the same emphasis upon the building of legal ideology in city after city during the 1000s and 1100s as the bourgeoisie gained the upper hand and then certified its accession to power by drafting a local set of customs. In contrast to non-Western modes of thought, the early bourgeoisie believed that detailing the ways in which law would operate was the essence of fairness, personal security, and liberty. The desire for predictability, and for formal means of assuring it, had been an element of Roman law since about the second century A.D., when the *praetor*'s edict began to remain virtually unchanged from year to year, and the opinions of professional jurists and writings of emperors began to be woven into a systematic body of doctrine. This was the moment when Rome's commercial hegemony was at last assured, and the Empire's commerce demanded stability.

The building of systems as a protective device is well adapted to the progress of bourgeois interests, as we have seen. One of the hardest points to grasp in discussing the law of other places—as Victor Li has noted in a fine study of Chinese criminal law—is that system-building of this kind is not essential to guaranteeing personal liberty, except the specific form of liberty embodied in Western bourgeois contract and commercial law and property relations.

In all cases of system-building, the legal rules and principles are justified by resort to sources that are accepted because of their reputed age and authenticity and to principles of social theory that are believed to be self-evidently valid but that in fact merely express the aspirations of the group which has for the moment achieved dominance. Thus, systems of legal rules expressed as legal ideology were not only predictions as to how state power—that is to say, organized violence—would be used in the future: they carried within them justifications of the legitimacy of the exercise of that power.

Because a legal ideology thus created is separate from the system of social relations which it regulates, it seems—both to those to whom it is promulgated and, in time, to those who made it up—to take on a life of its own. The practical consequences of this are soon evident. Warring factions are invited, indeed commanded, to subdue their rivalry and are drawn instead to the interpretation of rules and laws to determine how they shall be applied in particular cases. The warfare moves off the streets to the tribunals. This aspect of legal ideology was described by Engels in *The Origin of the Family, Private Property and the State*:

> In possession of the public power and the right of taxation, the officials now present themselves as organs of society standing above society. The free, willing respect accorded to the organs of the gentile constitution is not enough for them, even if they could have it. Representatives of a power which estranges them from society, they have to be given prestige by means of special decrees which invest them with a peculiar sanctity and inviolability. The lowest police officer of the civilized state has more "authority" than all the organs of gentile society put together. But the mightiest prince and the greatest statesman or general of civilization might envy the humblest of the gentile chiefs, the unforced and unquestioned respect accorded to him. The one stands in the midst of society, the other is forced to pose as something outside and above it.

The claim that state legal ideology stands outside and above the social classes that it governs is characteristic of all successful aspirants to state power in the period we have been studying. Legal ideology took the form of detailed and increasingly—as the bourgeoisie gained in strength—comprehensive and highly structured systems of positive law. These systems were counterposed to the "anarchy" of feudal law, which was either actively hostile to commerce or was simply too incomplete and chaotic to permit predictable reliance upon it. Even the laissez-faire idealism of the young American nation was only a superideology, within which the highly refined, centuries-old customary law merchant was received and attentively applied.

LEGAL IDEOLOGY, JURISPRUDENCE, AND INSURGENCY: SOME DEFINITIONS

We cannot clearly set out our theory that social struggle motivates changes in legal structure, nor contrast it with alternative ways of looking at law, unless we define our terms.

A legal ideology is a statement, in terms of a system of rules of law, of the aspirations, goals, and values of a social group.

It is not, however, the property solely of the group possessing effective control. To the contrary, as we have seen, groups that aspire to state power have formulated their attack in terms of systems of legal rules and principles. But when a group does possess state power—defined as effective control over a particular territory—its legal ideology is "the law." The question of how much territory or control is necessary need not detain us, for it is answered in each historical period by the effective units of production, exchange, and political viability: it may be a city in one historical period, a nation-state in another.

A legal ideology may consist of a number of different kinds of explicit and implicit statements. It may include "rules of recognition," which define the competence of certain persons to exercise legislative and judicial functions. The term may include such general ideological assertions as "the lawmaking body of the city should represent all the citizens." The ideology may encompass both individually and generally addressed commands, to adopt a distinction commonly used in the writings of legal positivists. The former are, in John Austin's words, "occasional or particular," in the sense that they "oblige . . . to a specific act or forbearance, or to acts or forbearances which it determines specifically and individually," such as judicial judgments. The latter are legislative commands, which speak in general terms and are addressed to unnamed persons at large. A legal ideology may be expressed as volumes of laws, rules, and judgments; or, as was the case in the earliest urban communes, it may consist of a few simple precepts and then the all-important provision of *who* is competent to make rules and issue orders.

The distinction between types of commands does not, in the development of bourgeois law, necessarily follow the line between legislative and judicial branches so familiar to modern bourgeois democratic theory. Decisions in individual cases, leading to individually addressed commands to pay money, restore certain property, or suffer a certain punishment, developed into a system of generally addressed "legislative" rules. This type of customary law is not based on ancient usage (usually fictitious), but on decisions made within living memory and having the force of precedent. The bourgeoisie, in all the regions we have examined, was unremitting in the cultivation and elaboration of legal ideology in this form.

We use the term "jurisprudence" to describe the process by which legal ideology is created and elaborated. The term "jurisprudence of insurgency" describes a certain kind of jurisprudential activity, in which a group challenging the prevailing system of social relations no longer seeks to reform it but rather to overthrow it and replace it with another.

We have seen the process of jurisprudence at work in the previous chapters: when the merchant traders of the 1000s and 1100s wished to put their activity on a firm legal basis, they embodied their demands and later their victories in the form of charters and treaties, in effect creating for themselves a place in the feudal legal order. The task of the lawyers for this upstart group was to find texts that would appear authoritative to even the most recalcitrant lord or reactionary prelate and use them as justification for the existence and operation of artisanal and merchant activity.

The merchants sought only a small place within the feudal system, however, and few if any realized the corrosive effects that would ultimately result from granting them this place. This was not a jurisprudence of insurgency, a fact that is reflected in the life histories of merchant families across several generations: the bourgeois aspirations to noble status acknowledged that the system of nobility was dominant, and the large number of merchants who took vows of poverty and ended their days in monasteries demonstrated the grip that the ideology of the organized Church still had upon them.

Because an ideology is a time-bound system of words and phrases crystallized out of human conflict, and because the legal ideology of a group holding state power is (as we have said) designed to subdue rivalries and turn the people's attention to interpreting the "system" of rules, there will always be room for interpreting the rules in different ways. As time goes on, more and more contradictions may develop between the prevailing system of social relations and the content of the formal rules that purport to govern it, and one early task of a dissident group is to explore the limits of the dominant legal ideology in order to see how much can be accomplished within those limits.

In every movement we can thus see the stage at which it accepts the dominant assumptions of the governing class and seeks to use them to its own advantage. The richly varied and highly developed legal ideology of the West, after the rediscovery—or reimportation—of Roman law, permitted and encouraged such an approach.

If the ideology has the relatively unstructured character of much European feudalism between 1000 and about 1350, the process is easy—if at times entailing some disorder. Open, ill-defined systems of authority, with emphasis upon the person entitled to make rules and binding judgments rather than upon the content of the rules themselves, leave more space for changes which do not appear to depart from the basic norms of the existing ideology.

This is not, however, a "jurisprudence of insurgency" as we have defined it, but in making this distinction we do not mean to deny the effect on the dominant legal ideology of jurisprudence sponsored by groups that are not opposed to the existing regime and that do not wish to achieve state power. It will remain to consider how to distinguish dissident groups which are insurgent from those which are not.

LEGAL IDEOLOGY AND ECONOMIC INTEREST

Throughout this book we have tried to show the relationship between legal ideology and the system of social relations from which it springs. We have provided some evidence for the view, set forth in the writings of Marx and Engels, that the state imposes itself as the agent of one class in dominating the other classes in a society, and that the maintenance and regulation of relations of production in the interest of the dominant class is the primary goal of legal ideology in the hands of the holders of state power.

Why, then, if the root of legal ideology is economic self-interest, put so much stress upon the content and development of the ideology itself? Our concern is due in part to the central role played by legal ideology in the justification for the sovereigns' exercise of state power and for their challengers' resort to arms. Legal ideology was the popular justification for controlling the daily lives of men and women and for the official violence visited upon them. Calls for social change were phrased as legal ideologies.

However, to assert that the origin and eventual justification of legal ideology is in economic self-interest does not mean that there is a direct and immediate relationship between each element of legal ideology—or even each individually addressed command—and the economic self-interest of a particular group. To the contrary, it is precisely the contradictions between ideology and self-interest that permit insurgent groups to win partial and temporary victories within the parameters of existing law.

These contradictions may arise from several sources.

As legal ideology takes on a life of its own, it becomes subject to interpretation and application, and the decisions of those applying it must bear at least some relationship to the ideology as initially stated, regardless of their particular interests. The possibility of contradictions between official jurisprudence and class interest is increased if the task of formulating individually and generally addressed commands is handed over to a specially trained class of jurisprudents who are accustomed to think in terms of the ideology itself, rather than in terms of the class interest.

Another source of contradiction lies in the fact that legal ideology is formulated at a given moment, while the underlying social relations are constantly changing. The result is that the ideology tends to become an empty form—which is what happened to the democratic features of the early city charters. Further, a rising class may seize an old ideology and turn it against its perpetrators, which is exactly what occurred when the European bourgeoisie used the Roman law—already semisanctified by the Church—to batter down legal barriers to commerce. In the same way, the dominant class, confronted by displeasing elements of its own ideology, may cast them aside and rely instead upon sheer class interest.

Legal ideologies may also contain gaps, or uncertainties, that are filled in and clarified to suit the insistent demands of powerful forces. We observed this suppleness in feudal customary law, which was not based on any detailed set of written customs and was largely administered personally by the lord. The same kind of exploitation of open spaces in the law occurred in England: when the semifeudal town charters proved too restrictive to permit introduction of new technology and larger units of production by the new entrepreneurs, the latter simply bought up land outside the cities and obtained favorable legislative treatment to begin building their enterprises.

21.

LEADING SCHOOLS OF LEGAL THOUGHT

To set our theory of the relationship between social struggle and legal change apart from other ways of looking at law, we must critically examine the leading schools of Western jurisprudence: positivism, natural law, sociological theory and legal realism, as well as describe the position taken by the Austrian legal writer, Karl Renner, whose attempt to summarize Marxian concepts of law and the state was a pioneering effort in this field.

POSITIVISM

Legal positivism flourished at the time of the scientific positivism of August Comte. Its leading nineteenth-century exponent was John Austin, who was anxious to distinguish temporal law "properly so called" from God's law and from those moral values that had a binding force unsupported by the imposition of sovereign power. For positivists, the task of jurisprudence is simply to identify which rules are predictably enforced by the power of the state.

Austin's theory was distinctively nineteenth-century English. He argued that one might criticize a particular law as good or bad, moral or immoral, but that the proper province of jurisprudence was to study the system of generally addressed commands enforced—in the form of individually addressed commands—by an identifiable sovereign. Who holds the power of the state and what does that person do with it are questions asked in all periods of history, but to make them, as Austin does, the sole legitimate inquiries of jurisprudence bespeaks a confidence in the bourgeoisie's ability to hold power and to establish its claim to the legal order. Any challengers—frame-breakers, Chartists, strikers, and others—had been firmly put down. Political quarrels might erupt over improving the conditions of workers in the cities and on the farms, but the power and unity of the class which had sponsored the world's first industrial revolution was unmistakable. Legal philosophy was thus focused upon the mechanics of power.

Later legal positivists have been less rigid. Hans Kelsen has taken into account the way in which a legal ideology may cease to be "the law" due either to desuetude or to public indifference to the sovereign command, and has described the way in which moral principles at large in a given society may influence the concretization of generally addressed commands. But the basic focus of legal positivism is upon an identifiable sovereign, who may be called by different names, and upon his or her creation of legal ideology as the justification and explanation of the exercise of state power.

Positivist legal theory does not profess to be uninterested in the internal law of groups other than states, nor to be unconcerned with changes in legal ideology. But in describing what is and is not "law," these things are by definition to be excluded, because the very task of jurisprudence is to isolate legal rules from other kinds of commands and requests. Such an approach may be faulted on its own terms, for it does not even permit understanding of the sovereign's legal ideology at a given moment, let alone the mechanism by which it changes.

Law is not, as we have seen, a *thing*, such as a brick or a rock or a scaffolding. Nor is state power (or sovereign power) a substance or object. One root fault of the positivist approach is that it reifies law and state power; it does so ostensibly in order to describe them better, but it ends up with a description of law that is distorted because the reification itself becomes integrated into the understanding of law.

State power is never absolute in the sense that its minions punish every infraction. More important, state power is continually subject to challenges from groups that want to see the dominant legal ideology interpreted in different ways, or even to overthrow it and replace it with another. In the former case, a group—through legislative petitions, lawsuits, or in other ways—demands that the dominant legal ideology be made concrete in a particular way. But if the demand is not met and the movement breaks into open revolt, it is neither seeking to "influence" or even to "seize" state power, but is destroying it through its own organized violence in order to install a new legal ideology and state power, also backed with violence. A reified theory of law cannot describe the process of rising up to gain social control, nor the impact of that *process* upon the content of the dominant legal ideology.

Nor do revolutionaries wait until they are in the houses of government to pass laws defining their own legitimacy and setting out the commands that will be enforced in the future. We have seen that all revolutionary movements in the West have expressed their aspirations and demands in terms of legal ideology while they were still subjects of the regime they opposed. Beyond this, these movements—from the first secret societies in the early communes to the parties of the French Revolution—regulate their own affairs through rules of conduct. These internal rules are vitally important when they regulate the conduct of a group that aspires to state power. They foretell the ideology that the group will impose on society at large if it is successful in obtaining state power, and give clues to the economic interests from which this ideology springs.

We are saying, in short, that legal ideology and state power can never be studied "by themselves," for to do so only gives a false picture. Legal ideology and state power are always in the process of coming into being, changing and being changed, and being swept out of existence. The positivists look only at the *structure* of social relations, while the important inquiry is into their *motion*.

We can see here why legal positivism has been so congenial a posture to the jurisprudence of the bourgeoisie since the 1800s. A social class so well established, and yet so fearful of its challengers, will find particularly useful a system of thought that denies its own revolutionary past and focuses on the concrete, present-tense character of its power. Once there was history, the positivists say, but now there isn't any.

THE NATURAL-LAW THEORIES

A reliance upon the natural order was typical of the jurisprudence of the insurgent bourgeoisie, and its ideologists were not bashful about claiming divine inspiration. Natural-law theories are judgmental; they are normative, in the sense that they ascribe validity or rightfulness to legal ideologies based upon "God, Nature, Reason, Intuition, or Recognition." "Nature and . . . Nature's God" reads the Declaration of Independence, and the French Declaration of the Rights of Man and Citizens modestly asserts that the National Assembly is acting only as God's publicist in issuing its list of liberties.

Even though we can recognize natural-law jurisprudence in the writings of the revolutionary bourgeoisie at an advanced stage of its move toward state power, it would be a mistake to attempt to equate natural-law jurisprudence with revolutionary ideology. As Max Weber wrote:

> Natural law has thus been the collective term for those norms which owe their legitimacy not to their origin from a legitimate lawgiver, but to their immanent and teleological qualities. Natural law has thus been the specific form of legitimacy of a revolutionarily created order. The invocation of natural law has repeatedly been the method by which classes in revolt have legitimated their aspirations, in so far as they did not, or could not, base their claims upon positive religious norms or revelation. Not every natural law, however, has been "revolutionary" in its intentions in the sense that it would provide the justification for the realization of certain norms by violence or by passive disobedience against an existing order. Indeed, natural law has also served to legitimate authoritarian powers of the most diverse types.

Whether used by a revolutionary class seeking power or an established one holding it, a natural-law legal ideology posits a validating norm that is outside—in the sense of above, or pre-existent to—the system. Whatever form it takes, this norm is inherently unverifiable, although natural-law theorists have sought various means to overcome this objection. Kant proposed that each person should act as though the basis of his or her actions should, by an act of will, be general law. Bentham attempted a calculus of pleasure and pain, and counseled a jurisprudence of the greatest good for the greatest number. Neither effort seems a credible solution to the problem. Both Kant and Bentham wrote within and for their times, and did not stand at all outside the social system of which they were a part. They assumed the validity of the fundamental postulates of their society, and failed to understand the developing character of human wants and needs. Neither saw the way in which needs and wants, and perceptions of them, are conditioned by contemporary society and by social class.

Some modern natural-law writers seek to verify their choice of a fundamental legal ideology by resorting to first principles which are claimed to be so generally accepted as not to require proof. They may also, like Lon Fuller of Harvard Law School, refer to a popular sense of justice which encourages obedience only to rules conforming to certain fundamental values. Such theories tend to assume only one sense of justice, taking no account of the way social position shapes outlook; they treat legal ideology as the substance, rather than the reflection, of social struggle.

The similarities, and increasing rapport, between the natural-law and positivist schools reflect their fundamental identity of purpose. The natural-law theorists of the modern West, like the positivists, work with the same material—the legal ideology of the triumphant bourgeoisie. While the positivists stress the system of coercion which enforces ideology, natural-law advocates focus upon the promises of human liberty which that ideology inescapably makes; both come at the same problem but from different directions. Both stand inside rather than outside the systems they are examining.

We should note, however, a special case among natural-law jurisprudents: Sir Henry Maine, whose *Ancient Law* is considered a classic on the development of English law. Although Maine is usually considered to represent the English historical school, like the Germans who sought the essence of the law in a *Volksgeist* or popular spirit, he clearly relies upon a validating norm, which puts him among natural-law writers. (Indeed, the historical school itself is better placed in the natural-law tradition because of the normative quality it attached to the customary, popular law of Germany.)

Maine's interest ranged over primitive legal systems, Roman law, feudalism, and the bourgeois law of his own time. Although his practical insights were many and his historical research extensive, he is best known for a single line from *Ancient Law* which expressed his attitude: "The movement of the progressive societies has hitherto been a movement from *Status to Contract*." Maine meant that the gradual, ineluctable development of the world legal order had been to cast off definitions of legal obligation based upon social position (and ultimately upon family ties) and to replace them by assertedly free bargains (contracts) concluded between individuals.

It is true that the growing strength of the bourgeoisie brought about the gradual expansion of the domain of contract. Why, then, do we describe Maine as a natural-law writer? First, he believed that this historical process was inherently good and right; by identifying contractual, capitalist society with self-evident good he adopted a position as idealistic as that of John Locke or the framers of the Declaration of Independence. Second, by this assertion Maine took his place firmly within his own national system. He could not envision that British capitalism and its laws were anything but the highest and final form, rather than a historical stage that would someday pass.

Finally, Maine adopted the mythology of free contract so popular in nineteenth-century England, when it had long ceased to have any relationship to reality. He wrote not of real, historical contracts concluded in the 1300s between peasants who walked a day to the village to meet the notary of their absentee landlord, or even the nineteenth-century contracts between Manchester workers and the mills that employed them. He was concerned with idealized contracts between hypothetical people with equal bargaining power and equal freedom to refuse to bargain.

It is disconcerting that a learned man could write such a book in the nineteenth century, not far from the din of social struggles and the widely reported work of the factory inspectors. It is surprising that *Ancient Law* remains a standard work in today's law schools. But lawyers are trained to deal in concepts rather than realities, to strip situations of their human element to get at the legal issues in which A and B are buying and selling in some abstract situation. This fascination with abstraction makes Western lawyers excellent ideologues. They keep alive the mythology of the crusading early days of bourgeois power, for they continue to treat seriously the conceptual framework of those times.

John Locke wrote that property was a human institution justified by a natural law. In a state of nature, a man went into the forest and began to grow plants. He mixed his labor with the earth and produced a crop. Another man killed deer, and mixed his labor with the meat and skin to make food and clothing. These two men, by means of their labor, created values which had not existed before, and therefore had a natural right to their product. What could be more naturally right than for them to trade their property as equals?

By the time Maine wrote, however, the greater part of English manufacture—rural and urban—was in the hands of the bourgeoisie, which owned the means of production and hired others to work it. Workers making cloth still mixed their labor with the fibers and cotton and wool, but they did not thereby own the product. They had contracted to sell their labor-power, which was all they possessed. The price at which they sold it was determined by market forces they did not control, and their choice of trade and place of work was limited by practical necessity. Challenges to this system by artisans, crofters, villagers, and small farmers had been eliminated one by one, as we have seen.

Maine's gift to British jurisprudence was to refine out of all consideration these human features of natural-law contract and property, and to sketch a garden of historical oddities in which the process of conceptualist decision-making could go on.

LEGAL REALISM AND SOCIOLOGICAL THEORIES

In reaction to positivist rigor and the natural law's unverifiability, the late nineteenth and early twentieth centuries produced two closely related schools of thought, legal realism and the sociological school.

The legal realists are exemplified by the patrician Supreme Court Justice Oliver Wendell Holmes, Jr., and, more recently, by commercial-law specialist Karl Llewellyn and Judge Jerome Frank. The realists' principal influence has been in the Anglo-American system, with its express reliance upon judicial decision and precedent as the means of elaborating legal ideology.

The realists were reacting to a common tendency of the positivist and natural-law schools to engage in abstract system-building. From Domat, Pufendorf, Grotius, and Montesquieu in the seventeenth century to Maine and Austin in the nineteenth, the legal ideology of the bourgeoisie, when formally elaborated, was stated as a coherent system of interrelated legal principles. This system was, for each of these authors, "The Law," and the task of a court in fashioning an individually addressed command was simply to find some relevant principle from this corpus and apply it to the dispute before it. Against this notion of law as a sort of "brooding omnipresence" the realists rebelled.

Realists look for law in the judgments of courts. "The prophecies of what the courts will do in fact and nothing more pretentious, are what I mean by law," Holmes wrote. This building up of the image of law from individually addressed commands made to litigants has the advantage of demystifying law to some extent by disregarding the stated rationale and ostensible judicial deference to legal theory for rules in practice. Rather than contemplating the generalizations of jurisprudential writing, or of a constitution, or the terse-or verbose, but always incomplete—enactments of the legislators, the realists were anxious to see how law worked when brought to bear against people in judicial judgments.

The realist school simply would not accept even the judges' statements of the reasons for their decisions. To know what courts will do one must search the "true rule," wrote Llewellyn, and Frank sought to bring psychiatric insight into the process of discovering that rule.

Although this practical approach might appear to permit realist jurisprudence to analyze the interests behind the rules as they are applied in individual cases—and thus perhaps to discover the moving principles of a legal order—the social attitudes of the realists themselves kept their analysis of social policy within narrow bounds. Realist writing mind-reads judicial opinions, and is therefore locked in by the walls of judges' minds.

Realists have been apt at pointing out the gaps between official statements of legal ideology and the actual system of law as enforced under pressure from social forces seeking to bend it in different ways. Legal realism contributed to the breakdown of formalistic, mechanistic theories of contract and property rights, which culminated in the late 1930s' and early 1940s' decisions of the United States Supreme Court upholding New Deal and other Depression-era social legislation. Legal realism is to legal ideology as Keynesianism is to political economy.

There are clear limitations in basing legal ideology on the decided case. The world of litigation is not the real world. Not all problems, not all arguable violations of law, find their way before tribunals. Quite the contrary: police in the streets, for example, exercise force against citizens many times each day and are seldom called to account. As Engels remarked, "The lowest police officer of the civilized state has more 'authority' than all the organs of . . . [primitive] society put together." Judicial decisions, even those declaring fundamental principles, only settle rights and wrongs between the two parties involved. They set precedent only to the extent that they say that if two parties with the same sort of dispute hire lawyers and bring the matter to a high enough appellate court, the odds are that they will receive the same judgment. For example, after the United States Supreme Court decision in *Brown v. Board of Education*, which declared segregation of the races in public schools unconstitutional, individual suits in countless school districts were necessary to secure judgments against each segregated school system. Then the long and often futile process of enforcement began, again on a district basis. In the same vein, how many copyhold tenants in the 1500s were driven off their land for each one who had the means to hire a lawyer and go to Westminster, there to help make "the law"?

The realists, of course, recognize the limited character of judicial judgment derived from one case. They concede that such decisions cannot claim to regulate the conduct of parties not before the court. The point is that a view of law which focuses on predicting the outcome of individual cases, and uncovering the reasons for these decisions, can state only a fraction of the truth about a society's legal ideology. It is equally a part of a legal ideology to define the permitted applications of state power in nonjudicial settings. Understanding informally applied administrative sanctions or decisions informally and often unconsciously made by state officials who are unaware of judicial decisions that deal with the conduct of other officials similarly situated, is often a far more important task than the analysis of judicial decisions and official texts.

Moreover, any system of jurisprudence that focuses on what judges will do applies only to a single society at one period of its development. Reform—new faces in old molds, the gradual accretion of new principles on old policies—is the material of the realist social outlook. Even the trenchant and biting criticisms that Jerome Frank leveled at the common-law system were directed at no more than reform in the light of principles then accepted in many political circles. The realist view is not suited to description of fundamental social change, but must treat such change as a discontinuous event, not part of jurisprudential concerns.

Distinguishing itself from both the positivists and the realists, the sociological school has undertaken to study law in a broader perspective. This view traces its origins to Max Weber. Max Rheinstein, editor of Weber's most significant works on the sociology of law, has summarized Weber's fundamental terms:

> The starting point is the concept of *social conduct* which is defined . . . as that kind of human conduct which is related to the conduct of others and in its course oriented to it. Social conduct can be oriented to the idea that there exists some *legitimate order*. Such an order does, in turn, effectively exist or, which means the same, possess validity in exactly the measure in which social conduct is actually oriented to it. An order is called (by Weber) *convention* when its validity is guaranteed by the likelihood that conduct which does not

> conform to the order will meet with the (relatively) general and actual disapproval of some given group of people. An order shall be called *law* where it is guaranteed by the likelihood that (physical or psychological) coercion, aimed at bringing about conduct in conformity with the order, or at avenging its violation, will be exercised by a staff of people especially holding themselves ready for this purpose.

Weber's definition of law is followed more or less rigidly in his work, and passes no judgment on the rightness of a legal ideology (which he would call a legitimate order) as a precondition to its being regarded as *convention* or *law*. The sociological study of law, at least in its descriptive work, is value-free.

Other sociologists of law have continued and complemented the work begun by Weber in *Economy and Society*, though with less historical and comparative breadth. The great merit of such study is that it reveals the impact of legal ideology on the lives of people and lays bare the elements that enter into choices of whether and how sanctions and vengeance will be visited upon them. Exponents of the sociological school have intensely studied the impact of group and individual interest upon the exercise of state power, and the use of legal ideology in expressing and codifying social relationships.

So diverse are the works reflecting the influence of the sociological school that we cannot in this short space either summarize or criticize them. Of Weber we can say that his claim to be value-free, seen in the light of his work, was false.

For the sake of a uniform terminology and a clean conceptual framework, he sketches and compares legal ideas divorced from the societies which gave them birth. Legal ideology becomes a tree cut off at the trunk, the better to study each branch, twig, and leaf, and to compare it with other trees brought from afar. Thus he sought to isolate methods of jurisprudence and elements of legal ideology in widely different times and places. In one five-page subsection, for instance, he compares the exercise of legislative power by medieval princes, the medieval Church, the Roman senate, and imperial Germany. He casts an eye on the use of popular acclaim as a means of approving judgments in the German customary law, and notes that the Roman *populus* had no such power save when the judgment of the magistrates was death. The difference between the Roman and German rules on this subject, he then says, may be traced to the relative lack of military discipline in German society. By a remorseless eclecticism, incomparable situations are compared, leading to the conclusion that everything is related to everything else but nothing is caused by or emerges from anything wise.

Weber's insights cannot be divorced from his basic concern as a sociologist—to demonstrate the increasing rationality of Western societies in the context of the increasingly bureaucratic state, with its power to co-opt, absorb, and manipulate. Further, he regarded all interests (other than that of the state) as functionally equivalent and therefore neglected to examine which interests, expressed on behalf of which groups, might pose more than a bureaucratic problem of accommodation for the state. He paid little attention to insurrectionary, struggling elements—including those that had begun to appear in his own society.

We must be grateful, however, for Weber's study of law for, as Loysel said of Beaumanoir, he "broke the mirror and opened the way." We must not, as the positivists would have us, narrow our concern to those legal ideologies that state power invests with its sanction and turns into "law." We must understand the interests that put pressure on a dominant legal ideology, and study the sets of rules that Weber terms *convention*—gang law, law merchant, ecclesiastical law—paying particular attention to those which aspire to replace the existing system of state law.

But we must at the same time examine the relation law has to the social system it purports to regulate, and discover which among the competing legal ideologies reflects the interests of groups that wish to change the system fundamentally. Weber focused upon law as administration, and therefore—despite the wealth of comparative and historical knowledge—he could not deal with the possibility of fundamental social change. He could study the past as done, but could not view the present as history.

KARL RENNER: THE INSTITUTIONS OF PRIVATE LAW AND THEIR SOCIAL FUNCTIONS

Karl Renner's work deserves close attention in any study of political economy and law. Renner set out to show the relationship between legal forms and what he termed the "economic substratum" that endows those forms with their specific historical character. Though he was a lawyer, his knowledge of economics was extensive. In *The Institutions of Private Law* he sought "to utilize the Marxist system of sociology for the construction of a theory of law." Though we disagree with several of his major premises, his work ranks with (and should be read with) Paul Sweezy's *Theory of Capitalist Development* as an indispensable introduction to the relation between law and society.

Renner was concerned only with "private law"—with those principles of legal order which regulate the relations between persons and between persons and things. Moreover, he focused on certain categories of the civil law of property and contract that dated to the late Roman period and were still in use among European lawyers. He included family law and the law of succession, although to a lesser extent and only in broad outline. The variations in property law which accompanied capitalist development, and particularly the elaboration of corporation law, law merchant, bills and notes, insurance, and devices for pooling risks and capital, interested him only marginally. This limitation is one of the major strengths of the book, but it is also its principal weakness.

Renner wrote in the positivist tradition in the sense that he accepted as "law" only those commands made by sovereigns. A typical argument takes a principle of law—for example, the contract of employment—and analyzes its change in function due to changes in economic circumstances. In bourgeois theory, as we noted in discussing the work of Sir Henry Maine, the two parties to such a contract confronted one another as equals. In feudal legal ideology, by contrast, the obligation to labor, and even the character of the labor each party was to perform, were the subject of the most detailed rules of law. This law was "public law," in the sense that the state enforced the obligations of each party to perform its assigned task.

Bourgeois legal ideology turns the matter into one of private choice and calls the change a move toward freedom: no one need work, and those who do settle the terms by bargain. Renner seeks to penetrate this fiction. Quoting Marx, he writes:

> The juridical relation, which thus expresses itself in a contract, whether this contract be part of a developed legal system or not, is a relation between two wills, and is but the reflex of the real economical relation between the two. It is this economical relation that determines the subject matter comprised in each such juridical act.

Since, whatever the ideology says, "society must be able to dispose of the working power of the individual," the fiction of free choice masks the reality that the wage-laborer's lack of property compels him to hire out at wage-work. To put it another way, the notion that property is no more than a relationship between a person (*persona*) and a thing (*res*), and therefore involves no domination of person over person, is a fiction. Control of property—when property consists of means of production—is converted into control over persons through the medium of the contract to work; thus the idea of contract as free bargain is itself rendered illusory.

Pursuing his point, Renner distinguishes capitalist from feudal property law:

> At this stage it is useful to realize the original implications of the institution of property: it is not a mere order of goods. It is just in respect of the deliberate planned social distribution of goods that it first abdicates. It merely protects him who has possession by virtue of an unassailable title, but it does not distribute goods according to a plan. Contrast with this the law of property of the feudal epoch. How richly diversified was its catalogue of *jura in rem* [rights in things, used here as meaning the right to use a thing in a socially prescribed way]. The property law of bourgeois society leaves the order of the goods to the goods themselves. It is only thus that they organize themselves and accumulate in accordance with the specific laws of capitalist circulation. At this stage we see already that this anonymous and anarchical regulation of "goods" becomes control over men in their capacity as potential labor.

By stating that people are free, the bourgeois legal code says only that the owners of property are free to organize systems of production and exchange typical of capitalist society at a given stage of development, and that they use the power their property confers to organize the rest of the population into the system of production.

> It is not the law or a legal privilege which endows property with this function of regulating distribution, but the quiet force of facts. Yet it is not a process against or outside the law, but a process which occurs on the basis of the very norms which in the past corresponded with the period of simple commodity production. The legal content of the right of ownership is neither enlarged nor restricted; nor is it abused. It is not even necessary to invent a new complementary institution to supplement the institution of property. There is nothing special in the power to alienate one's own property and to spend money as an equivalent for hired labor, nor is the power to hire out one's own labor an abnormal exercise of personal freedom. There has been no change in the content of either institution.

To emphasize the connection between economics and legal ideology, Renner again quotes Marx:

> The original conversion of money into capital thus proceeds in strict accordance with the economic laws of commodity production and with the laws of property derived therefrom. Nevertheless, its outcome is (1) that the product belongs to the capitalist, not to the worker; (2) that the value of this product . . . is inclusive of a surplus value on which the worker has expended labor and the capitalist nothing whatever, but which nevertheless becomes the legal property of the capitalist; (3) that the worker has preserved his labor-power and can sell it anew if he finds a buyer. . . . In other words, the law is not broken, rather it is given the opportunity for perpetual operation.

The elements of economic life associate according to forms prescribed by the law, which is part of the ideology of a dominant class. As Renner puts it, "In their own imagination, they are autonomous, but in reality they are dominated by a social power."

Renner undertook to show in careful detail that legal forms were the superstructure under which the real relations of capitalist production went on, and that these forms were used to serve and foster those relations. He also demonstrated that these forms, grouped together as bourgeois legal ideology, mask the constraint in fact exercised by the bourgeoisie as entrepreneurs and finance capitalists. This description echoes the writings of the young Marx, as well as the modern concern of radical psychiatrists with alienation. In the words of R. D. Laing:

> Men have . . . always been weighed down not only by their sense of subordination to fate and chance, to ordained external necessities or contingencies, but by a sense that their very own thoughts and feelings, in their most intimate interstices, are the outcome, the resultant of processes which they undergo.

In spite of Renner's unique and important contribution to the study of bourgeois legal ideology, his view that legal norms remain the same while their content changes according to social conditions is mistaken. While legal norms are indeed the product of—and are shaped by—the economic substratum, the bourgeoisie manipulates these legal norms and the state power in order to realize its goals. If we concentrate solely on the contract of employment and the concept of ownership of property, and if we use, as Renner does, Roman-law ideas about these operations, we can say that certain legal categories remained unchanged for centuries. But this creates a false impression: while the private-law contract of employment did not change, *public law* was used to drive workers off the land and into the cities, and to enforce the obligation to work. This, like the drastic rearrangement of the poor laws under bourgeois influence, certainly involved the use of legal ideology to influence the progress of economic relations. More, these actions required the creation and enforcement of legal forms. The contract of employment cannot be seen—as Renner sees it—in isolation from its social context. Further, Renner pays only slight attention to those auxiliary institutions that were crucial to bourgeois legal ideology, thus implying that the basic legal definition of law of property did not change. But through the conscious formulation of legal ideology, means were found to build up systems of banking, corporations, and so on.

There is another troubling aspect of Renner's choice of legal norms. His concentration on categories of legal norms drawn from the Roman law isolates such principles from the general legal ideology of which they are a part at each period. These categories become universal in the sense that they have survived as "pure" legal ideas, expressing in a few Latin words a relationship that in fact occurs in many social contexts over a period of a thousand years. In the early medieval cities, the bourgeois codes, as we saw, provided for the employment of labor, and thus for the contract *locatio conductio operarum*; this same contract is at the heart of the nineteenth-century employment relationship as well. But in the 1000s, the municipal code invested the employment contract, expressly as a matter of law, with certain social content—no more than one worker per master, and so on. The permissible extent of the contract of employment as a device for social regulation was a matter of legal ideology, an ideology that contained at least one myth: the assumption that legal restrictions could halt the natural process of capitalist accumulation.

In the nineteenth century the legal ideology of triumphant capitalism gave practically unlimited scope to the employment contract, and it contained a different myth: the myth of freedom that Renner unmasks so well. Only by viewing legal ideology as a whole is it possible to identify its true social function. Renner speaks of legal rules that lose their social function and die. This is not, however, the fate of the most important functionless elements of legal ideology. In France, the bourgeoisie could have staggered into the nineteenth century paying the nobility tributes that were defined and exacted according to a legal ideology that had lost its social function and become a hindrance to progress. But because it was backed by state power and supported by force, the old ideology did not "die." It had to be killed.

Finally, Renner's concentration upon private law has made his book less useful than it might be. Revealing the social function performed by institutions of private law is a valuable task; exposing the reality of coercion behind the legal facade of free choice and fairness is an indispensable part of what we call the jurisprudence of insurgency. A detailed consideration of the bourgeoisie's increasing reliance upon public-law institutions to protect its interests and to foster the increasing concentration of capital would have given the lie most convincingly to the pretense of bourgeois legal ideology that the state is neutral arbiter of individual relations between and among equals. Some attention to public law would have pointed up the error in insisting that legal forms of bourgeois private law remain relatively unchanged at widely different historical periods in the development of capitalist institutions.

Renner did, however, pose a most important series of questions, which appear in the last two paragraphs of his book:

> Given that, like all else under the sun, norms have their causes, wherein do these lie? Given that they enjoy a real existence, what are its characteristics, what is the mode of their existence and how do they change? Given that their origin lies in the conditions of life of the human race, that they are nothing more than a means of preserving human society, what part do they actually play in the existence and development of our own generation?

These are open questions of jurisprudence. The time has come to engage in an attempt at their solution.

22.

THE JURISPRUDENCE OF INSURGENCY

Neither the sterile rigors of the positivists, nor the dreams of the natural-law enthusiasts, nor the restricted vision of the realists and sociologists serves to describe, much less to explain, the means by which the bourgeoisie first accommodated, then openly confronted, then overthrew the legal ideology of feudalism. And none of these theories of law explains the sharpening contradictions now appearing in the legal systems of the West.

All of these schools either describe the legal system constructed by the victorious bourgeoisie as a static institution, or in some measure seek to justify it, or attempt to explain those of its inner workings that have to do with adjusting internal conflict. None is concerned with analyzing the revolutionary beginnings of legal ideology, or with identifying those social forces which may—also by revolutionary means—bring into being a newly dominant legal ideology based upon a different system of social relations.

Though this book has been about the bourgeois revolutionaries themselves, we are interested as well in the use of legal ideology in the struggle for social change. We think a theory of jurisprudence should make such a study its primary concern. In this connection we may recall the words of another former law student, Karl Marx, writing in the preface to *A Contribution to the Critique of Political Economy*:

> I was led by my studies to the conclusion that legal relations as well as forms of state could neither be understood by themselves, nor explained by the so-called general progress of the human mind, but that they are rooted in the

> material conditions of life which are summed up by Hegel after the fashion of the English and French of the eighteenth century under the name "civil society"; the anatomy of that civil society is to be sought in political economy. The study of the latter which I had taken up in Paris, I continued at Brussels. . . . The general conclusion at which I arrived and which, once reached, continued to serve as the leading thread in my studies, may be briefly summed up as follows: In the social production which men carry on they enter into definite relations that are independent of their will; these relations of production correspond to a definite stage of development of their material powers of production. The sum total of these relations of production constitutes the economic structure of society—the real foundation on which rise legal and political superstructures and to which correspond definite forms of social consciousness. The mode of production in material life determines the general character of the social, political, and spiritual processes of life. It is not the consciousness of men that determines their existence, but, on the contrary, their social existence that determines their consciousness. At a certain stage of their development, the material forces of production in society come in conflict with the existing relations of production, or—what is but a legal expression for the same thing—with the property relations within which they had been at work before. From forms of development of the forces of production these relations turn into their fetters. Then comes the period of social revolution. With the change of the economic foundation the entire immense superstructure is more or less rapidly transformed.

Although in reading this paragraph we might get the impression that Marx thought that the legal ideology of a given system of social relations always, in every detail, supported that system, his intense study of reform legislation in nineteenth-century England, in the first volume of *Capital*, should dispel any such notion. In any case, we have seen that the contradiction between old forms and new social forces does not reach a critical state—that of social revolution—suddenly. From the dawn of bourgeois urban power to the French Revolution was a period of eight hundred years. In that period, is it fair to say that the dominant legal ideologies were the product of systems of economic relations; and that the champions of this or that ideology were in the service of economic interests? We think so.

We have watched the bourgeoisie at each period consolidate its power and, through changes in the law, bring elements of its legal ideology under the aegis of the state. As this happened, the legal definition of social relations changed: land that had been held in feudal tenure became the subject of contract; land that had been held in common was fenced and former yeomen worked it for wages or went to the city. The farmer or worker had little choice as to the type of social relation into which he entered. He could work for one proprietor or another, but the form of the bargain—contract or not, feudal or not—was determined for him.

Bourgeois ideas of contract and property in land did not spread over wider areas because they were necessarily better than other ideas; they spread from the urban nuclei of bourgeois power because they represented a system of economic relations uniquely adapted to the level of technology and learning of a certain time. Their implacable tendency was to dissolve old relations of production and exchange. As Marx also wrote: "Agriculture comes to be more and more merely a branch of industry and is completely dominated by capital. . . . Capital is the all-dominating power of bourgeois society."

In this process, the attitudes and goals of the bourgeoisie continually changed, as the horizons of its members broadened. Its demands changed as well, and we have seen that it was far from unified at most stages of its development. Urban artisanal commerce gave way before the international trading companies, and the legal ideologies of local bourgeois groups came into conflict with those of the more powerful long-distance traders. The protective shield of the guilds only temporarily resisted the force of new techniques of production and new means of legal organization of production, exchange, and distribution.

All of these changes took place within a framework of political organization which at least outwardly had maintained its essential elements unchanged since the eleventh century. Monarchs, to be sure, had enlarged their power and the military function of the feudal system had largely fallen into disuse. Princes formed alliances of mutual advantage with sections of the bourgeoisie, exacting financial support in exchange for legal concessions. Within the old legal ideology, room was found for innovations favorable to the growth and maintenance of trade.

How can we best describe this process of change? We have pointed to stages in the growth of bourgeois consciousness, and of the gradual formulation of a jurisprudence of insurgency in the process of struggle against hostile ideology. Our task now is to formulate a theory of legal ideology and of jurisprudence which correctly describes these changes, lays bare the connection between legal ideology and the system of social relations, and permits us to analyze movements for social change in light of their revolutionary potential.

We must make a distinction between opposition to specific parts of the legal ideology of a state, seeking change through the existing, dominant organs of state power, and, on the other hand, rejecting the entire system as illegitimate. This distinction is the subject of two of Plato's dialogues, *Apology* and *Crito*. In the *Apology*, Socrates rebukes the Athenians, defends his right to have taught and spoken as he did, and pronounces unworthy of respect any legal ideology which does not permit behavior such as his, though it be said to have corrupted the youth and to have defiled the gods. At the same time, perhaps foreshadowing the position he is to take in *Crito*, he defends his conduct as lawful under the laws of Athens and denies the specific charges against him. Socrates is nonetheless condemned to death.

Later, Crito comes to the condemned Socrates in his cell to tell him that his friends have a plan to spirit him away. Socrates refuses their aid and discourses upon the importance of the state. It has educated him, it has given him a place in the world, it has defined in some sense the terms of his existence, and he owes it obedience though it has unjustly condemned him to death. One may seek to change the existing order, but one must accept defeat at its hands in acknowledging the legitimacy of its claim to rule. Socrates, therefore, took a position far from insurgent, while seeking to change the ideology of the state whose power he acknowledged.

Consider again the case we described earlier, of a peaceful valley taken over by brigands. The chief brigand and his henchmen impose a system of rules upon the populace, guaranteeing rights and setting out certain duties. Everyone clearly understands which commands, in what form, are to be regarded as authoritative, both in the case of generalized commands and of those addressed to individuals. The system of rules established by the chief brigand and enforced by his henchmen would, in a positivist description, be termed "law"—a legal system, or a legal ideology backed by state power—and this would be enough, for we would know who has sovereign power and the monopoly on legitimate violence. But this analysis would not get us very far, even in a descriptive sense. For the populace, which might begin after a time to chafe under the brigands' rule and to organize resistance to it, conduct may not be governed by the brigands' rules in quite the way it appears to be, even when most citizens appear to be law-abiding.

There may, for instance, be a period during which the flexibility of the brigands' legal ideology is tested. Attempts will be made to modify its substance, or to apply its terms (when ambiguities appear) in ways that are to the populace's advantage. More or less room will be found in the dominant legal ideology to accommodate these claims for justice; if less, the claim of the brigands to obedience will begin to erode in practice.

Later, perhaps, the populace, or a dissident section of it, may reformulate the formal laws as "maxims of prudence" designed to minimize the harmful consequences of lawlessness. For example, if the rule is "no three or more persons shall conduct political meetings without the consent of the chief brigand," dissidents may take precautions of secrecy. The rule is recast in practice as the maxim of prudence that "no three or more persons shall conduct a political meeting so that the authorities will be able to prove, by the accepted means of proof and a sufficient quantum of evidence, that the meeting took place and who was present." Yet the dissidents engaged in organizing such meetings may be prepared to accept the legitimacy of the state's punishment if they are found out, though they will strenuously argue in the brigands' tribunal that they ought not be convicted, for want of evidence or because the rule against meetings does not comport with, or is not essential to, the main principles of the brigands' legal system. In this process, legal ideology meets legal ideology; the exposition of competing claims in tribunals, as well as the formulation of intelligent maxims of prudence, falls to those trained in the law. It may even be that a shared professed regard for a common legal tradition unites the brigands and the populace and forms the basis for the latter's demands that the former behave in certain ways.

The lawyers for the dissidents will also be seeking to show the true social function—repressive—of the brigands' ostensibly neutral commands. Jurisprudents and legal ideologists—who may in this case be called lawyers—will be called upon by dissidents to evaluate the extent to which the brigands' rules can accommodate the claims for justice of the populace. Eventually, however, the process of accommodation may come to be seen as futile if the brigands' legal ideology cannot change sufficiently to encompass the fundamental demands of the populace.

When this evaluation—that there can be no lasting compromise—becomes part of the dissidents' legal ideology, it serves as an argument for social revolution. We saw something of this in the debates of the Estates-General before they transformed themselves into the National Assembly. The legal ideologists of the new regime said, in effect: "The old regime, with its *Parlements* and courtiers and hangers-on, has given us all it can. Its offers of compromise are illusions; its legal ideology tells us that further progress is possible, but that is only a sign that law has become a lie the regime tells the people." The Assembly only formulated what great numbers of people had come to believe and act upon.

There is another way in which legal ideology and lawyers can be important to the process of revolutionary change: those trained in the law assist the insurgent group to build its internal legal ideology. The dissidents develop styles of life and work and relationships to one another built upon mutual confidence and the shared experience of a common endeavor. Some of these work-styles and relationships may be granted recognition by the governing legal ideology—thus political parties, corporations, intentional communities—giving the dissidents an area of autonomy within which to further shape and test their principles. Where such recognition is not granted, and even where any counter-organization is expressly forbidden, dissidents relate to one another in ways that they determine as a group. They have an internal legal ideology, and discuss and live out the juridical principles of a social organization alternative to the one under which they live. Such activity can lay the foundation for the principles of the state legal ideology that will be enforced if the brigands are overthrown.

The working out by members of the resistance of the extent to which claims for justice can be accommodated within the brigands' rules, the way in which members of the resistance behave toward one another, and the alternative forms of social organization foreshadowed by their conduct—all these are different in principle from the operation of those voluntary organizations that acknowledge the supremacy of the brigands' rules. And they are different from ordinary aggregates of criminals, both in the content of their proposals for social organization—their legal ideology—and in the revolutionary function which their resistance assumes and the role it plays historically.

When we look at this resistance activity from outside the valley, we can analyze it from several perspectives. We can question the values of the resisters. We can challenge their judgment about the extent to which the brigands' rules can be bent to their demands. We can regard the call for revolution as doomed to failure. But if we recognize that the resistance has at least the prospect of success, and particularly if we are looking back at the history of a resistance movement that has come to power, we must recognize that it is wrong to describe as "law" only those commands issued by the brigands and enforced at a given time. While those commands presuppose a monopoly of violence on the brigands' part, the power of the resistance, by virtue of its strength of numbers and its tenacity, is equally a part of the process of making law—by which we mean the rules by which people live in organized society and which are backed up by the power of the state. What we call "law" is, in short, not a system but a process. To describe law as a system is useful only if we recall that we are describing a stop-action photograph, useful to record a state of events at a given moment but not to tell us about the direction or speed of change.

Once we have recognized the tentative character of any description of a legal ideology, even one backed by state power, we must ask a further question. In any social system there are rebels and social bandits, all of whom exert pressure on the state legal ideology and all of whom formulate, more or less expressly, legal ideologies of their own. Are we, like Weber, to put them in one group for purposes of analysis, and call all of their legal ideologies "convention"?

If we want to understand the dynamics of jurisprudence, of changes in legal ideology, and if we want to grasp the essential meaning of the jurisprudence of insurgency, then the answer must be no. During the period we have studied, countless aspirants to state power sought to influence the dominant legal ideology, and even regarded themselves as being in fundamental conflict with the state. Think, for instance, of the communal movements which occasionally sprang up in the Western European countryside, or of the bands of brigands in the wake of the plague in southern France which succeeded in setting back the march of the bourgeoisie toward economic domination of the region. All these failed, while the bourgeoisie succeeded; indeed, the bourgeoisie was sometimes able to invoke the aid of the existing state to destroy these very groups. What, then, must we study, beyond the content and contradictions in legal ideology, in order to classify these different sorts of dissidence?

We must discover which legal ideology at a particular time expresses the aspirations of the class or group that eventually takes power and which represents the fundamental contradiction between an existing system of social relations and that which replaces it. In retrospect, we can see the triumph of the capitalist organization of production. This, and only this, divides the bourgeoisie from the bandits and the communalists. As the consciousness of fundamental contradictions grew, the legal ideology built up within the dissident bourgeoisie became subject to numerous variations. Dictated by the technological and economic situation, by the influences exercised for centuries by the then dominant ideology, by its internal conflicts, and by its formulation of its own goals, the bourgeoisie in each country made choices. The different paths taken by the French and English bourgeoisies make this point clear, and the failure of attempts by the Italian and German bourgeoisies to unify their countries until relatively late is only further evidence.

It was not that no means could be found in 1789 to mediate the differences between the French nobility and the bourgeoisie, but that the price of accommodation had become so great that the latter group determined to move into an insurrectionary posture. This point is well made by Louis Boudin:

> According to the Marxian philosophy a system of production can only last as long as it helps, or at least does not hinder, the unfolding and full exploitation of the productive forces of society, and must give way to another system when it becomes a hindrance, a *fetter*, to production. That a system has become a hindrance, and a fetter to production, when it can only exist by preventing production, and by *wasting* what it has already produced, goes without saying. Such a system cannot therefore last very long, quite irrespective of the purely mechanical possibility or impossibility of its continuance. Such a system has become *historically* impossible, even though mechanically it may still be possible.

The decision no longer to move within the old ideology, to perform the "mechanically" possible, is insurgent. Such a decision, although taken by a *class*, crystallizes around those few leaders who take the first steps; it has, therefore, no precise historical moment.

And what role does the lawyer play in this process? A more contradictory figure could hardly be found. Since the founding of the legal profession, or its refounding in the wake of the Crusades, the lawyer's role has become increasingly ambiguous. Lawyers have always been in the service of those who could pay—the lords, the princes, the Church, the bourgeoisie. They are committed to elaborating legal doctrine under the aegis of state power. There were lawyers who ably served their masters. There were scriveners who wrote in contracts what they interpreted the law to be on behalf of whoever could pay a fee. And there were lawyers who identified with the rising class and pressed for reform. When lawyers worked for the bourgeois institutions created by urban revolt or carved out in a charter of liberty, their role was reasonably straightforward, but when, in the great movement toward monarchical control begun in the 1200s, they were drawn increasingly into "national service," contradictions arose.

If a lawyer's oaths of loyalty to a prince were called into question by his view that a particular law was so bad for commerce that it must be changed—and if not changed, evaded, and if not evadable, resisted—what then? Many lawyers resolved this contradiction by doing nothing, and thereby casting their lot with the status quo. This is not surprising: nonlawyer bourgeois could be found enjoying the perquisites of royal sponsorship as well.

But other lawyers, in the service of other bourgeois, worked to devise principles of legal ideology in the service of insurgency. A lawyer could always be found to resolve contradictions to a client's satisfaction. If the challenge to the state posed by the lawyer and the client proved serious enough, both risked punishment. There is no doubt that this kind of lawyering was useful in the bourgeoisie's progress toward power; nor is there any doubt that an open break between the bourgeois lawyers and the feudal and royal systems which gave them that title was sure to come.

INSURGENCY IN MODERN DRESS

Revolutionary movements now challenge the system of social relations built by the insurgent bourgeoisie and we can observe a new jurisprudence of insurgency at work. These movements have a history which parallels the rise to power of the bourgeoisie, and have faced the same problems of attempting to accommodate their demands to aspects of bourgeois legal ideology before breaking into open conflict with it.

The possibility of accommodation is enhanced by the dual nature of bourgeois legal ideology—that it ostensibly protects both property-related interests and an abstract "human" interest in freedom from arbitrary power. The struggle of modern revolutionary movements also seeks, as did the bourgeoisie, to turn elements of the dominant legal ideology to its own purposes. In this section, we examine the duality of bourgeois legal ideology and the jurisprudence of its principal challenger and probable successor, socialist legal ideology.

The American, French, and British constitutions declare that liberty, fairness, and justice *ought to be* protected by a regime's legislature and its judicial tribunals. They establish such principles as freedom of speech and press, the right to a fair trial, and liberty of property and contract. In the American case, certain of these commitments are the product of a revolutionary past, while others were added in the wake of a civil war in which the system of slavery was defeated.

We can speak with some certainty about the origins of these freedoms and the reasons why they developed. The ideals of property and contract were central to the bourgeoisie's rise to power. As Engels wrote:

> All revolutions hitherto have been revolutions to protect one kind of property against another kind of property. They cannot protect the one without violating the other. In the great French Revolution feudal property was sacrificed to save bourgeois property.

When it abolished feudalism, the National Assembly was careful to throw the feudal estates into the hands of the nobility's creditors. This was accomplished by regarding expropriatory decrees as not affecting the interests in feudal property which had been created by the bourgeoisie as means of securing their loans to the nobility. The triumph of the bourgeoisie was marked, however, by a series of contests with the feudal state, carving out here and there areas where its interests would dominate. It was not just at the revolutionary moment of expropriation by a victorious National Assembly, but in the long march from the days of urban communes, that the bourgeoisie enlarged the scope of action of congenial legal ideologies of property, and of the techniques—contractual—of dealing in such interests.

That section of the bourgeoisie which at any time was in revolt—often against a coalition which included those bourgeois who had made their peace with the dominant legal ideology—formulated principles in the interest of its own drive for freedom of property and contract. It demanded freedom of speech and of worship, the better to organize and maintain solidarity in a time when an official church served as a means of social control. Because they were early regarded as conspirators and therefore dangerous—witness the writings of Beaumanoir in 1283 and the inquests into urban revolts beginning in the 1100s—the insurgent bourgeoisie resisted the rigorous and often barbaric systems of criminal justice and took a critical stance toward them.

Two conclusions emerge from the study of the rise of the bourgeoisie: first, legal ideology is the expression of social struggle, and specific elements of a group's legal ideology are the outcome of struggles in which that group is engaged and has been engaged. Second, and of vital importance to present-day jurisprudence and its challenge to bourgeois legal ideology, the system of bourgeois freedom, in its grand outlines, separates into two fairly distinct parts. One reifies into ideology the principles of property and contract upon which the capitalist system rests, and predictably allows for the use of state power to protect those freedoms. The other consists of those legal principles which the bourgeoisie promoted as essential to the political task of winning power. Both sets of principles were justified by reference to the natural-law ideology which was the peculiar emblem of the bourgeoisie at the period of its final move toward state power.

We might expect to find quite different jurisprudential attitudes toward these two trends in bourgeois legal ideology; and this is in fact the case. Theories of property and contract have been reworked and elaborated according to the needs of an increasingly centralized, monopolized system of production. The principles of personal freedom and of fairness to individuals have come under increasing attack from elements within the ruling class as it has shed its revolutionary sentiments and itself been challenged; needless to say, the bourgeoisie has no desire to see itself displaced by a group taking advantage of the very freedoms it once relied upon and championed. The challengers to bourgeois power have been many, but it is now clear that of the many contenders, Marxian socialism, which set the pattern of world revolution in this century, is the most likely to succeed in replacing it.

When Marx described the immanent tendencies of capitalism to irrationality and collapse, the matter was perhaps in doubt. This is no longer the case.

In the following pages, we briefly discuss some of the challenges to bourgeois legal ideology and the issues to which a new jurisprudence of insurgency addresses itself. (A detailed consideration of these issues is outside the scope of this book.)

We are today witnessing a process parallel to the one we sketched in our study of the bourgeoisie's rise to power. Claims for justice are being framed by dissident groups in terms of demands that the dominant legal ideology be interpreted in particular ways. In the domain of contract and property, claims to equal access to national wealth are being presented to tribunals and legislatures. These demands emphasize the antimonopoly, egalitarian values of the bourgeois legal ideology. In the domain of personal liberty, the dissidents cite the dominant legal ideology's claims of freedom of association and procedural fairness to protect their right to organize and proselytize, and to defend themselves against attack from the institutions of state power.

Professor Arthur Kinoy, in an essay published in 1972, analyzed the lawyer's role in this process:

> The lawyer's particular role in the system is to make it look good, to provide at least the appearance of justice, as one Supreme Court opinion so candidly put it. But it is this very role assigned to the lawyer which enables the lawyer to be particularly effective at the present moment in a struggle to safeguard and to preserve these forms as the ruling class moves, out of fear and desperation, to abandon them and destroy them. But this requires flexibility, skill, and above all, understanding on the part of the radical lawyer. He or she must find every opportunity to expose, within the framework of the judicial arena itself, the extraordinary fact that the rulers and their servants in the judicial system, be they prosecutors or judges, are turning upon their own system, are abandoning their own stated rules, designed once in a bygone age to embody the then revolutionary principles of fairness, equality, justice, and liberty.

Kinoy cites the example of Fidel Castro's two involvements with Cuban justice in 1952 and 1953. Two weeks before Fulgencio Batista's coup d'état in 1952, Castro, as a lawyer, filed a petition with the court in Havana demanding that Batista and his accomplices be arrested and charged with violations of the Code of Social Defense for preparing an armed insurrection. The petition was ignored. One year later, after the Batista coup, Castro was taken prisoner in his unsuccessful military raid on the Moncada barracks. At his trial, he spoke in defense of the right of revolution, and recalled that he had attempted to bring to the attention of the authorities in lawful ways the grievances that motivated the Moncada attackers. He said:

> You will answer that on the former occasion the court failed to act because force prevented them from doing so. Well then—confess: this time force will oblige you to condemn me. The first time you were unable to punish the guilty! now you will be compelled to punish the innocent. The maiden of justice twice raped by force!

Castro's subsequent conviction by the military court was a dramatic affirmation that the system of state power had cast aside a portion of its own legal ideology. The claims for justice of that part of the Cuban population that shared Castro's view could no longer be accommodated within the official legal ideology. The period of revolutionary activity that followed saw the construction not only of an armed revolutionary force, but the institution in successively larger areas of the country of an alternative legal ideology backed by this force.

One can find the same progression from accommodation to a dominant legal ideology, to a struggle to shape the ideology to meet the demands of dissidents, to a posture of open revolt in a number of Third World countries, and more recently in Portugal.

In the United States, the Left—black, brown and other Third World as well as white—devoted great energy in the past few decades to forcing the institutions charged with interpreting and applying legal ideology to honor basic guarantees of freedom and fairness. The lawsuit, often in the form of a "test case," was a principal means of struggle. As the prospect dimmed of meeting the Left's claims for justice by such means, and as the state's apparatus of repression dishonored even those rules which were formally and explicitly part of the bourgeoisie's legal ideology, the American Left began to elaborate a critique of bourgeois legal ideology and an alternative to it.

The Left's demands have been directed at both public and private wielders of power, and this fact is central to a critical analysis of bourgeois legal ideology. Public power-wielders are, of course, presumptively subject to constitutional commands relating to, for example, nondiscrimination on the basis of race, and under some circumstances have been held to be under an affirmative obligation to remedy the impact of past discrimination. But this obligation does not generally encompass the duty of invading the public purse to finance affirmative programs of assistance. The constitutional command of equal protection does not, in general, apply to the conduct of private persons, and the "duty" of employers, even corporate employers, is customarily limited to obeying the commands of state nondiscrimination statutes, and such contribution to the public weal as may be made by paying one's taxes. Black organizations have challenged the notion that private wielders of power are not accountable to those whose lives they affect. Their critique of American society as essentially racist in character calls upon the great corporations equally with public authorities to redress the impact of years of discrimination, and to create new economic and political forms to ensure that both public and private aggregations of power are accountable to the victims of power's exercise. These demands rest in part also upon the assertion that American economic and social institutions have reaped the advantages of racism for the past hundred years through the superexploitation of blacks, and that this conduct creates an obligation in a quite specific sense to repay to this generation of blacks the toll exacted from prior generations. The statement that owners of private property have an obligation to use their property accountably rests, therefore, upon qualitatively different implicit premises than a statement that the state must ensure as a matter of constitutional principle that its power is used in a nondiscriminatory manner when it influences or supports the acts of private proprietors.

Rejection of the notion that the "privateness " of property insulates it from claims that it be used responsibly was accompanied by recognition that state power stands presumptively behind all private owners' desires to do as they wish with that which is "his" or "hers," a presumption overcome only by specific and limited legislative and judicial declarations restraining the alienation or use of one's "own" property. Capitalists, as we have seen, exercise enormous power. Behind the private-law claim of property stands an impressive array of police and other public force to preserve to them what is "theirs." Both northern and southern blacks in the movement for social change picture the state, therefore, not as neutral arbiter of contending social forces, but as protector of those who possess the ostensibly private means of exploitation and repression. For this reason, their struggle reveals at first an alliance with the forces of "state," or positive, law, and then a growing realization that a demand for "justice for blacks" is inherently revolutionary in today's America.

We could cite many examples of confrontation between bourgeois legal ideology as administered today and the insistent demands of various dissidents: student and youth groups, young workers in urban areas; and so on.

The details may vary, but the picture remains the same: the system of organization of production for private profit is unable to meet the needs of the people, and the legal ideology of the dominant group is unable to accommodate their demands for freedom and fairness. Few of these movements for change are class conscious or class-based, and we do not suggest that their struggles are more than the precursor of class conflict. As with the bourgeois challenge to feudalism, consciousness may be expected to develop slowly, in the process of confronting the legal ideology of the dominant class.

The pace and nature of change in the United States is greatly influenced by events taking place outside the United States, particularly in the Third World. As former colonial possessions begin to control the export of their own raw material, the threat of economic crisis increases in the more "advanced" countries. In these countries, economic difficulties—unemployment and inflation—make it more difficult for the holders of state power to meet—to buy off—the demands of dissidents. It is in this sense that the fight against American imperialism—and its economic domination of Third World countries—is crucial to the struggle at home.

This heightened tension produces for modern jurisprudents the contradictions we discussed earlier for early bourgeois jurisprudents. Litigating lawyers—jurisprudents in battle dress—begin to draw careful distinctions. While the legal obligations of workers and owners are defined by the dominant ideology, lawyers attempt to change and adapt them, to adjust differences without disturbing the integrity of the ideological system as a whole. Real improvements in the lives of ordinary people come about through these changes: consumer credit legislation to prevent gouging and unfair practices; fair housing legislation; equal employment projects mandating compensatory treatment for blacks, Chicanos, and women. They come about because jurisprudents penetrate the legal ideology and its norms and expose the interests they protect, thus clarifying and helping to justify the demand that public law be changed to curb the domain of the "freedom" of contract. In the battle for the freedoms of speech and association, and for due process of law, the lawyer demands that constitutional principle be honored and constitutional promises be kept.

In both realms, the jurisprudent carefully studies the legal ideology of the dominant group, taking into account its historical origins in order to understand the basis of particular rules and systems. He or she identifies specific contradictions between the interests of the dominant group and its ideology, and turns these to the advantage of those demanding social change. At the same time, as Kinoy points out, in order not to become merely a mouthpiece for the dominant ideology—maintaining the façade that any right worth having can be won within it—the lawyer points out the ways in which the dominant group departs from its own ideology.

But he or she does more than this. Lawyers truly committed to social change will follow the example of their predecessors in the bourgeois revolution and take a clearly revolutionary position. They will study and counsel "maxims of prudence" in the sense we described earlier, to blunt the impact of obdurate state power upon their clients' political activities. More important, they will work with their clients to formulate an alternative legal ideology.

The decision to side with the movement for social change may resolve contradictions in the interior being but those in the realm of social action remain and are, indeed, intensified. This is particularly true for jurisprudents. The ideology that the dissidents collectively elaborate and individually accept when they move to an insurgent position is what Weber called a "convention," in the sense that it governs the conduct of the group. It is, however, more than that: it embodies the claims for justice that the group makes upon the dominant legal ideology, and it begins to describe the principles of law that will be put into practice when and if the group achieves state power.

The kind of society you get after a revolution is the kind you deserve, its legal ideology built upon the foundations of that which preceded it and embodying the principles by which the group that wanted change lived when it was contending for power. So in today's revolutionary movements in the West, racism, sexism, bureaucratization, establishing mutual love and trust—all the problems that a movement for change must regulate in its internal affairs—must be dealt with as though the principles of decision were to be those which will govern an entire society at some future time. For in reality, and subject always to the possibility of the need for change and correction of mistakes, this will indeed be the case. The wiser and more observant jurisprudents will know these things as they solve, each on its own terms, the contradictions which their profession imposes upon them. They are perhaps aided in knowing that these same problems have been faced by others of their number in the service of an earlier revolution whose time, we trust, is about to pass. As Shelley wrote in his introduction to *Prometheus Unbound*: "The cloud of mind is discharging its collective lightning, and the equilibrium between institutions and opinions is now restoring, or about to be restored."

AFTERWORD

LEGAL IDEOLOGY TODAY

The twenty-three years since *Law and the Rise of Capitalism* have witnessed events that call for a renewed analysis of the relationship between legal ideology and insurgency—what I termed the jurisprudence of insurgency. Some account of the changing context of radical legal practice is needed, to provide a basis on which the historical analysis presented in this book can be expanded and, if need be, modified.

Events during recent decades cannot be fitted into any uniform pattern. In Chile, a coalition government led by Socialist Party member Salvador Allende was brought down in 1973 by a military coup. In the wake of the coup, a military junta enforced its rule by repression, disappearances, and murder. Challenges to the junta's power focused attention on significant issues of international human rights law. This culminated in the arrest of Chilean junta leader Augusto Pinochet and path-breaking judicial decisions that he is subject to trial for human rights abuses committed during the junta's reign.

In South Africa, a mass movement compelled the release from prison of Nelson Mandela and the dismantling of apartheid, and was seeking ways to satisfy long-suppressed claims for justice by the majority of South Africa's people.

In Eastern Europe and the former Soviet Union, a legal and governmental system that surrounded socialist economic institutions seemed to crumble overnight, to be supplanted by legal ideologies that tolerated, perhaps encouraged, greed, racism, and irredentism. Yet in the ensuing years, popular movements embracing a socialist ideology began to gain ground as people saw the consequences of the "free market." I could cite other examples of ferment in which legal ideology continues to play a major role—for example, in Palestine, Namibia and Haiti. Most of the world lives in poverty. The economic "boom time" of the metropolitan countries does not even reach down to improve standards for huge numbers of these countries' own residents. This situation cannot continue indefinitely, because its victims will not permit it to do so.

Yet, one cannot overlook the conservative trend in American law, with diminishing protection for the economic and political rights of people of color, and assaults upon the rights of the accused in the criminal justice system. Because people of color are disproportionately caught up in the criminal justice system, such assaults have the dual effect of enhancing state power generally and of legitimizing racism. Two egregious examples of such reasoning, which I discuss later, are the Supreme Court's holdings that "money is first-amendment protected speech," and that the promises of racial justice in the Fourteenth Amendment may be turned on their head to protect white privilege. To put it another way, we know that bourgeois declarations of rights are double-edged.

All of these episodes seem to illustrate the fragility of legal ideology and legal institutions, in the sense that what seemed so solid and sure turns out to be so vulnerable. South African scholar and jurist Albie Sachs has written, "All social revolutions are impossible, until they happen; then they become inevitable." One might say that most great social changes are impossible, until they happen. Great changes seem impossible because people mistakenly reify legal ideology. They fail, as Paul Sweezy has reminded us, to see "the present as history." People are constantly reinterpreting legal ideology, and demanding of the state that it respect certain claims for justice that are presented as demands that legal ideology be construed and applied in a certain way. In this process of struggle, people, individually and in groups, become aware that a given legal ideology contains two kinds of rules: those that entrench and advance the prevailing system of social relations, and those that purport to embody neutral or even progressive principles.

So legal ideology is twice fragile. First, its forms may be made to accept new content, to meet demands for justice. There is value to struggle that seeks to maximize well-being within the existing social system.

Second, to the extent that citizens test the limits of an existing and dominant legal ideology, a movement for change begins to develop a new ideology within the framework of the old, waiting for a shift in the institutions of state power. When that shift comes, it may seem sudden, so that what yesterday seemed so solid and secure today seems to crumble at a touch. Of course both perceptions—of solidity and of fragility—are ahistorical, for change is but the expression of a dialectical process, as is evident from the historical analysis presented in this book. This seeming fragility is key to understanding both the power of expressing claims for justice in terms of legal ideology and the limits on struggle conducted in a legal forum.

Can this description be matched with the turbulent and fast-changing conditions of this decade? I think so, although many serious questions may justly be raised. The collapse of the former Soviet Union led many observers to conclude that a Marxist theory of history, as well as a particular form of social organization, had failed. As time has gone by, that swift conclusion, whether expressed with a grimace or a smile, has become questionable. In fact, the changes in Eastern Europe, like those elsewhere, are part of a dialectical process in which sometimes one end of a contradiction is emphasized, and sometimes another.

It is true that in the United States today we have seen ostensibly neutral legal rules distorted to serve dominant interests and progressive principles viewed through the prism of bourgeois interest. Distressingly, political leaders have rejected principles of international human rights as simply being irrelevant to the actions of the world's remaining superpower.

Despite this reality, the significance of legal ideology is demonstrated in case after case. All criminal cases, indeed all lawsuits, involve decisions about boundaries in some sense of that word. Did the defendant do the act, or not? The advocate marshals evidence and argument to convince the jury to decide in a particular way.

The most effective and moving advocacy, however, deals with boundaries between certain types of fundamental values and the power of the state to punish. This is so because, to a greater or lesser degree, jurors have internalized the legal ideology of bourgeois democracy, including principles of freedom and fairness. Judges contribute to the importance of boundary exploration to the extent that they echo these values and instruct the jury about them.

Take an "ordinary" criminal case: A defense lawyer will seek not only to "argue the facts," but to put the jury's factual decision in the context of "reasonable doubt," and if possible, she will allude to the government's obligation to conduct its investigation fairly. When she argues in this vein, she is trying to make the jury realize that a guilty verdict is not simply a reflection of a decision about "facts," but rather an exercise in defining a constitutional right: the right not to be convicted save upon reliable and properly obtained evidence that demonstrates guilt beyond a reasonable doubt. And, if the jurors have a reasonable doubt, they are reminded that another fundamental value requires them to acquit.

In case after case, I have seen the jurors' own sense of justice mediating the insistent demands of state power. I have even seen judges struggling to play the relatively neutral role assigned to them in bourgeois legal ideology. To deny that such victories are possible is as irresponsible as it would be to claim that they tell us everything we need to know about the bourgeois state.

But in arguing that law matters, we need to guard against at least three myths which are often associated with it. The first is the myth of the benign state (that the state can be neutral and still do its job, any job). The second is the myth of neutral principles, that is, that the state can be counted on to apply rules consistently toward the ruling class and the ruled. This entire book is refutation of that myth, and this Afterword adds further evidence. The third is the myth of legal process, the idea that courts are the sole or principal arena of meaningful change. In fact, courts respond only when claims for justice are demonstrably part of a broader people's movement. In order to make effective use of the law, we need to act always on the basis of a clear understanding of the decisive features of the legal ideology of our time.

In this respect, an important development during recent decades has been the growth of an increasingly broad, although still contested, consensus that there exists a legal ideology of human rights, independent of the will of any given state or group of states. One might, carelessly and inaccurately, think of this as a kind of "natural law" development, a purely idealistic exercise that is neither verifiable nor enforceable. In fact, the developing international human rights consensus arises from the actual experiences of people and is increasingly enforceable in measurable ways. Moreover, this consensus represents a collective "claim for justice"—one element of a transnational ideology that motivates struggles for change.

The major constituents of this consensus are:

1) reaffirmation of the progressive elements of bourgeois legal ideology, such as respect for the opinions of others, restraint of arbitrary state power, prohibition of arbitrary discrimination, and the guarantee of access to impartial tribunals to resolve disputes;

2) recognition of prohibitions of genocide, racism, and other crimes against humanity, enforceable even against an assertion that the alleged offender was acting under superior orders or in pursuit of a policy of state power;

3) recognition of "second generation" rights of individuals—with correlative duties imposed on the state—to education, employment, and shelter;

4) recognition, although more tentative at this point, of "third generation" rights to environmental protection, development and social identity. Formulating these rights into discrete claims for justice remains a principal task of Third World societies.

If I am correct in saying that these are decisive features of legal ideology today, the struggle over their content and application is by definition transnational. This leads us to an examination of the historical emergence of human rights within the broader field of international law.

HUMAN RIGHTS, THE NATION-STATE, AND INTERNATIONAL LAW: FROM GROTIUS TO BENTHAM

Bourgeois victories were accomplished in the context of nation-states, in which state power is, by definition, limited as to area and population. So a victory that installed bourgeois legal ideology as state legal ideology—that is, as law—was confined within given borders. Yet, as we have seen, the bourgeoisie claimed a global reach for its ideology. And, as we have also seen, the basic norms of bourgeois legal ideology, are, in their most abstract form, of a universal character. In Chapter 18, we saw the use of purportedly universal themes in the works of Domat, Loyseau, and Loisel. The work of Lord Coke in England, discussed in Chapter 19, illustrates the same tendencies. These writers were, however, concerned mainly with transnational principles of so-called private law: the principles of obligation and property that governed commercial transactions. To the extent they considered public law, they addressed mainly the proper relation of their own sovereigns to the people within a given nation-state.

In the same period, however, other writers were also formulating universal theories of legal ideology that more broadly addressed issues of public international law. Such writers considered the proper relation of sovereigns to one another, but also posited universal norms that bound even sovereigns in their treatment of individuals. Today's legal ideology of human rights can be traced back to this context.

This ideology had its beginnings in the contradictory aspirations of bourgeois legal ideology on the eve of the bourgeois revolutions in Europe. Bourgeois legal ideology found both historical and divine support for its proclaimed universals of contract and property right. Yet, the bourgeoisie had come to recognize that its desire to see these allegedly universal principles put into practical application depended on the existence of a state apparatus that would enforce them. Legitimating these claims in this way meant—in that time and place—securing their adoption as the legal ideology of a nation-state in which the bourgeoisie controlled state power.

Yet therein lay a serious contradiction—once thus codified, the principles were no longer universal, they were simply the law of a particular place. They were not principles of a transnational class, but rules established to protect a particular group. That group needed protection against its erstwhile feudal opponents, and against those within the nation-state whose interests were in opposition to the newly victorious bourgeoisie. Among the latter were the peasants forcibly displaced from the land in order to create an urban work force, and to destroy customary barriers to the unfettered right of property by eliminating peasants' use-rights.

But the bourgeoisie of one nation-state also looked to the state for protection against the bourgeoisie of other states. The contradictions between different national groupings triumphed over their common interest in establishing and defending transnational principles favorable to commerce.

These contradictions had, of course, begun to appear even as the bourgeoisie was beginning to form alliances with royal power. Colonial conflicts began shortly after the voyages of discovery and conquest in the fifteenth century, and international conflict was of course a continuous feature of European life.

By 1600, the Spanish and Portuguese (united at that time under a single monarch) had colonized large parts of the Americas, and monopolized the rich trade between Europe and Asia around the Cape of Good Hope. The King of Spain and Portugal claimed sovereignty (awarded originally by the Pope) over large expanses of the seas, and therefore the right to interdict and seize, or to tax and license, vessels flying other flags. Spain claimed the Pacific Ocean and the Gulf of Mexico, and Portugal the Atlantic south of Morocco and the Indian Ocean. The Dutch, having thwarted the reconquest of their homeland by the Hapsburg monarch of Spain and Portugal (with whom they were still at war), began to send fleets around the Cape of Good Hope to tap the rich trade of the Indies. The fleets returned with stupendous cargoes, bringing great wealth to the investors who had sent them out. England and France had just made peace with the Spanish King, and pressure was building upon the Dutch to do likewise. But the ministers of the Spanish King insisted most vehemently on the right to control trade in the oceans over which he claimed sovereignty, and the issue was certain to be at the heart of peace negotiations between the Dutch and the Hapsburgs. Into this controversy, and on behalf of the Dutch East India Company, strode young Hugo Grotius, with a tract entitled *Mare Liberum*, or "Freedom of the Seas," and subtitled, "The Right which Belongs to the Dutch to Take Part in the East Indian Trade."

Grotius's tract was published in Leiden in 1609 (the year that the Dutch first negotiated a truce with Spain that recognized their independence), but not conclusively attributed to him for centuries. Grotius' argument was that the seas cannot by their nature be anyone's property, nor subject to anyone's sovereign power. By amassing authorities from ancient times down to his own day, Grotius argued that the seas—beyond a narrow territorial area adjacent to a sovereign's land-based holdings—were never subject to capture or to acquisition by possession. Even adjacent seas were subject to a right of free passage. Grotius' tract was thus progressive in that it opposed the early colonial powers dividing up the waters as well as the land, and argued on the basis of transnational universal norms.

As a young lawyer, Grotius was involved in litigation as lawyer for the Dutch East India Company, in a celebrated case concerning capture of a Portuguese vessel in the Indian Ocean by a Dutch vessel. The case involved significant questions under the law of nations, in a time of colonial conflict between various seaborne powers. From this early experience, Grotius took an active interest first in the law of the sea and then in the larger questions to which his masterwork, *Of the Law of War and Peace*, is dedicated. In this work, which first appeared in 1625, Grotius brought together diverse streams of authority in a single treatise that purported to state universal principles applicable not only within states but among them. It was an effort to restate a general theory of law beginning with the basic question whether "law" as such could be said to exist, and what was its essential nature and function. That is, Grotius well understood the operation of state power within nation-states, but insisted that the exercise of such power was mediated by norms originating outside of the state.

While Grotius took aim (anonymously) at the Portuguese claims to sovereignty over the Indian Ocean, he struck a target of equal economic importance closer to home. The North Sea was the site of the great herring fishery, the economic base of Dutch prosperity. The Dutch claimed the right not only to trade anywhere, but, of equal importance, to fish anywhere (including off the coast of Scotland and England). As long as Scotland was independent and of little significance as a naval power, the Dutch could ignore its claims. But in 1603 James VI of Scotland became, in addition, James I of England.

The year 1609 also marked the start of a determined British campaign to license boats engaged in the herring fishery, the great majority of which were Dutch. John Selden, a lawyer's lawyer and in domestic English constitutional matters a determined opponent of the Stuart monarchs, took on the job of crafting the argument for the British case in the fisheries dispute.

Selden's celebrated response to *Mare Liberum* (and Selden had no doubt as to the identity of Grotius as the anonymous author) was entitled *Mare Clausum*, or "Closed Seas," written first in 1619, though the version known to us was not published until 1635 when the fisheries issue was again a hot dispute.

Selden argued, on behalf of the English Crown, "that the sea, by the law or nature or nations, is not common to all men, but capable of private dominion or property as well as the land," and "that the King of Great Britain is lord of the sea flowing about, as an inseparable and perpetual appendant of the British Empire." That is, Selden argued that just as land can become subjected to the property norm discussed in Chapter 16 by purchase or conquest, so can the seas. Selden's argument was yet more historical than that of Grotius, detailing the actual domination of largely enclosed seas—like the North Sea—such as that of the Adriatic by Venice, the Baltic by the Scandinavian states, and back to the first historical dominion of the seas, the Minoan Cretan domination of the eastern Mediterranean. Notably Selden ignored the question of the unenclosed ocean, for the English also had a prosperous East Indies Company.

Grotius never answered Selden. By the time of the 1635 publication of *Mare Clausum* he was in the employ of Sweden, which claimed sovereignty over the Baltic. It is not necessary to trace the details of the debate in any detail. Selden's views did not prevail overall, even in Great Britain. The principles of equality of states and of freedom of the seas were an integral part of victorious bourgeois legal ideology, and so the analogy to the property norm that was employed to justify colonization was deemed irrelevant.

Grotius' major work, *Of the Law of War and Peace*, was the first systematic attempt to take account of the conflicts between universal principle and narrow state interest based on the accepted categories of private law, and to harmonize the asserted universality of bourgeois legal ideology with the particularism of nation-states. If we are to grasp the subsequent development of this relation of universal aspiration and nationally specific jurisdiction, it is worth reconstructing his argument more fully. His work differed from legal theorists such as Domat by the breadth of his discussion: He purported to deal with the general principles that transcended national boundaries and the barriers between fields of law. He differed from political philosophers such as Hobbes, Locke, and Montesquieu by going well beyond political theory to set out with precision the way in which state power should be organized and administered. He is the first eminent figure in an unbroken line of jurists whose work has dominated transnational law. The influence of Grotius and his followers is particularly marked because *opinio juris*, the opinion of jurists, is regarded as persuasive authority before international tribunals.

Grotius' work is ostensibly devoted to "the law of nations," "the body of law which is maintained between states," rather than to domestic law or the "natural" basis of law in general. Yet the structure of his argument assumes the validity of Roman-law-based concepts of legal ideology, and the text itself contains detailed consideration of property, contract, and penal law in a domestic law setting. He understood that the nation-state was becoming the dominant form of political organization in Europe, and sought a basis from which to argue that even national sovereigns were subject to overarching norms of conduct respecting the earth and the human condition.

Grotius begins by asking whether "law" exists, as distinct from a reflexive series of principles based upon a supposed human tendency to pursue self-interest. He answers "yes," based upon two sets of arguments. One of these arguments is essentially religious—law exists because God wills it so, and because God has created people with an innate sense of social life, with the gift of speech to express themselves, and with an innate sense of justice that tempers self-interest.

This branch of the argument is not, however, Grotius' first or main justification. He denies that "every animal is impelled by nature to seek only its own good," based on the evidence of social organization that he observes. That is, "even if we should concede . . . that there is no God, one can observe that people have a strong bent towards social life," the power of speech, and "a power of discrimination which enables [them] to decide what things are agreeable or harmful (as to both things present and things to come)." He opposes this view to that of philosophers who argued that law is only a set of arbitrary principles, and that for any such principle an opposite one can as easily be invented and defended. As he acknowledges, this way of arriving at conclusions owes much to the work of Aristotle.

Grotius' argument suggests that people have these tendencies and capacities, yet he does not assert that these are innate and eternal. That is, although he does not explicitly say it, his argument is consistent with the fact that social existence, speech, and a power to make ideological choices are themselves the products of a certain stage of human development. As he says, "History in relation to our subject is useful in two ways: it supplies both illustrations and judgments."

Grotius underscores the historical character of his argument by noting the sources of secular authority on which he relies, to varying extents, in deriving the principles of Roman law on which his work is largely based. He places "great weight" upon the codification of Justinian and related writings from antiquity. Of the twelfth and thirteenth century commentators upon the Roman texts, whose explications were often supplemented with references to canon law principles, Grotius says they paid "no heed to divine law or to ancient history," and were hampered by a lack of historical knowledge and understanding. He also rejects those more contemporary writers who "confine themselves within the limits of Roman law."

Grotius does, however, acknowledge that French legal scholars such as Bodin—upon whom Loyseau relied—have valuable insights because they "have tried rather to introduce history into their study of laws." In short, Grotius claimed to stand at a vantage point of recorded history, and to have derived from that history, as well as from the teaching of his religious faith, the fundamental lessons of world social order. His method resembles that of Lord Coke, but takes a broader perspective than a single country. Grotius argues that "the source of law properly so called" is the maintenance of a social order "consonant with human intelligence," and that this implies "abstaining from that which is another's, the restoration to another of anything of his which we may have, together with any gain we have received from it; the obligation to fulfill promises, and making good of a loss incurred through our own fault, and the inflicting of penalties upon me according to their deserts." There is a distinctly non-idealistic edge to this mode of argument. Grotius is seeking to justify ostensibly moral choices in terms that permit rational argument.

Grotius insists that rules of law and justice are applicable among nations as well as within nations. Indeed, he says, "Least of all should that be admitted which some people imagine, that in war all laws are in abeyance." That is, there is a law of nations that should be observed in times of war and peace, contrary even to that maxim attributed to Cicero—*silent enim leges inter arma*, in time of war the laws are silent. Much of *Of the Law of War and Peace* deals with the obligations of states in time of war, with respect to such things as the right of capturing enemy vessels, the conditions under which war may be undertaken, and the limits on permissible hostilities, for example, against noncombatants.

The influence of Grotius and those who followed him was at its height toward the end of the 1700s. We can now begin to see how the division into nation-states helped to submerge the idea of "human" rights, that is, of claims for justice based on "dialectical arguments that have their roots in experience, to a definite view of human flourishing and good human functioning," that is, upon the view that humans have needs for such things as political rights, money, shelter, and respect. The nation-state, by claiming the right to a monopoly of force within its borders, as extended by its colonial claims, asserted that the only valid claims for such things were those that it recognized as such.

This departure from the theory of universal and natural right was not completely surprising. Although Grotius traced the details, Jean Bodin had foretold it in his 1576 treatise on sovereignty, arguing that "all men are linked to one another and participate marvelously in the universal Republic," while at the same time acknowledging that this "empire of reason" has been weakened in such a way that "one cannot know how to bring together all nations in one single republic." Instead their relations are governed by "arms and treaties."

From here we can trace the ways in which Grotius' universal norms were traduced by the victorious bourgeoisie. This discussion is a necessary prelude to showing how the human rights movements of our own day seek to transcend such contradictions in a new synthesis of new and old ideology.

The political victory of the bourgeoisie was embodied in the nation-state, a particular constellation of political power. The nation-state, in its typical bourgeois form, perpetuated a legal ideology based on the ostensibly universal principles of freedom that were part of the bourgeois program. In seeking to displace predecessor forms of state power, bourgeois ideologists proclaimed the theory that rights "belong" to each person, and that the content of this packet of rights may be deduced from reason. Bourgeois legal scholars continued to reassert such claims as a matter of rhetoric, even after the bourgeois state had undermined them as a matter of fact.

Bourgeois legal ideology began, as we have seen, as transnational: in the service of a class whose activities did not respect frontiers. There is not now, and has not been, any reason why a market should be coterminous with a political frontier. To take a modern example, today's multinational corporations use their simultaneous presence in many countries to outflank the effort of any individual sovereign to control their fraud, pollution, and exploitation. In the earliest centuries of merchant activity, the bourgeoisie accepted political frontiers as efficient mechanisms for obtaining access to state power. Their shifting alliances with temporal and ecclesiastical authorities show just how little they scrupled over the particular form of state power with which they were allied. Only in later centuries did bourgeois political economy unite political and economic liberty into a consistent theory. The nation-state was a logical expression of that theory. It was an instrument to crush the bourgeoisie's opponents by using the state's monopoly of organized violence.

But what of this idea of individual self-realization, of "natural rights," and of a transcendent natural law or "right reason" justification for such a view? In the domestic realm, these principles provided a basis for claims for justice against state power, of which the American struggles for civil rights and civil liberties are a modern example. Such claims share a characteristic with those made by the bourgeoisie as it battled for access to state power, and that is their duality: On the one hand, these claims are based on principles of justice deduced from principles that are independent of any given arrangement of state power. On the other hand, these claims are addressed to the wielders of state power, and claimed to be guaranteed by the dominant legal ideology; in this form, the claims for justice might be phrased as arguments about "legal rights."

The claim of bourgeois ideologists, at least from Grotius' time forward, was that individuals possess rights as a consequence of simply "being," or could be considered by historical materialist arguments as entitled to justice, personal security, and kindred benefits. To put matters in older language, there was a true "*jus gentium*," in the literal sense of those words, a "law of all peoples."

The bourgeois nation-states moved quickly to dispel any such theory. In the late eighteenth century, Sir William Blackstone, in his influential *Commentaries on the Laws of England*, had spoken of the "law of nations" as

> a system of rules, deducible by natural reason, and established by universal consent among the civilized inhabitants of the world; in order to decide all disputes, to regulate all ceremonies and civilities, and to ensure the observance of justice and good faith, in that intercourse which must frequently occur between two or more independent states, and the individuals belonging to each.

For Blackstone, the "law of nations" included provisions relating to individual rights, at least with respect to mercantile transactions and the rights of hostages. Moreover, Blackstone wrote that the law of nations had been incorporated into the law of England, and was therefore part of "the law of the land," to be applied by English courts in deciding cases between individuals. That is, there were certain transcendent norms that a legitimate sovereign was bound to respect.

In a sense, Blackstone's definition was true when he wrote it, and continued to be true. British courts did apply general principles of transnational law in deciding certain private law questions, and in admiralty cases, as did courts of most other countries. In the nineteenth century, judges and legal scholars continued to think of mercantile law principles as transnational in character, and to look to the old merchant law sources.

But the dominant themes of nineteenth century legal writing were that the nation-state was the exclusive source of rights, and that any transnational or supranational rules were the product of consent given by treaty or custom. In 1776, the English legal philosopher Jeremy Bentham penned an influential statement of this view. Indeed, Bentham is credited with having coined the word "international," in discussing the law of nations in his book *Principles of Morals and Legislation*. Two brief passages from that book summarize Bentham's view, which was also the dominant theme of international law for more than a century. Bentham acknowledged that the word "international" was "a new one; though, it is hoped, sufficiently analogous and intelligible" to describe "in a more significant way, the branch of the law which goes commonly under the name of the law of nations."

Bentham makes his point again by saying that dealings between individuals from different states are a matter of the internal law of one or the other of those states, as indeed are dealings between sovereigns in their private capacity. Then, he says, "[t]here remain then the mutual transactions between sovereigns as such, for the subject of that branch of jurisprudence which may be properly and exclusively termed international."

Lest one mistake Bentham's intention, one can look at the writings of d'Aguesseau on which he relies. D'Aguesseau wrote that the terms "law of nations," "law of all peoples," and "*jus gentium*" were misleading, for they did not describe the legal relationships involved. One should rather speak of "law among peoples," because the legal relationships were between nation and nation, rather than involving the rights of individuals as such.

Bentham had prefigured his views in an essay he wrote between 1774 and 1776, criticizing lectures given at Oxford by Sir William Blackstone, whose *Commentaries on the Laws of England* were part of English and American lawyers' staple diet. The young Bentham concluded that, in great measure, the "law of nations" "isn't law at all." In a further discussion of Blackstone's views, John Lind, Bentham's collaborator in a systematic critique of Blackstone, wrote in a passage reviewed and probably approved by Bentham:

> The fact is, the term, law of nations, however allowable in common conversation, should never find a place in a philosophical discussion of law: and that for this plain reason, that nations have no common superior upon earth, from whom they can receive a law. 'Tis strange how this confusion of terms disfigures even arguments which would otherwise have merit. Even Montesquieu falls into the same error as our Author [Blackstone] in confounding compacts and principles with Laws. There is a difference, however: the mistakes of Montesquieu are the mistakes of a man of genius: whilst those of our Author speak only of the servile copyist.

The theory of "international law" made clear that sovereigns were arbiters of their own conduct within their borders, and that no individual had rights against any sovereign except as the sovereign should decide to accord. Relations among sovereigns were to be regulated by treaties and other instruments, by observance of customary law norms based on tacit consent of states as shown by their consistent practice, and by warfare as a sanction or as an instrument of policy.

In such a system, there was no basis for speaking of "international human rights" except as any particular sovereign chose to interpret and apply them. As we shall see, this method of analysis effectively fettered all progress toward enforcing rights within the framework of bourgeois legal institutions, as that framework was established by the great powers that had amassed colonial empires

U.S. CONSTITUTIONALISM AND ITS ANOMALIES

Let us examine these principles in operation, first to see their details, and then to discuss the sovereign behavior they were used to justify. The most dramatic example was the international concern about slavery. The American

Constitution of 1787 had expressly recognized the slave-owners' interests. The federal Congress was forbidden by article 1, section 9 from interfering with the slave trade until 1808. Article 4, section 2, in effect obliged each state to deliver fugitive slaves, at least absent federal legislation. And in article 1, section 2, slaves and Indians were counted as three-fifths of a person.

While federal fugitive slave laws persisted until the Civil War, despite efforts by some states to prevent their enforcement, United States law after 1808 forbade American citizens from engaging in the slave trade and even termed such action piracy. The slave trade had also been condemned by a number of other countries. There matters stood in 1825, when the United States Supreme Court decided a case called the *Antelope*, that being the name of a slave-carrying ship found off the Georgia coast and brought into port by a U.S. naval vessel.

On board were 225 Africans who had been captured for sale as slaves. Some of these men and women had originally been taken from the shores of Africa by Spanish and Portuguese slave traders. The Supreme Court convened to decide who, if anyone, had a property right to these people.

The Spanish and Portuguese consuls argued that their respective countries should receive the slaves. For the slaves, it was argued that the slave trade was an offense to the law of nations and that they should be freed. After all, the United States, while maintaining the institution of slavery, had declared the slave trade as such to be "contrary to the principles of humanity and justice," that is, against universal principles binding on all states. Great Britain had also forbidden slavery and the slave trade, after a public campaign that exposed its horrors.

The Supreme Court was not moved by these arguments. Chief Justice Marshall's decision shows just how far the Bentham view expressed the tenor of bourgeois thought. Marshall began by noting that the case presented "the sacred rights of liberty and of property . . . in conflict with each other"—the slaves' liberty and the slave traders' property. Having said that, Marshall —a Virginia slave-owner—cautioned that "the Court must not yield to feelings which might seduce it from the path of duty."

Marshall conceded that "the opinion is extensively, if not universally entertained, that this unnatural traffic ought to be suppressed." In addition, one could turn to ancient texts and find condemnation of slavery save in limited circumstances such as the aftermath of war. Indeed, the institution was itself at war with some fundamental premises of capitalist social relations. Yet Spain and Portugal had continued the trade.

From all of this, Marshall concluded:

> That the course of opinion on the slave trade should be unsettled, ought to excite no surprise. The Christian and civilized nations of the world, with which we have most intercourse, have all been engaged in it. However abhorrent this traffic may be to a mind whose original feelings are not blunted by familiarity with the practice, it has been sanctioned in modern times by the laws of all nations who possess distant colonies, each of whom has engaged in it as a common commercial business which no other could rightly interrupt. It has claimed all the sanction which could be derived from long usage and general acquiescence. That trade could not be considered as contrary to the law of nations which was authorized and protected by the laws of all commercial nations; the right to carry on which was claimed by each, and allowed by each.

Marshall's argument thus rejected the overwhelming public outcry against the slave trade, the developing consensus among sovereign states that it was wrong, and the mounting evidence of its fundamental inhumanity. He even acknowledged that slavery was "contrary to the law of nature."

He also ignored that fact that those states that had abolished the slave trade had termed it "piracy." Piracy was, by the eighteenth century, generally regarded not simply as a crime against the country whose ships were attacked and the people and goods on board. It was a crime against all humanity. Hence, any nation who acquired jurisdiction of a pirate might, indeed was obliged to, try him for that crime regardless of the nationality of the pirate's victims. In an important precedent for our own day, piracy was a crime as to which there was "universal jurisdiction." As to most crimes, a nation-state would try an offender only if the offense was committed in its territory, or by or against its nationals.

Marshall turned away from this impressive body of evidence. Rather, he found "international law" in the past practices of "Christian and civilized," that is bourgeois, states, and in the fact that a few of those states still continued the trade. In his view, all states are equal. "It results from this equality, that no one can rightfully impose a rule on another. Each legislates for itself, but its legislation can operate on itself alone. . . . [T]his trade, in which all have participated, must remain lawful to those who cannot be induced to relinquish it."

Under this view, international law is a race to the bottom. Whatever discredited practice may persist in one state cannot be contradicted by any other state. Marshall extended this principle so far that even in the United States, where the slave trade was a crime, the Supreme Court yielded to the legal rules of Spain and Portugal. This is Bentham's theory with a vengeance.

In addition, Marshall's theory turns Grotius' theory on its head. Universal principles, said Grotius, dictate freedom of the seas. Grotius would have argued that the same universal principles forbid the form of chattel slavery practiced by the United States, Spain, and Portugal—or at least that a developing international consensus could establish such principles. For Marshall, however, freedom of the seas meant the freedom of each seaborne power to do as it wishes, based on a particularistic idea of individual national sovereignty.

Only when Spain had itself abolished the slave trade, and declared all slaves setting foot on Spanish territory to be free, was the Supreme Court able to hold that slaves captured by Spanish traders had the right to be free.

Another nineteenth century "international law" issue of note concerned the status of Native Americans. When European settlers arrived in the Western Hemisphere, they encountered groups of Native Americans organized into civil societies. The relations between the invaders and the native peoples have been chronicled. I wish simply to signal the kind of legal ideology that United States courts constructed to characterize those relations.

The respective rights of occupiers and natives were established in a series of treaties. The tribes were to retain sovereignty over their land and people, as there defined. In a series of decisions, again under the leadership of Chief Justice John Marshall, the Supreme Court eviscerated treaty rights and relegated tribal sovereignty to the status of historical curiosity.

In 1823, the Supreme Court decided *Johnson v. McIntosh*, a case involving disputed title to land. One party claimed through deeds given by the Piankeshaw tribe during the Revolutionary War era. The other party claimed under a deed issued by the United States government, after the war and after the government had forced the Piankeshaw off the land.

Chief Justice Marshall again sought a principle of "international law" and found it in something called "the doctrine of discovery." Under this doctrine, the occupying European powers acquired "the exclusive right to extinguish the Indian title of occupancy, either by purchase or by conquest." Thus, the Native Americans did not have title to their land, such that they could sell or otherwise dispose of it as they chose. They could validly convey it only to the occupying power.

This invented principle of international law, an "exception" to the principle expressed in the *Antelope* that nation-states had equal rights, has several interesting aspects. First, it is based on the consensus of colonial powers. Unlike the slave trade rules, there is no dissent among the metropolitan countries. Here then is a reaffirmation that international law is not only based on consent but that the only relevant givers of consent are bourgeois states. Neither the opinions of individuals, nor of other nations, matter.

Second, the doctrine of discovery, considered as a part of legal ideology, reflects the bourgeois property norm. The Native Americans occupied and used land; they did not "own" it in the bourgeois fashion. They were in this sense like persons who exercise customary use rights. As we saw in Chapters 15, 16, and 21, the rising bourgeoisie had sundered all claims to customary rights of use in favor of establishing the exclusive right to possess and use property. Indeed, in Native American legal ideology, the idea that any person or group of people could "own" a portion of the earth was thought absurd. Considered in this way, the fate of Native Americans was but a more extreme and deadly case of that of peasant groups in England and elsewhere who held out against the bourgeois effort to drive them from land where they had been accustomed to hunt and pasture.

Some Native Americans fought back, invoking "legal" rules to defend their rights. The Cherokee Nation of Georgia adopted a written constitution and asserted sovereignty over its land. The Georgia legislature responded by declaring Cherokee laws and customs void and opening Cherokee land to settlement. The federal Congress, at the urging of President Andrew Jackson, passed legislation seeking to compel Native Americans to give up and move westward. Georgia authorities arrested, tried, and hanged a Cherokee for an offense allegedly committed on Cherokee territory.

The Cherokee Nation sought relief in the courts. They were, after all, a nation. They sought to restrain the enforcement of Georgia laws which "go directly to annihilate the Cherokees as a political society, and to seize, for the use of Georgia, the lands of the nation which have been assured to them by the United States in solemn treaties reportedly made and still in force." The Cherokees' lawyer invoked the Supreme Court's power, saying that the lawsuit was between a foreign nation—the Cherokee—and the state of Georgia. Under the United States Constitution, the Supreme Court could exercise its original jurisdiction over such a lawsuit without waiting for lower courts to decide it and then hearing the case on appeal.

Chief Justice Marshall looked to the constitutional grant to Congress of the power to regulate commerce with "foreign nations, and among the several states, and with the Indian tribes." He found the Cherokee to be "a domestic, dependent nation" that was "in a state of pupilage," like "that of a ward to his guardian." It was not, he said, for the Court a true "foreign nation." Thus, the Cherokee Nation had no legal existence. It could not even come to a federal court to vindicate its treaty rights.

The Supreme Court decided *Cherokee Nation v. Georgia* in 1830, over the dissents of Justices Story and Thompson. Two years later, in *Worcester v. Georgia*, Chief Justice Marshall retreated a bit, and held that Georgia did not have the right to regulate activities on the Cherokee lands. He did not reach this result by recognizing the position of the Cherokee Nation, but by denying the right of a state such as Georgia to interfere in matters that are essentially federal. That is, the national government had the constitutional power to deal with Native Americans and the states had only a limited role to play.

The Cherokee Nation case prefigured another discreditable event in American constitutional development. In 1857, the Supreme Court decided the infamous *Dred Scott* case. Scott, a former slave who claimed his freedom, sued his former master for assaulting him, his wife, and his child. The Supreme Court held that Scott could not bring a suit in federal court because he was not, and, as a black, could never be, a "citizen" of the United States. The Court, in an opinion by Chief Justice Roger Taney, held that the United States Constitution had enshrined the principle of black inferiority. In Taney's notorious words describing "the Negro race":

> They had for more than a century before been regarded as beings of an inferior order, and altogether unfit to associate with the white race, either in social or political relations; and so far inferior, that they had no rights which the white man was bound to respect; and that the negro might justly and lawfully be reduced to slavery for his benefit.

Not only did the American Constitution afford Scott no protection; this conclusion was said to follow from universal historical experience. Taney's opinion was undone by the Fourteenth Amendment, adopted in the wake of the Civil War. But it is remarkable for its breadth and audacity. No African-American could ever claim justice in a federal court, because they were not "citizens" of any state and could never be. Supreme Court Justice Grier leaked advance news of the impending *Dred Scott* decision to President-elect Buchanan, who used this knowledge to assure Americans in his inaugural address that the issue of slavery was about to be resolved by the Supreme Court.

These brief accounts illustrate the way in which positivist doctrine swamped all pretension of progressive, popular, and universal principle. Claims for justice were to be judged by positive national law, and the United States courts would even yield to inhumane claims of other sovereigns. This was the story of international law in the nineteenth century. It was made by great powers in their interest. It conferred rights on such powers, and not on individuals, smaller states, or colonized peoples.

For nineteenth century judges, finding norms of "international law" did not involve much of a search. They paid little attention to the aspirational words of natural law scholars; some judges, such as Joseph Story, railed against such limitations, but to little effect. The judges did not engage in any of the historical analysis that characterized the work of Grotius. Rather their judgments were based on examining the practices of the "Christian and civilized states" with which the United States dealt. That is, the so-called great powers dictated international law by their common practices and by their mutual agreement.

Under this system, nineteenth century legal ideology built a systematic justification for colonialism, and the great powers divided up the world. Even when the colonies were accorded nominal independence, their political and economic affairs were in fact controlled from Europe or North America. And, as students of economic history know, financial means of dominance were at least as important to imperialism as political ones.

In this essentially positivist climate of legal reasoning, even purely domestic claims about rights fared poorly. The courts were hostile to freedom of speech, freedom to organize, and the equality promised by the constitutional Civil War amendments.

ENFORCING HUMAN RIGHTS INTERNATIONALLY: FROM NUREMBERG TO PINOCHET

Against this backdrop, one must ask how in this century one could develop and advance a progressive legal ideology. The answer comes in two parts: one dealing with transnational legal principles and the other with American domestic law.

The Russian Revolution signaled a major shift in world power. The Soviet government insisted on the equality of states, and that protection of private property was not a fundamental principle of international law. That is, each nation-state might or might not have a system based on private ownership of means of production, but no state or group of states could impose that system on others. The Soviets and capitalist powers debated for nearly two decades over whether socialist expropriations gave rise to claims under "international law." The Soviet insistence on equality contrasts with Chief Justice Marshall's "equality" analysis in the *Antelope*. Marshall invoked equality to protect slavery against the demands of progressive legal ideology. The Soviets invoked it to defend the legal ideology of revolutionary change. It is important to say that equality as a norm is valueless unless one asks what must be equivalent to what. Like the norms discussed in Chapter 21, equality is an empty category which can be filled with differing content.

Soviet legal ideology also rejected the legitimacy of colonialism, whether of the political type or the form of economic domination that Lenin had termed imperialism. And while the Soviet Union was relatively isolated and weak for the first decades of its existence, these views began to change the way in which scholars and international jurists thought about such issues.

The Second World War and its aftermath saw another major leap forward. First, the victorious powers adopted treaties that codified the principle of crimes against humanity. This was not a new concept. That is, launching aggressive war, using force against civilian populations, and genocide had been termed international crimes at least since the early 1900s. None of the great powers had done much to punish such behavior, however.

The trials of Nazi perpetrators changed that. From those trials onwards, a steady stream of events has undermined the Bentham formulation of "international" law, including treaties defining international crimes such as genocide and torture, and large-scale adoption by individual states of internal penal laws permitting punishment of such crimes by domestic tribunals.

At the same time, colonial liberation has brought more than one hundred new voices to the deliberations of international bodies. Thus, the expressed will of the global community has a different character. The United Nations, through its various organs, has been responsible for formulating sets of human rights norms, of which the most influential has been the Universal Declaration of Human Rights.

No longer can it be said that a nation-state is the final arbiter of what happens within its borders. Apartheid, genocide, and torture can be condemned and punished by legitimate international institutions. Nor can a nation-state's leaders proclaim that they, like the sovereigns of old, are immune from prosecution and punishment. From 1945 onwards, it has been recognized more and more that even heads of state can be found guilty of crimes against humanity. Moreover, there is increasing recognition that the "race to the bottom" analysis that Chief Justice Marshall used to justify the slave trade no longer holds. That is, there are peremptory norms of international law binding on nation-states even without their consent. This view owes a great deal to Soviet theorists such as G. I. Tunkin, and even more to the work of human rights activists in the former colonies.

Finally, and perhaps most important, it is now clear that international law is no longer "inter-national" in the sense of being only rules that govern relations between and among states. Individuals are recognized as possessing international rights, enforceable against their own sovereigns. In former days, an individual's claims could be heard by an international tribunal only if sponsored by that person's sovereign, or by some other sovereign who would sponsor the individual's claim. Today, there are even multinational forums, such as the European Court of Human Rights, in which individuals can sue their own sovereigns for violations of international human rights. Among the European Court's accomplishments has been denunciation of British torture of Irish prisoners and forced relocations carried out by the Turkish government. The United States has campaigned against the creation and operation of such forums, not wishing to have its own actions judged by "outsiders," but its opposition has only slowed progress, not halted it.

This perceptual shift opens up avenues of struggle for justice. Of course, struggle remains the operative word. The great powers continue to manipulate principles of international law in their own interest. For example, the North Atlantic Treaty Organization states conducted a brutal bombing campaign against Yugoslavia in 1999. This campaign—which cost thousands of civilian lives and destroyed Yugoslavia's economic infrastructure—was undertaken ostensibly to protect the rights of ethnic Albanians in the province of Kosovo. It is clear that Yugoslav Serb troops and militias had engaged in brutal acts in Kosovo. However, the NATO powers had themselves recognized Yugoslav sovereignty over the province when it was in their strategic interest to do so. Hypocrisy aside, NATO deliberately bypassed the truly transnational United Nations mechanisms for resolving the conflict, thus violating the NATO members' treaty obligations. The bombing campaign triggered waves of violence, and created scenes of destruction, more widespread than would have occurred if an alternative and truly transnational solution were to have been sought. As the atrocity propaganda smoke clears it now appears quite possible that more civilians have been slaughtered by NATO bombing and Albanian nationalist armed groups than by Serbian troops and militia. Thus claims that "human rights violations" override "outdated" notions of sovereignty or the binding nature of multilateral treaties can be used to prettify policies of the most powerful states, based on the old-fashioned dictum that might makes right.

In short, the term "universal" can and has been appropriated by powerful countries to achieve decidedly non-universal ends. It taxes credulity to term NATO bombing raids as an "enforcement mechanism" of the "international legal community." No trial in any fair forum ever decided that such a thing should happen. The findings of alleged fact that preceded the raid were sharply contested from many reliable quarters, and the military response was incompatible with the basic objectives of an international legal system—which is to preserve and protect life and not to take it.

This contradiction lies at the heart of our present struggle for international human rights. We are at times drawn into a Faustian bargain. We take our claims to national tribunals, which may later convert our expressions of principle into results that are not consistent with human rights.

We do not want for examples of how claims for justice may be presented based on the rediscovered norms of human rights. In assessing these stories, one must keep in mind that using legal ideology to present claims for justice is not an end in itself. That is, the claims are made by and on behalf of a movement for change, and the purely "legal" maneuvers are but one element of the movement's activity. To see matters otherwise puts law and lawyers too much in the center of things, and risks both reification of the norms and trivialization of the movement's popular base.

As one episode, consider the case of Chile. In 1973, the government of Socialist Party leader Salvador Allende was overthrown by a military junta, led by General Augusto Pinochet. Pinochet became leader of a government that ruled until 1990. The junta was responsible for thousands of disappearances, tens of thousands of tortures, and for political assassinations of its opponents in Chile and abroad.

On September 21, 1976, former Chilean Foreign Minister and ambassador to the United States Orlando Letelier and his American associate Ronni Karpen Moffitt were killed by a car bomb in Washington, D.C. Letelier, who had served in the Allende government, was an effective opponent of the junta on the international scene. The bomb was planted and detonated by Cuban-Americans hired by the Chilean secret police agency DINA and its successor, CNI.

My partners and I sued the Chilean junta and won a judgment declaring it responsible for the killings. The damage award was eventually paid. This case thus helped to establish the principle of state responsibility for acts of terrorism conducted against political opponents. It was, of course, no secret that agents of reactionary governments used the United States as a base for operations against their own nationals. This was a pathbreaking decision on state liability for such conduct.

In the meantime, with renewed vigor after the junta yielded power, lawyers in Chile brought cases dealing with the junta's abuses. General Manuel Contreras, head of the secret police, was tried and convicted by a military court. He then gave a statement implicating Pinochet in all the murders and tortures and disappearances. This statement added to a considerable body of evidence of Pinochet's personal involvement in those crimes. After all, Pinochet's favorite expression was "not a leaf moves in Chile but that I know of it."

The question was: Could progressives make Pinochet personally accountable? To be sure, the principle of accountability for crimes against humanity had been reaffirmed by the post–Second World War Nuremberg prosecutions of Nazi leaders. In France, persecutors of the Resistance—including one former Gaullist cabinet minister—had been prosecuted. The United Nations had established war crimes tribunals for the former Yugoslavia and Rwanda.

A Spanish lawyer and academic, Dr. Juan Garces, brought together these strands of doctrine and filed criminal charges against Pinochet in the Spanish courts. His theory was this: systematic torture of one's political opponents—because of their politics—is regarded under international law as a kind of genocide. Spanish criminal law expressly defines this kind of torture as the serious crime of genocide.

Even though some Spanish nationals were tortured and killed, this is not necessary for Spain to have power over the case. Crimes against humanity are like the crime of piracy in traditional international law—any nation that captured a pirate could try him, for his crime was said to be committed "against all humankind." This is known as the principle of universal jurisdiction. Most criminal offenses are prosecuted based on territoriality: where the crime was committed. Some states also punish their own nationals for crimes committed anywhere: the principle of active nationality. And a state may punish those who commit crimes against its nationals anywhere in the world: the principle of passive nationality. This principle of universal jurisdiction is well enough established that the courts of Spain upheld the notion of prosecuting Pinochet.

So in October 1998, while Pinochet was visiting London, he was arrested on a Spanish warrant, seeking his extradition. His case wound up before Britain's highest court, the law lords or Lords of Appeal, of the House of Lords. Those of us who had brought the Letelier-Moffitt case were called into service. Pinochet claimed that under British and international law, he was immune from prosecution for any acts he had committed while head of state. This principle of head of state immunity, like the similar idea of diplomatic immunity, is well established.

But the Nuremberg principles, a host of treaties signed since the Second World War, and many judicial decisions, most of them from the United States, have established an important exception to this immunity. The head of state is immune from prosecution only for ordinary wrongs, and not for crimes against humanity such as torture and genocide. The House of Lords recognized this exception, albeit in a limited way. It held that Pinochet could be prosecuted for tortures committed between December 1988 and the time he left power in 1990. The lords chose this date because it was the date on which Britain had become a party to a treaty, the Torture Convention, which expressly denied immunity for torture. A London magistrate, Roland Bartle, then held that Pinochet could be extradited to Spain if Britain's Home Secretary approved, for extradition is ultimately a matter for the political branch of government to decide. Remarkably, magistrate Bartle had been regarded by the pro-Pinochet forces as a potential ally, due to his pro-empire political affiliations. However, his judgment against Pinochet was based upon an announced recognition that in the field of human rights, there must be "one law for one world."

Britain's Home Secretary ultimately freed Pinochet to return to Chile, on grounds of ill health. Nonetheless, a point had been made. This account shows how claims for justice can find open space even in the legal ideology of bourgeois states. The erosion of state and head of state immunity, and the growing consensus that torture and genocide are crimes against the whole of humanity, are instances of international solidarity.

The Pinochet case illustrates the Faustian bargain of which I spoke earlier. The principle of universal jurisdiction over human rights offenses puts a weapon in the hands of every country. Any nation can, in its own courts, accuse the leader of any other nation, claiming that he or she is guilty of such offenses. Powerful nations can particularly invoke this weapon against weaker ones. This difficulty will endure until the creation of genuine international tribunals. Indeed, even after such tribunals are created, there will remain problems of "prosecutorial discretion." That is, prosecutors may choose the wrong targets, as prosecutors have done time out of mind.

The answer to such difficulties lies in the relationship between law and movements for social change. The Pinochet litigation in London and Spain would not have had a lasting effect unless a movement in Chile had taken up the call to bring him to justice. All of our work on the Pinochet matter, from 1976 forward, has been done in close collaboration with the movement for change in Chile. That movement redoubled its efforts when Pinochet was released in Britain, and the Chilean courts have now stripped him of his immunity from suit and prosecution. In the same vein, aberrational invocations of human rights and universal jurisdiction principles will be countered by responses from the people affected by the alleged conduct. If no movement for change responds to an initiative, it will lose force.

Other examples of progressive use of human rights norms are not hard to find. In October 1999, a welfare rights group filed a petition with the Inter-American Commission on Human Rights, claiming that United States welfare policy violates international human rights norms. The United States Supreme Court has held that the U.S. Constitution does not obligate the federal or state governments to provide minimal subsistence, nor to create the economic conditions necessary to protect social and economic rights. Thus, the Court has held that legislatures may terminate social welfare programs at will, even while recognizing that when such programs are funded benefits may not be withheld on prohibited grounds such as race.

While American courts have taken this view, international treaties and customary international human rights law have increasingly recognized economic and social rights to subsistence, to work, to organize, to education, to health, and to maintain family life. These rights are enshrined in, for example, the Universal Declaration of Human Rights, and the American Declaration of Human Rights, which is applicable to members of the Organization of American States.

The petition was filed by several groups of poor working people, and their individual members, as well as law reform groups such as the Center for Constitutional Rights. It describes in detail how "welfare reform" legislation in fact pushes people below subsistence income levels, undermines family life, shuts off educational opportunities, and endangers the health and safety of children in poor families. Organizations of working poor and welfare recipients have battled for years against the injustices of the social welfare system. In this respect, the petition's claims are not new.

What is new is the assertion that transnational norms that the United States is obligated to respect require major changes in how the welfare system is financed and administered. That is, the petitioners are looking to the progressive elements of legal ideology to formulate claims for justice. And they are explicitly recognizing that United States domestic law provides them no relief.

The use of international norms as the basis to attack United States policy is a progressive development, for it enlarges the field of struggle and provides a coherent set of critical norms: critical in the sense that they judge the strictly domestic standards, and find them wanting.

The ultimate success of this petition in an international judicial tribunal is, once again, not decisive. The United States has repeatedly refused to obey decrees of the Inter-American Commission on Human Rights or even to recognize the jurisdiction of the affiliated Inter-American Court of Human Rights. It has, for example, continued to execute juveniles, and to deny basic procedural fairness in capital cases generally. But as was the case with the campaign against apartheid and other human rights struggles, raising claims for justice as international human violations provided a rallying cry for the movement, and eventually influenced institutions.

Principles of legal ideology, reflecting international consensus, become the basis for demands for change. And if the change does not come, the insistent argument that this represents a betrayal of "the law" helps to galvanize the movement for change. One need only look at the struggles for civil rights and against apartheid to see the point. To say that one desires change is one thing. To say that one is entitled to change, and to back that argument up by appeals to legal ideology, makes the demand clearer. And, as I noted above, the great powers no longer possess a monopoly on formulating principles of legal ideology. Thus, the conduct of the most reactionary government—as in Chief Justice Marshall's day—is no longer the defining principle of international norms.

The availability of international forums in which to arraign domestic exercise of state power does not mean that purely domestic or internal legal ideology has become irrelevant. Struggle over the meaning and interpretation of key bourgeois democratic constitutional principles still has a role to play.

THE JURISPRUDENCE OF INSURGENCY REVISITED

The legal ideology of bourgeois states has proven remarkably flexible in accommodating claims for justice phrased as demands for legal rights. This flexibility is not natural or inherent; rather it is the product of social struggles. It is commonplace, however, to note that the bourgeois definition of freedom contains inherent contradictions. The freedom of property is an instrument of social domination when the means of production are owned by a few. In such a system, freedom of contract is a means to regulate the hiring of labor of the workers by the owners. Even the formal guarantees of political freedom are largely illusory when private ownership of means of communication cuts off the free flow of discourse and debate. The gathering places where communication may take place—streets and parks—are subjected to restrictions in the name of private property and social control. It is, unfortunately, easy to see how nominally neutral or even progressive rules take on a reactionary aspect in the hands of judges. Two examples tell the story.

The First Amendment to the United States Constitution guarantees freedom of speech and press. Today, moneyed interests dominate electoral politics, drowning out less-well-financed voices. The sensible citizen wonders if campaign finance reform would help even things out. That citizen even asks whether the dominance of money so erodes the freedom of speech that government has an affirmative duty to see that all voices can participate in the process.

That citizen, reading current Supreme Court decisions, will be disappointed. The Court has held that limits on individual contributions to influence elections, and contributions to office holders for increased access, are forms of speech protected by the First Amendment. Only few and ineffective restraints on money in politics are found to be constitutional.

Thus, the Supreme Court sees the First Amendment through the prism of bourgeois ideology. Money, the universal commodity, enables speech. It pays for the means by which a message is delivered. Therefore, money and speech are in a sense equivalents. The Constitution places no inhibition on people spending their own money. By this reasoning, money is speech. The wealthy person does not want to talk, or hand out leaflets. But because money is the equivalent of all things, he or she can pay for others to do those things.

While some aspects of finance reform will no doubt survive constitutional analysis, the "money is speech" equivalence seems likely to persist as long as the system of social relations that gave it birth. This is one of the boundaries on change in legal institutions of which I spoke before.

Another frustration in constitutional argument has been in the field of racial justice. In the Civil War's wake, the Thirteenth Amendment abolished slavery, the Fifteenth Amendment guaranteed former slaves the right to vote, and the Fourteenth Amendment broadly commanded the states to provide due process and "equal protection of the laws."

Under the banner of equal protection, the civil rights movement has championed the rights of African-Americans, women, gays, and others. But reactionary jurists have stood equal protection on its head, invoking it to protect white privilege. The legal legerdemain works like this: The equal protection guarantee of the Fourteenth Amendment was designed to ensure formal equality to the former slaves. By extension, it forbade any invidious discrimination against any identifiable class or group.

However, for nearly 100 years, with few exceptions, the Supreme Court accepted a strained interpretation of equal protection that left southern Jim Crow legislation and customs untouched. The desegregation decisions from about 1950 onwards turned back toward the original intent of those who forced the Thirteenth, Fourteenth, and Fifteenth amendments upon the former rebel states and put them into the Constitution.

As one means to enforce the equal protection clause, the Supreme Court declared that race-based classifications are inherently suspect. This formulation was designed to foster elimination of the legal racial barriers to full participation by African-Americans in educational, political, and financial life. Of course, nothing in any of these developments struck directly at race and class-based economic discrimination conducted by nominally private entities.

Within the past decade, however, the Supreme Court has taken the "inherently suspect" label and turned it inside out. Thus, the Court, over the dissent of such justices as Thurgood Marshall and William J. Brennan, Jr., has said that many affirmative action programs violate the equal protection clause. The reasoning of these decisions is that affirmative action seeks to remedy the legacy of slavery and racism by recognizing that African-Americans should be given preferences in hiring, education, and other fields, and that such conscious use of race as a criterion is "inherently suspect" and therefore almost never justifiable. The same "reasoning" has been used to strike down laws and programs that benefit Hispanics, women, and other historically disadvantaged groups.

Thus, the historic lesson of equal protection, that a just society should strive to mend its ways, is sacrificed in the name of an ahistorical and fundamentally reactionary interpretation that has no basis in the history, and very little in the text, of the Constitution. And because much racial, ethnic, and gender discrimination proxies for class-based discrimination, the effect is to reinforce bourgeois power.

Let me explain that last statement. Racial antagonism has been a traditional bourgeois weapon in dividing the working class. Discrimination against women in the workplace reinforces the "typical," which is to say stereotypical, image of the family that Marx and Engels described and critiqued in the Communist Manifesto.

The answer to reactionary textual misreading of constitutional principle is several-fold. First, no subjects of judicial decision making are more politicized than those related to race and gender. Therefore, one must use the political process to see that progressive judges are appointed. Second, some race and gender preferences will "win" if the lawyers can prove specific present inequities linked to specific past injustice. Second, even these latest distortions of equal protection leave room for argument—for manipulation of legal ideology. Because race and gender classifications often proxies for or correlate to other characteristics, preferences based on those other characteristics can be used and justified. For example, a state university that gave an admission preference to African-Americans would face legal challenges that might well succeed—at least without a winning demonstration of the absolute necessity of using such a means to redress past discrimination. An admission preference based on poverty and lack of educational opportunity would, however, fare better.

These illustrations of limits on constitutional argument in the bourgeois nation-state are not intended to suggest the irrelevance of rights rhetoric or the futility of making claims for justice based on purely domestic norms. Victories for the right to organize and to speak are still possible. And claims for justice play a vital role in resisting brutal exercises of state power.

In the Introduction, I referred to the racial disparity in prosecution and sentencing. In addition, the courts have refused to put meaningful limits on prosecutorial and police misconduct. There remains, as I noted, the right to jury trial. While that right is often meaningless because defense counsel is inadequately prepared, it exercises a vital popular control still effective in the face of ever more powerful means of fashioning public opinion through the highly concentrated mass media. Even in the case of Oklahoma bombing suspect Terry Lynn Nichols, the subject of hostile media coverage of extraordinary scope and intensity, a Denver jury acquitted him of all first and second degree murder charges and acquitted him of arson and use of a weapon of mass destruction. Jurors interviewed after the trial voiced their distrust of the prosecutors, and their chagrin and anger at the prosecution and FBI tactics. In a nation so bombarded with pro-prosecution rhetoric, these expressions were all the more remarkable.

It may still be asked whether these legal avenues amount to a jurisprudence of insurgency, as described in the first edition of this book—that is, whether they form part of a direct challenge to existing state power. Often, these avenues are followed within a much larger, transnational terrain than the insurgency of the 1970s. Within that terrain, there are many pockets of insurgency, and sometimes—as in the Seattle protests against the World Trade Organization of 1999—they are brought together around a single issue. But capitalism—in part by shifting to this global terrain in the aftermath of the Cold War—has averted a threat to the national bases of its power in the West and in the Third World, and is newly ascendant in the former Soviet bloc. The pace of change has been slower than was hoped during the 1970s, and the power and resourcefulness of international capital has sometimes been greater. But the direction of history, and its motive power, remain as they have been.

Like all other arguments, the argument I made in 1977 for a jurisprudence of insurgency was a product of its time. However the times may have changed, there is hardly a word in it which I would retract now. It has become fashionable in some quarters to say that there is no alternative to capitalism. I could not agree with such a view, given the way in which most of the world's people are compelled to live. Even the vaunted "freedom" of post–Soviet Russia has become a cruel joke for most people. For example, in the Soviet Union, women's salaries were about 75% of men's for equivalent work. Today, that number is about 40%. The relative condition of women has worsened. And this is merely one example. As the editors of *Monthly Review* wrote in September 2000, "we must not waver as we continue to study [and] educate . . . for the transcendence of the social system of capitalism and the development eventually in its place of a society of equals."

Our hope for change is dimmed by seeing the suffering and carnage being wrought in the former Soviet Union, the former Federal Republic of Yugoslavia, in Southern Africa and elsewhere. How, one must ask, can it seem that all the progress toward more equality and justice, even though that progress was marked and scarred by injustice and repression, is being swept aside so easily and quickly? How do we account for the recrudescence of older ideas that justify hatred and killing?

You can cover up the old ideas with decades of new society, and a thousand pages of laws, but their latent traces remain in the attitudes and ideas of people. Why and how did we forget this lesson? We see national and religious groups reenact in myriad ways the rituals of the old Roman seeker after justice, who after stating his claim repeated the talismanic words, "and I claim this by my right as a Roman citizen." In the West, the deeply held and passionately expressed beliefs, given as the reason for killing or dying, turn out to be the remnants of some half-forgotten theory of law and justice.

These events help us to detect fallacies and flaws in a theory of social development that sees revolutionary change as discontinuous, able to surmount old ideologies without integrating them into new ones. Such hopes have repeatedly been proven vain. Just as the new may grow at the center of the old, and one day burst the bonds that constrain it, so the old will exist within the new. Elements of the old ideology may, indeed, be progressive and indeed essential.

After all, state power cannot enforce all legal rules simply by application of continuous force. The ongoing stability of a regime depends in great measure on habitual, not to say voluntary, compliance with laws. Law as ideology persists across fundamental social change, because people are "used to things." As I wrote several years ago:

> The lesson of past changes in the social system is that rights rhetoric persists across the replacement of one ruling class by another. This persistence is not, I would argue, solely a matter of false consciousness, nor a sort of collective hangover that people wake up with the morning after the revolution. People will continue to believe, based on their experience, that certain "rights" are "due."

That is, fundamental change involves both transformation and continuity, as the old and new interact. Every successful social revolution in recorded history has nonetheless been followed by a frank recognition—more or less delayed—that large portions of the old regime's legal ideology will continue to affect the attitudes of people toward events, and to influence their conduct.

A central element of dialectical theory is interpenetration of opposites. Yet, many socialist leaders and thinkers have assumed that with a new society comes the obliteration or effacement of opposites, They have assumed that after a relatively brief period in which old "vices" are suppressed, new ideologies will take root and flourish. These ideologies, in turn, are thought to be nourished by the new social relations that are being formed. Such views have repeatedly been proved wrong.

If an old ideology is persistent, despite fundamental change, one must examine and classify its elements. The old and meretricious must be guarded against, and its supporters isolated. The old and progressive, such as the persistent themes of free expression and fairness in exercise of state power, must be identified and preserved.

Thus the "how" is based upon an understanding of two significant considerations—one about the new international context in which claims for justice are formulated, justified, and asserted, and the other about the context in which successful claims must be safeguarded.

I would generalize John Mage's observation, quoted in the Introduction, that in the United States, "all significant legal and political questions are given legal form." In all cultures, people claim "justice" and "right." They phrase their demands for change in terms of entitlements. They seek to change the way in which state power is exercised, therefore they are inevitably speaking in terms of legal ideology. One is reminded of Molière's character, who exclaimed, *Par ma foi! Il y a plus de quarante ans que je dis de la prose sans que j'en susse rien*. "For forty years I have been speaking prose without even knowing it."

The entire lesson of this book in 1977 was and remains that history may move fitfully, but (to paraphrase Galileo's alleged remark on the laws of physical motion) "it still moves." We are still in the period where the movement for change seeks open spaces in bourgeois legal ideology that can be filled up with progressive content, and points up contradictions between that ideology's formal guarantees and the way in which state power is actually being used. At the same time, movements for change are formulating new claims for justice and insisting that institutions of bourgeois state power recognize them. This process openly tests the limits of bourgeois legal ideology, and hence the very legitimacy of its asserted neutrality and right to rule.

In sum, the old avenues of struggle remain open in some measure, while new avenues are opening before us.

APPENDIX:

FOREWORD TO THE FIRST EDITION BY THOMAS I. EMERSON

In this book Michael Tigar and Madeleine Levy undertake to trace the origins and development of our present legal system in terms of the struggle between a rising capitalist society and a declining feudal structure. The story begins as early as the eleventh century, with the commencement of mercantile life in the cities, and carries through the triumph of bourgeois jurisprudence in the eighteenth century. The focus is on the manner in which law and legal institutions reflect the interests of the dominant class and how they are changed as a new social class gradually replaces its predecessor. As history, it is an absorbing account. It will add to the understanding of all lawyers and law students, and they would do well to be familiar with it.

The book also has broader implications. Those of us who are concerned with social change in the United States, and most of all the legal profession, have largely ignored some central questions. Plainly our nation, like most of the Western industrial world, is in a period of transition. Problems mount day by day and the solutions do not seem possible within the framework of traditional capitalist institutions. Whether or not the new order will be Marxian socialist, as Tigar and Levy believe, it will certainly be more collective, will rest on a new consciousness, and hopefully will embody a system of individual freedom. This process of social change, and the shaping of our ultimate destiny, give rise to the crucial issues of the day.

What role can rules of law and legal institutions play in the period of transition and what will be their place in the new scheme of things? Without doubt our system of law has been a major feature of Western society. And, as Tigar and Levy point out, legal ideology has not been the sole property of the dominant group within society; on the contrary, groups that aspire to state power have formulated their attack in terms of systems of legal rules and principles. This is not likely to change. The new order cannot represent a total break with the past. It must develop out of existing arrangements and in the end many of the old ideas, attitudes, and institutions will be merged into the future order. We may therefore expect that the new society will be distinctly Western, rather than, say, Chinese, in its dependence on law as a vital means of social control.

How then can law be utilized within the existing system to effectuate social change? Tigar and Levy make clear that our system of law lends itself to this use. The rights asserted under the prevailing legal ideology, both with respect to property and contract rights and with respect to individual rights, are stated in universal terms; they may be claimed by all elements in the society. There are necessarily gaps and uncertainties in the system, which make for a certain flexibility. As the original factual basis for the law changes, the law gets out of joint and develops contradictions, which call for resolution by change. The legal rules are interpreted by a specially trained class of jurists, who tend to develop their own momentum. A rising group can take advantage of these features of the legal system and develop what Tigar and Levy call a "jurisprudence of insurgency." But just how should this be done? What will advance the process of social change and what will merely shore up existing outworn institutions?

What is the position of the individual lawyer participating in such a process? Certainly it is ambiguous. On the one hand, the lawyer must operate within the existing system, or lose all influence and perhaps the status of lawyer itself. On the other hand, he or she has a commitment to serious social change. Many lawyers have agonized over this problem, but it remains a serious dilemma.

How does a group challenging the old order begin to formulate its own jurisprudence? That it must do so is clear, given the central role of law in Western society. And again as Tigar and Levy observe, the ideology of a growing dissident movement will greatly influence the legal system that it will put into effect when it achieves state power. By what means, then, can it begin to introduce into the ongoing system its ideas of how the productive forces of society should be ordered, how a system of individual rights can be maintained in a collectivist society, and how a sense of community can be developed?

What about the advisability of pressing in the courts for a distinction in the role of the judiciary between property and contract rights on the one hand, and individual rights on the other? The legal ideology of the rising capitalist class placed emphasis on securing bourgeois interests in both areas, in the former to achieve material supremacy, in the latter as essential to obtaining state power. Now it is the capitalist establishment which seeks to curtail the system of individual rights and the dissident groups which have a stake in maintaining and expanding it. Is this ground for seeing the role of the courts in this period as primarily concerned with the system of individual rights? Are the courts powerless to introduce changes into the system of property and contract rights? Or can they respond to claims, extrapolated from bourgeois ideology, for material equality and a share in the national wealth?

Finally, is it enough to ask the courts to protect citizens in their traditional rights against government interference with their freedom of expression and religion, against unfairness in their dealings with government, and against unequal treatment under the law? Or should the legal system now be geared to affirmative action if the ideals of the system of individual rights are to be achieved in reality?

Law and the Rise of Capitalism does not answer all these questions. In tracing the part played by law and lawyers in the transition from feudalism to capitalism, however, the book does throw a great deal of light upon them. Every person seriously interested in social change, whether student, legal practitioner, or simply citizen, should find it stimulating and suggestive reading.

New Haven, Connecticut
January 1977

SELECTED BIBLIOGRAPHY

We decided against including footnotes, preferring to make clear from the text our debts to other writers, and to place at the end the full reference to the works we consulted or which we recommend. We are including only those primary sources on which we particularly relied and secondary sources which are generally available. The citation of works consulted is in the form prescribed by *A Uniform System of Citation*, 11th ed., published by the editors of the Columbia, Harvard, Pennsylvania, and Yale law reviews. Dates given are those of the editions consulted.

H. Adams, *Mont-Saint-Michel and Chartres* (1961)

C. L. Appleton, *Histoire de la compensation en droit romain* (1895)

Assises du royaume de Jerusalem (V. Foucher ed. 2d ed. 1839)

W. Atkinson, *A History of Spain and Portugal* (1960)

J. Austin, *The Province of Jurisprudence Determined and the Uses of the Study of Jurisprudence* (H.L.A. Hart ed. 1954)

R. Baillet, *L'Ancien Cabris et l'Actuel* (1920)

Basic Documents in Medieval History (N. Downs ed. 1959)

M. Bateson, *Borough Customs* (1904–06) (Selden Soc. ed.)

M. Bateson, *Laws of Breteuil*, 15 Eng. Hist. Rev. 76 (1901)

H. Battifol, *Droit international privé* (4th ed. 1967)

J. Beames, *A translation of Glanville* (1900)

P. Beaumanoir, *Les Coutumes de Beauvaisis* (P. Salmon ed. 1899–1901 and J. Beugnot ed. 1842)

G. J. Bell, *Commentaries on the Law of Scotland* (5th ed. 1870)
J. Bernard, *Trade and Finance in the Middle Ages*, 900–1500 (1971)
W. Bewes, *The Romance of the Law Merchant* (1923)
M. Bloch, *Feudal Society* (L. Manyon trans. 1961)
M. Bloch, *French Rural History* (J. Sondheimer traps. 1966)
W. Boak, *A History of Rome to 565 A.D.* (4th ed. 1955)
J. Bobé, *Notes sur la coutume de Paris* (1683)
R. Bolt, *A Man For All Seasons* (1960)
L. B. Boudin, *The Theoretical System of Karl Marx* (1907)
Bourdot de Richebourg, *Nouveau coutumier general* (1724)
F. Bourjon, *Le Droit commun de la France* (3d ed. 1770)
F. Braudel, *Capitalism and Material Life 1400–1800* (M. Kochan traps. 1973)
J. A. Brillat-Savarin, *The Philosopher in the Kitchen* (A. Drayton trans. 1970)
J. B. Brissaud, *A History of French Private Law* (1912)
W. Buckland, *A Manual of Roman Private Law* (2d ed. 1939)
W. Buckland, *A Text-Book of Roman Law* (2d ed. 1932)
W. Buckland and A. McNair, *Roman Law and Common Law* (2d ed. 1952)
J. Burckhardt, *The Age of Constantine the Great* (M. Hadas trans. 1949)
E. Burke, *Selected Writings of Edmund Burke* (W. Bate ed. 1960)
R. Busquet, V.-L. Bourilly and M. Agulhon, *Histoire de la Provence* (5th ed. 1972)
J. Campbell, *The Lives of the Lord Chancellors* (1845)
Capitalism and the Reformation (M. J. Kitch ed. 1967)
M.-L. Carlin, *La Penetration du droit romain dans les actes de la pratique Provençal* (1967)
E. Carus-Wilson, *Medieval Merchant Venturers* (2d ed. 1967)
R. Chambers, *Thomas More* (1935)
The Code Napoléon (B. Schwartz ed. 1956)
Conseil d'Etat Français, *Conference du Code Civil* (1805)
Conseil d'Etat Français, *Discussion du Code Civil* (1850)
Conseil d'Etat Français, *Discussion du Projet du Code Civil* (1803–08)
Corpus Juris Canonici (A. Friedberg ed. 1879–81)
B. Croce, *History of the Kingdom of Naples* (H. S. Hughes trans. 1965)
R. David, *Les Grands systèmes de droit contemporains* (4th ed. 1971)
J. Dawson, *The Oracles of the Law* (1968)
G. de Bruges, *The Murder of Charles the Good, Count of Flanders* (J. Ross trans. 1959)
L. de Hericourt, *Les Loix ecclésiastiques de France dans leur ordre naturel* (3d ed. 1771)
F. A. De Smith, *The Prerogative Writs*, 11 Cambridge L.J. 40 (1951)

J. Des Graviers, *Le Droit canonique* (2d ed. 1967)

D. Diderot, *Rameau's Nephew and D'Alembert's Dream* (L. W. Tancock trans. 1966)

M. Dobb, *Studies in the Development of Capitalism* (1963)

A Documentary History of England, 1066–1540 (J. Bagley and P. B. Rowley eds. 1966)

P. Dollinger, *The German Hansa* (D. Ault and S. Steinberg trans. 1970)

J. Domat, *Les Loix civiles dans leur ordre naturel* (nouv. ed. 1745)

C. Dumoulin, 2 *Omnia Quae Extant Opera* (1681)

B. Dunham, *Heroes and Heretics, A Social History of Dissent* (1964)

A. Ehrenzweig, *Private International Law* (1967)

A. Ehrenzweig, *Psychoanalytic Jurisprudence* (1971)

J. Ellul, 3, 4 & 5 *Histoire des Institutions* (6th ed. 1969)

F. Engels, *The Origin of the Family, Private Property and the State* (E. Leacock ed. 1972)

A. Esmein, *Cours élémentaire d'histoire du droit français* (11th ed. 1912)

A. Esmein, *A History of Continental Criminal Procedure* (J. Simpson trans. 1914)

J. Evans, *Life in Medieval France* (3d ed. 1969)

P. Faure, *La Renaissance* (5th ed. 1969)

C. Ferrière, *Corps et compilation de tous les commentateurs anciens et modernes sur la coutume de Paris* (2d ed. 1724)

C. Ferrière, *Dictionnaire analytique de la coutume de Normandie* (1780)

C. Ferrière, *Dictionnaire de droit et de pratique* (nouv. ed. 1769)

J. Fortescue, *De Laudibus Legum Anglie* (S. B. Chrimes ed. and trans. 1942

The French Revolution: Conflicting Interpretations (F. Kafker and J. Laux eds. 1968)

Gaius, *Institutes* (F. de Zulueta trans. 1946)

G. Gilbert, *The History and Practice of the High Court of Chancery* (1758)

C. Gilliard, *Histoire de la Suisse* (5th ed. 1968)

P. Goubert, *Louis XIV and Twenty Million Frenchmen* (A. Carter trans. 1970)

M. Grandclaude, *Etude critique sur les livres des assises de Jerusalem* (1923)

J.A.C. Grant, *The Anglo-American Legal System* (rev. ed. 1947)

J. and E. Green, *The Legal Profession and the Process of Social Change: Legal Services in England and the United States*, 21 Hast. L.J. 563 (1970)

F. Guicciardini, *The History of Florence* (M. Domandi trans. 1970)

P. Guichonnet, *Histoire de l'Italie* (1969)

R. Hailey, *Comparative Development of Theories of Self-Incrimination in England and France* unpubl. seminar paper 1971)

W. Harpsfield, *The Life and Death of Sir Thomas More* (Everyman's Library ed. 1963)

C. Hill, *Reformation to Industrial Revolution* (1967)

E. Hobsbawm, *Industry and Empire* (1968)

W. S. Holdsworth, *A History of English Law* (various dates 1922–1938)

E. Jenks, *Law and Politics in the Middle Ages* (2d ed. 1913)

J. Joinville, *History of St. Louis*, in *Memoirs of the Crusades* (F. Marzials trans. 1958)

F. Joüon des Longrais, *La Conception anglaise de la saisine du XIIe au XIVe siècle* (1924)

M. Keen, *The Pelican History of Medieval Europe* (1969)

A. Kinoy, *The Radical Lawyer and Teacher of Law*, in *Law Against the People* (R. Lefcourt ed. 1971)

P. Kropotkin, *The Great French Revolution, 1789–1793* (N. Dryhurst trans. 1971)

R. D. Laing, *The Politics of Experience* (1967)

G. Lancellotti, *Institutiones Juris Canonici* (1704)

The Legacy of the Middle Ages (C. Crump and E. Jacob eds. 1926)

J. LeGoff, *Marchands et Banquiers du Moyen Age* (5th ed. 1972)

J. LeGoff, *The Town as an Agent of Civilization, 1200–1500* (1971)

W. Leslie, *Similarities in Lord Mansfield's and Joseph Story's View of Fundamental Law*, 1 Am. J. Legal Hist. 278 (1957)

E. Levy, *West Roman Vulgar Law: The Law of Property* (1951)

L. Levy, *The Origins of the Fifth Amendment* (1969)

Li Livres de jostice et de plet (P. Rapetti ed. 1850)

A. Loisel, *Les Institutes Coutumières* (1608)

J. D. Mackie, *A History of Scotland* (rev. ed. 1969)

H. Maine, *Ancient Law* (1861)

F. Maitland, *Township and Borough* (1898)

P.-L. Malausséna, *Commerce et crédit à Nice à la fin du XIIIe siècle, Nice Historique*, June 1970, p. 1

P.-L. Malausséna, *Promissio Redemptionis: Le Rachat des captifs chretiens en pays musulmans à la fin du XIVe siècle*, 80 *Annales du Midi* 255 (1968)

P.-L. Malausséna, *La Vie en Provence orientale aux XIVe et XVe siècles* (1969)

C. McEvedy, *The Penguin Atlas of Medieval History* (1961)

W. McGovern, *Materials on Legal History* (mimeo ed. 1973)

B. Mitchell, *Statistical Appendix, 1700–1914* (1971)

T. More, *Utopia* (P. Turner trans. 1965)

J. Mundy and P. Riesenberg, *The Medieval Town* (1958)

G. Nogent, *Self and Society in Medieval France* (J. Benton ed. C. Bland trans. 1970)

P. Ourliac and J. Malafosse, *Histoire du droit privé* (2d ed. 1971)

R. Pernoud, *Histoire de la bourgeoisie en France* (1960–62) (2 vols.)

C. Petit-Dutaillis, *Les Communes Françaises* (1970)
H. Pirenne, *Early Democracies in the Low Countries* (J. Saunders trans. 1963)
H. Pirenne, *Economic and Social History of Medieval Europe* (1936)
H. Pirenne, *Medieval Cities: Their Origins and the Revival of Trade* (F. Halsey trans. 1952)
B. Pitti and G. Dati, *Two Memoirs of Renaissance Florence* (J. Martines trans. 1967)
T.F.T. Plucknett, *Bonham's Case and Judicial Review*, 40 Harv. L. Rev. 50 (1926)
T.F.T. Plucknett, *A Concise History of the Common Law* (5th ed. 1956)
J.-R. Pothier, *Oeuvres* (J. Beugnot ed. 1861)
D. Powell, *The Marxist-Leninist Notion of the Withering Away of the State and Law* (unpubl. seminar paper 1971)
S. Pufendorf, *The Law of Nature and of Nations* (B. Kennett trans. 4th ed. 1729)
M. Radin, *The Myth of Magna Carta*, 60 Harv. L. Rev. 1061 (1947)
M. Radin, *Roman Law* (1927)
K. Renner, *The Institutions of Private Law and Their Social Functions* (1947)
Y. Renouard, *Les Hommes d'affaires italiens du moyen age* (nouv. ed. 1968)
E. Rice, Jr., *The Foundations of Early Modern Europe, 1460–1559* (1970)
M. Roblin, *Les Juifs de Paris* (1952)
E. Roll, *A History of Economic Thought* (2d ed. 1961)
W. Roper, *The Life of Sir Thomas More, Knight* (Everyman's Library ed. 1963)
C. Roth, *The History of the Jews in Italy* (1946)
S. Runciman, *A History of the Crusades* (1971)
C. St. Germain, *Doctor and Student* (facsimile ed. 1973)
F. Sanborn, *Origins of the Early English Maritime and Commercial Law* (1930)
F. I. Schecter, *Popular Law and Common Law in Medieval England*, 28 Colum. L. Rev. 269 (1928)
P. Senequier, *Cabris et Le Tignet* (1900)
C. Sherman, *Roman Law in the Modern World* (3d ed. 1937)
P.-A. Sigalas, *La Vie à Grasse en 1650* (1964)
J. J. Silke, *Ireland and Europe 1559–1607* (1966)
H. Silving, *The Oath*, 68 Yale L. J. 1329, 1527 (1959)
T. Smith, *The Assize of Jerusalem* (1842)
T. Smith, *De Republica Anglorum* (1573)
R. Sohm, *The Institutes: A Textbook of the History and System of Roman Private Law* (A. Ledlie trans. 3d ed. 1907)
J. Stair, *The Institutions of the Law of Scotland* (2d ed. 1693)
J. Stephen, *History of the Criminal Law of England* (1883)

J. Story, *Commentaries on Equity Jurisprudence* (2d ed. 1839)

P. Sweezy, *The Theory of Capitalist Development* (1942)

R. H. Tawney, *Religion and the Rise of Capitalism* (1926)

M. Tigar, *Automatic Extinction of Cross-Demands: Compensatio from Rome to California*, 53 Calif. L. Rev. 224 (1965)

M. Tigar, *Book Review*, 67 Mich. L. Rev. 612 (1969) [Civil Disobedience]

M. Tigar, *Book Review*, 78 Yale L. J. 892 (1969) [Civil Liberties]

M. Tigar, *Judicial Power, the "Political Question Doctrine," and Foreign Relations* 17 U.C.L.A. L. Rev. 1135 (1970), reprinted in *The Vietnam War and International Law* (R. Falk ed. 1972)

M. Tigar, *Socialist Law and Legal Institutions*, in *Law against the People* (R. Lefcourt ed. 1971)

M. Tigar, *Book Review*, 86 Harv. L. Rev. 785 (1973) [Psychoanalytic Jurisprudence]

P. Timbal, *Histoire des institutions et des faits sociaux* (4th ed. 1970)

J. Toubeau, *Les Institutes de droit consulaire, ou la jurisprudence des marchands* (2d ed. 1700)

P. Ure, *Justinian and His Age* (1951)

G. de Villehardouin, *The Conquest of Constantinople*, in *Memoirs of the Crusades* (F. Marzials trans. 1958)

P. Vinogradoff, *Roman Law in Medieval Europe* (2d ed. 1929)

P. Vinogradoff, *Some Considerations of the Method of Ascertaining Legal Customs* (1925)

Voltaire, *The Age of Louis XIV* (M. Pollack trans. 1926)

Voltaire, *Oeuvres Historiques* (1957)

C. Walford, *Fairs, Past and Present: A Chapter in the History of Commerce* (1883)

M. Weber, *The City* (D. Martindale and G. Neuwirth trans. 1962)

M. Weber, *From Max Weber: Essays in Sociology* (H. Gerth and C. W. Mills eds. 1946)

M. Weber, *Max Weber on Law in Economy and Society* (M. Rheinstein ed. 1954)

M. Weber, *The Protestant Ethic and the Spirit of Capitalism* (T. Parsons trans. 1930)

T. Westen, *Usury in the Conflict of Laws: The Doctrine of the Lex Debitoris*, 55 Calif. L. Rev. 123 (1967)

G. Woodward, *The Dissolution of the Monasteries* (1966)

BIBLIOGRAPHY FOR SECOND EDITION

BOOKS AND ARTICLES

Tariq Ali, *NATO's Balkan Adventure*, Monthly Review, June 1999, p. 9

Stephen B. Bright, *Can Judicial Independence Be Attained in the South?* 14 Ga. St. L. Rev. 817 (1998)

Alan E. Brownstein and Steven M. Hankins, *Pruning Pruneyard: Limiting Free Speech Rights*, 24 U.C. Davis L. Rev. 1073 (1991)(noting the contradictions inherent in supporting an ostensibly neutral value like freedom to protest)

Buergenthal and Harold G. Maier, *Public International Law* (2d ed. 1990)

J. H. Burns and H.L.A. Hart, eds., *Introduction to A Comment on the Commentaries and A Fragment on Government* (1977)

Julius L. Chambers, *Beyond Affirmative Action*, 27 Cap. U. L. Rev. 1 (1998)

Thomas Wemyss Fulton, *The Sovereignty of the Sea* (1911)(An Historical Account of the Claims of England to the Dominion of the British Seas, and of the Evolution of the Territorial Waters: with special reference to the Rights of Fishing and the Naval Salute)

Hugo Grotius, *The Freedom of the Seas* (Ralph Van Demean Magoffin trans.) (James Brown Scott ed.)(1916)

Hugo Grotius, *The Law of War and Peace* (Kelsey trans. 1925)

Mark W. Janis, *An Introduction to International Law* (2d ed. 1993)

Mark W. Janis, *Jeremy Bentham and the Fashioning of "International Law,"* 78 Am. J. Int'l L. 405 (1991)

Arthur Kinoy, *The Constitutional Right of Negro Freedom*, 21 Rutgers L. Rev. 387 (1967)

John Mage, Book Review, Monthly Review, Nov. 1996, p. 46

Martha Nussbaum, *Skepticism About Practical Reason in Literature and the Law*, 107 Harv. L. Rev. 714, 718 (1994)

Joseph A. Ranney, *Shaping Debate, Shaping Society: Three Wisconsin Chief Justices and Their Counterparts*, 81 Marquette L. Rev. 923 (1998)(valuable article on Wisconsin laws concerning fugitive slaves)

E. P. Thompson, *Whigs and Hunters: The Origin of the Black Act* (1975)(which shows how the English bourgeoisie land grabs affected the development of criminal law, and includes a valuable discussion of Marx's essay on the law relating to the theft of wood)

Michael E. Tigar, *Crime-Talk, Rights-Talk and Doubletalk*, 65 Texas Law Review 101 (1986)

Michael E. Tigar, *Defending*, 74 Texas Law Review 101 (1995)

Michael E. Tigar, *The Foreign Sovereign Immunities Act and the Pursued Refugee: Lessons from Letelier v. Chile*, 1982 Michigan Yearbook of International Legal Studies 421

Michael E. Tigar, *Haymarket: Whose Name the Few Still Say with Tears* (1987)(play)

Michael E. Tigar, *Original Understanding and the Constitution*, 22 Akron L. Rev. 1 (1988)

Michael E. Tigar, et al., *Paul Touvier and the Crime Against Humanity*, 30 Tex. Int'l L. J. 286 (1995)

Michael E. Tigar, *The Right of Property and the Law of Theft*, 62 Tex. L. Rev. 1443 (1984)

G. I. Tunkin, *Theory of International Law* (William E. Butler trans. 1974)

Robert A. Williams, Jr., *The American Indian in Western Legal Thought: The Discourses of Conquest* (1990)

Richard J. Wilson, *Prosecuting Pinochet: International Crimes in Spanish Domestic Law*, 21 Human Rts. Q. 927 (1999)

Comment, *Hopwood v. Texas: The Fifth Circuit Engages in Suspect Compelling Interest Analysis*, 34 Houston L. Rev. 871 (1997)

Native Americans and Public Policy (Fremont J. Lyden & Lyman L. Legsters eds. 1992)

New Left Review, Issue 234, *The Imperialism of Human Rights*, March/April 1999

Panel Discussion, *Human Rights and Human Wrongs: Is the United States Death Penalty System Inconsistent with International Human Rights Law*, 67 Fordham L. Rev. 2793 (1999)(including comments by Stephen B. Bright of the Southern Center for Human Rights and former death row inmate Rubin "Hurricane" Carter)

JUDICIAL DECISIONS

The Amistad, 40 U.S. 518 (1841)(this is the case about which the motion picture was made)

The Antelope, 23 U.S. 6 (1825)

Buckley v. Valeo, 424 U.S. 1 (1976)(Supreme Court holds that "money is speech," and that First Amendment puts sharp limits on regulating campaign finance)

Cherokee Nation v. Georgia, 30 U.S. 1 (1830)

DeShaney v. Winnebago County Dep't of Social Services, 489 U.S. 189 (1989)

Johnson v. McIntosh, 21 U.S. 543 (1823)

McCleskey v. Kemp, 481 U.S. 279 (1987)(by vote of 5–4, Supreme Court refuses to order inquiry into racial bias in death penalty prosecutions)

Scott v. Sandford, 60 U.S. 393 (1857)(the Dred Scott case)

United States v. Armstrong, 517 U.S. 456 (1996)(racial sentence disparity in narcotics cases upheld by Supreme Court majority)

United States v. Alvarez-Machain, 504 U.S. 655 (1992)(Supreme Court majority upholds kidnapping suspect in Mexico for trial in U.S.)

Worcester v. Georgia, 31 U.S. 515 (1832)

INDEX